Oz in Perspective

Oz in Perspective

Magic and Myth in the L. Frank Baum Books

RICHARD TUERK

McFarland & Company, Inc., Publishers
Jefferson, North Carolina, and London

Library of Congress Cataloguing-in-Publication Data

Tuerk, Richard, 1941–
    Oz in perspective : magic and myth in the L. Frank Baum books /
Richard Tuerk.
       p.   cm.
    Includes bibliographical references and index.

    ISBN-13: 978-0-7864-2899-1
    ISBN-10: 0-7864-2899-6
    (softcover : 50# alkaline paper) ∞

    1. Baum, L. Frank (Lyman Frank), 1856–1919 — Criticism and
interpretation.   2. Baum, L. Frank (Lyman Frank), 1856–1919. Wizard
of Oz.   3. Children's stories, American — History and criticism.
4. Fantasy fiction, American — History and criticism.   5. Oz (Imaginary
place).   6. Magic in literature.   7. Myth in literature.   8. Values in
literature.   I. Title.
    PS3503.A923Z88   2007
    813'4 — dc22   2006038829

British Library cataloguing data are available

Cover image ©2007 Digital Vision.

Manufactured in the United States of America

McFarland & Company, Inc., Publishers
  Box 611, Jefferson, North Carolina 28640
  www.mcfarlandpub.com

To the memory of two good
colleagues, mentors and friends,
James W. Byrd and Lee Dacus

Acknowledgments

In connection with my studies of L. Frank Baum I have many debts. I am especially grateful to the hundreds of students with whom I have discussed and studied his work over the last thirty plus years. They have pointed out many things in the books that I was unable to see myself. I also am grateful to audiences at meetings of professional organizations, especially those of the national and Texas/Southwest Regional Popular Culture Associations and the American Studies Association of Texas, who have listened to my ramblings about Baum and made constructive comments about them. I also owe a debt of gratitude to Harry Eiss, C. Jason Smith, Ximena Gallardo C., Peter Rollins, and Donna Walker-Nixon, who have repeatedly made room on programs for my presentations on Baum. In addition, my good friends C. Jason Smith, Ximena Gallardo C., and Robert Long very generously commented on manuscript versions of this book. Scott Downing, director of interlibrary loans at Gee Library of Texas A&M University–Commerce, repeatedly performed what seemed to be miracles in getting materials I needed; to him I am extremely grateful, as I am to Joe Shipman, Instructional Designer in Educational Media and Distance Education at Texas A&M University–Commerce, who reproduced the illustrations for me. Joe's ability to make clear illustrations from old, yellowed ones constantly amazed me.

A much shorter version of my chapter on *The Wonderful Wizard of Oz* was published in *Mythlore* in autumn of 1990 (and was reprinted in a collection of essays in 2003), and a shorter version of my chapter on *Dorothy and the Wizard in Oz* appeared in the *Baum Bugle* in winter of 1996. Both essays have been greatly revised in their new context in this book. I am grateful to the editors of those periodicals for allowing me to use those essays as a basis for parts of two chapters.

I owe thanks to many good friends for their support and encouragement during the time I was working on this study, including but not limited to Jim Adams, Gerald Duchovnay, Jon Jonz, Dorys Grover, Brian Philips, Marco Portales, my wife Roz, and my two children, Becky and Michael. I also thank Ray Brown for his advice on finding a publisher. I am also grateful to my late parents for introducing me to the Oz books when I was about four or five years old, so that I was able to enjoy them as both a young child and an adult. To all the people I mention here, I owe many good things in my study of Baum. Finally, I owe a debt of gratitude to my friends and colleagues who urged me to publish my Oz material in book form. As for my study's faults, they are entirely my own.

Table of Contents

L. Frank Baum's Fourteen Full-Length Oz Books

Preface

Oz in Perspective contains a series of essays on various aspects of L. Frank Baum's so-called canonical Oz books, that is, his fourteen full-length Oz books. Rather than try to approach each book and topic in the same way, in effect forcing them into the same mold, I try to use the theories and techniques that seem most appropriate to the works and ideas I explore, including close reading, myth and archetypal criticism, psychoanalytic and Jungian criticism, historicism and new historicism, history of ideas, intertextuality, feminist criticism, and deconstruction. Nonetheless, I find in each work at least one variation of the quest myth, so archetypal criticism is present in my discussion of each. At the heart of my work, however, lies the close study of a set of texts that many critics insist are not worthy of close examination. Careful study of the sort I provide, however, can help readers see how much of a literary artist Baum was and can help dispel some of the misconceptions based on cursory readings of his works.

Such a study is important for a number of reasons. First, Baum remains an extremely popular author. His Oz books continue to sell in large numbers year after year. He has also, as has been often shown, had a tremendous impact on American culture, especially through the 1939 movie version of *The Wizard of Oz* that is based on his first Oz book.

In addition, Baum's accomplishments as a writer are, I am convinced, underrated. He is often treated as a person who just happened, in spite of himself, to write a number of entertaining books. I hope that I can at least begin to dispel that idea and show that he was a better literary craftsman than many of his critics realize. In fact, I hope to show that his works are not "unliterary," as several of his critics say; quite the contrary.

I have loved Baum's Oz books since I was a child. I remember my pleasure when my mother read Oz books to me in the evenings. I rediscovered the Oz books as an adult when I started teaching children's literature as part of the English curriculum at what was then East Texas State University and is now Texas A&M University–Commerce. I taught *The Wonderful Wizard of Oz* in most of my undergraduate children's literature courses and managed to teach a number of Baum's Oz books in my graduate classes, both those involving children's literature and those involving the period of American literary Realism, to which Baum belongs. The more I examined the books along with my students, the more I became convinced that they are worthy of careful study and that they have an important place in the history of children's literature and American literature. Incidentally, not until I became an adult and an English professor did I realize that Baum wrote books other than ones about Oz. Still, I feel that the Oz books are his best, a feeling apparently shared by most of the reading public during Baum's time and ours.

I have presented many papers on Baum to groups at Texas A&M University–Commerce and at conferences of learned societies, including the American Studies Association of Texas, the Popular Culture Association, and the Southwest/Texas Popular Culture Association. These presentations challenged me to learn more about Oz. The discussions that resulted from them also forced me to add to my knowledge of Baum.

I have done extensive research on Baum, reading his works repeatedly, including his non–Oz fantasies and many of the series books that he wrote under pseudonyms for adolescents. I have also read the secondary works on him, many of which are excellent. In addition, I have traveled to the Library of Congress to work on Baum, reading, among other things, *Dot and Tot of Merryland* in the first edition in the Rare Book and Special Collections Reading Room. I also traveled to the University of Texas at Austin to work in the Harry Ransom Humanities Research Center, where I examined the manuscript of *The Tin Woodman of Oz* and a fragment of an unfinished book Baum was working on about Mary Louise, one of the heroines of a series of books he wrote pseudonymously for adolescents. (It is interesting to note that the typescript of the Mary Louise fragment is written on the verso of pages of the manuscript of *The Magic of Oz*.) I also made extensive use of the Interlibrary Loans department of Gee Library at Texas A&M University–Commerce.

Serious literary critics and scholars tend to neglect Baum. Yet during the last quarter or so of the twentieth century numerous serious essays about Baum's first Oz book, *The Wonderful Wizard of Oz*, began appearing, and a few critics, wrote book-length studies of Baum, beginning with Raylyn Moore's pioneering work published in 1974. I feel that they show that he is worthy of serious study, even though some critics still consider Baum essentially the author of one decent book.

Few book-length studies have been published on Baum's Oz books. Most of them are now out of date. The first, Edward Wagenknecht's *Utopia Americana* (1929), is really a pamphlet rather than a book. It briefly summarizes the Oz books and tries to show that Baum creates within them a kind of American eutopia, or good place. My book treats Baum's Oz books in much more depth and tries to show that in them Baum does not create a kind of American eutopia. Another book-length critical study is Raylyn Moore's excellent work *Wonderful Wizard Marvelous Land* (1974), which is now, of course, outdated. My book focuses far more attention on individual works than Moore's does. A third is Michael O. Riley's *Oz and Beyond* (1997), which, as its subtitle — *The Fantasy World of L. Frank Baum* — indicates, is mainly concerned with the worlds that Baum creates within his fantasy books, including several non–Oz books. My focus is on the Oz books, and I tend to be more concerned with Baum as a literary artist than Riley is and perhaps less concerned with landscape.

Other full-length works either are biographies, like Katharine M. Rogers' excellent study *Frank Baum: Creator of Oz* (2002); studies primarily of the first Oz book, *The Wonderful Wizard of Oz*, like Suzanne Rahn's The Wizard of Oz: *Shaping an Imaginary World* (1998); or essays appended to editions of Baum's books, such as Michael Patrick Hearn's comprehensive introduction and magnificently informative centennial edition of *The Annotated* Wizard of Oz.

My book is not a biography, nor is it an edition of any of Baum's works. Instead, it is an examination of each of Baum's Oz books in chronological order of publication. In addition, it concludes with one chapter that studies Oz as a place, and another that asks whether Oz is some kind of eutopia.

Introduction

Writing a book on Baum involves a number of risks. First, for serious students of literature, children's literature tends to be suspect. Writing in 1992 of the United States, Jerry Griswold in *Audacious Kids* claims to find evidence of "belated recognition that this country's Children's Literature is not marginal, but squarely within our central literary tradition" (241). Nonetheless, two years later, in *An Introduction to Children's Literature* Peter Hunt points out, "[A]dults are wary about approaching children's books critically [...]" (2). It is true that Hunt's book is devoted mostly to British literature. However, in 2003, in *Kiddie Lit*, a book that treats both British and American literature, Beverly Lyon Clark says that "contemporary critics have been slow to take children's literature seriously and treat it canonically" (2) and that "[c]hildren's literature has low status in literary criticism" (14). As Clark herself indicates in her discussion of Lewis Carroll, she slightly exaggerates here[1]: what matters is one's definition of children's literature. Some works of what are usually called children's literature, such as Jonathan Swift's *Gulliver's Travels* (1726) and Lewis Carroll's *Alice's Adventures in Wonderland* (1865), seem to be readily accepted as part of the canon of British literature, and works of Mark Twain often classified as children's literature, like *The Adventures of Tom Sawyer* (1876) and *Adventures of Huckleberry Finn* (1885), find ready acceptance in the canon of American literature. Many literary critics recognize that these books work on many levels and insist that they are aimed at both children and adults.

Most works of children's literature, however, are considered decidedly non-canonical, so much so that in a book published in 2002 Deborah Cogan Thacker has to argue in favor of the idea of reading them seriously, since "[t]he development of an understanding of the importance of these books as vehicles for artistic expression, or as expressions of aesthetic concerns common to all literature may challenge the remembered experience of reading 'as a child'" (Introduction 6). Nonetheless, as Thacker and a growing number of others demonstrate, many children's books are important as "vehicles for artistic expression" and "expressions of aesthetic concerns" of the sort readers take for granted in much so-called adult literature. Still, since Baum regarded himself primarily as a writer for children, and since people remember him primarily in that way, critics have tended and still tend to regard his works as having "low status."

C. S. Lewis writes of what he calls "three ways of writing for children": "writing for children as a special department of 'giving the public what it wants'"; writing for "a particular child"; and what Lewis calls the only way that he can write a children's story, "writing a children's story because a children's story is the best art-form for something you have to say [...]" (208). For our purposes, whether Lewis is entirely honest here — and I do not think he is — about his own method of writing is beside the point. What matters is that Baum unabashedly claimed to be writing for children, to give the child public, as Lewis says, "what it wants." In his note "To My Readers" in his fifth Oz book, *The Road to Oz*, for example, Baum states point blank, "[...] I write only to please children [...]" (n. pag.). According to Thacker, this statement and similar statements of Baum confirmed, "for the public, the status of children's literature as popular and unliterary" ("*Wonderful Wizard*" 90).

However, in his statement about writing "only to please children," Baum undoubtedly is distorting the truth. As Hunt indicates, "the writers and manipulators of children's books are adults" (*An Introduction* 2), and as Clark points out, "children's literature is always written for both children and adults; to be published it needs to please at least some adults" (96). Clark is basically correct. Hunt asserts that "the core of children's literature rests on those books that are primarily for children, but which satisfy adults, either when they are reading as quasi-children (taking on an implied role) or when they are responding as adults" (*An Introduction* 14). Baum's Oz books fit Hunt's category: they have things within them that satisfy child and adult readers, even if those adult readers respond as adults only. Baum certainly wrote to please both children and adults. In *As Far As Yesterday* Edward Wagenknecht understates when he writes, "I am not sure that the children understand all the humor and satire in the Oz books" (77). Wagenknecht's booklet about Oz, *Utopia Americana*, published in 1929, is the first study of the Oz books by a serious literary scholar. In that booklet is an earlier version of the sentence just quoted above; the 1929 version reads, "There is one element in the Oz books that the children probably do not get, and that is the element of satire" (33–34). The addition of "humor" in Wagenknecht's later book seems significant: it points to Wagenknecht's growing understanding of the sophistication of the Oz books. Still, though many adults read Baum's Oz books with great pleasure and though he undoubtedly did not write his books solely for the sake of children, Baum's contemporaries regarded him as primarily a writer of fairly simple books for children, and that is how he is largely regarded today.[2] Baum's Oz books, however, are not so simple and not so "unliterary" as they at first seem.

Although Baum wrote some books for adults, such as *The Book of the Hamburgs* (1886), a treatise on a kind of chicken, and *The Art of Decorating Dry Goods Windows and Interiors* (1900), and he wrote many non–Oz books for children, including many series books under such pseudonyms as Edith van Dyne, Laura Bancroft, Floyd Akers, and Schuyler Staunton, his Oz books were his most popular during his lifetime, and readers remember him today mainly, if not exclusively, for them. As Martin Gardner points out in his introduction to *The Surprising Adventures of the Magical Monarch of Mo*, " *The [Wonderful] Wizard [of Oz]* was the first of fourteen Oz books destined to propel Baum into the ranks of the world's greatest writers for children" (vii). Partly as a result of the popularity of the 1939 motion picture entitled *The Wizard of Oz*, the Land of Oz and some of the characters connected with it are extremely well known throughout America and indeed the world. On the other hand, places like Merryland that Baum created in *Dot and Tot of Merryland* (1901), the Island of Yew that Baum created in *The Enchanted Island of Yew* (1903), and Mo are largely unknown. In addition, his Oz books seem to generate a kind of excitement that his non–Oz books do not, possibly because Oz and its neighboring lands are more clearly delineated than his other imaginary kingdoms, possibly because the characters in the Oz books are so exciting, and possibly because of the universality of his Oz books, a universality that comes from Baum's having drawn extensively in creating the books on traditions of myth, folklore, and various other kinds of literature that have stood the test of time.

Many readers also think of Baum's Oz books as a unit that presents some kind of unified history and conception of a single fairyland, even though they are really full of contradictions. Nonetheless, they do in some ways form a unified whole. Thus, I concentrate on his Oz books rather than the whole body of his writings. Moreover, in this book I do not give extensive, separate plot summaries of Baum's works; I try to limit summaries to parts of plots that seem necessary for the points I make. Excellent individual plot summaries already exist in several book-length studies of Baum that can easily remind readers of what happens in the books.[3] Also, the books themselves are readily available and are easy to read in terms of their plots. I also do not explore in much detail Baum's extensive influence on American culture. That topic too has been explored at length and with excellence.[4] I do, however, treat at times the effect of American culture on Baum's books in attempts to understand many of the things that are going on in his works.

At least Baum's Oz books no longer seem considered by many people to be dangerous for children, even though there have been times when adults attempted to keep them out of children's hands and out of children's sections of libraries.[5] Some fairly recent critics still imply that children would do well to turn elsewhere for their amusement. For example, in an excellent work published in 1997, Margery Hourihan calls what critics recognize as Baum's best book, *The Wonderful Wizard of Oz*, a "banal and mechanistic story" with a "contrived and predictable" plot. Hourihan writes of a "whining Dorothy," whom she labels, "the girl-woman of Hollywood." The book, she says, "reinforces" "gender stereotypes" (209). In spite of her reference to Hollywood, Hourihan here indeed claims to be writing about the book rather than the 1939 movie. However, Baum's Dorothy rarely cries, and when she does, she quickly stops. Rather than lamenting her fate, she accepts her troubles in a matter-of-fact way. As Jordan Brotman points out, she "faces death time after time in Oz with philosophic calm" (71). Also, she certainly is not a "girl-woman"; she is a little girl throughout the entire series of Baum's Oz books, especially the first one.

However, as Clark points out, "there continues to be some discomfort with *Oz* among adult readers" (135). Even some lovers of Baum's Oz often spend more time in print criticizing him than praising him, thus implying that the Oz books are seriously flawed and unworthy of careful study. Perry Nodelman, an extremely astute critic of children's literature, writes that the Oz books "are, quite simply and purely, and quite literally, wonderful" (12). He writes, however, about the first Oz book, *The Wonderful Wizard of Oz*, that it "may now seem to be the least imaginative of the lot" but adds that it may seem that way since "we have become so familiar with Baum's inventions" in it. Nodelman says about the later Oz books that they have "inventions" in them unlike those in other writers' works. Baum "does not often," Nodelman insists, "create his fantasy worlds and characters out of his previous knowledge of literature and mythology," and he calls Baum's "fecund and quick imagination [...] the most notable factor of his work" (10–11). Thus, he adds to the idea that Baum's Oz books are basically "unliterary."

Nodelman finds that the tension "between delightful fantasies that give and are clearly meant to give readers pleasure, and a healthy, very practical, and very American cynicism about the usefulness of such meaningless frippery" makes *The Wonderful Wizard of Oz* "interesting." But he feels that that tension does not result from any "conscious decision" by Baum "to explore it. Its presence seems to be quite accidental [...]. Had it been intentional and more fully worked through the book and its situations, the combination of unique ideas and careful craftsmanship" might have made the book "one of the two or three greatest of children's books." But, alas, for Nodelman, Baum was not a conscious craftsman and consequently falls short of his potential. As a result, Nodelman considers *The Wonderful Wizard of Oz* "a flawed masterpiece" that nonetheless merits "more admiration" than it usually receives from children's literature specialists. Perhaps demanding that a masterpiece have no flaws is demanding too much. Yet that seems to be the exact demand that Nodelman places on Baum. At any rate, Nodelman adds to the idea that whatever is good in Baum's works appears there accidentally. Even though Baum was a professional man of letters, he apparently was, many critics feel, an accidental creator of at least one masterpiece. Nodelman nonetheless says that the later Oz books have what he calls "a freshness and flavor like no other children's books," and some "have an intricate and individual imaginative consistency of their own" (11–12).

In *Children's Literature: An Illustrated History* Peter Hunt and his collaborators too mix praise and damnation. They say very little about L. Frank Baum's works, but of *The Wonderful Wizard of Oz* they write that "some commentators have suggested [that it] owed its initial success to its illustrations. It is generally agreed to be no more than workmanlike in its prose, and pedestrian — not to say utilitarian — in its invention. But, like other great myths, it refuses to lie down" (241).[6] They give no explanation of what they mean by saying that it is "like other great myths." Are they saying that it too is a great myth? It seems that way. But what do they mean? Nor do they explain what they mean by saying that it "refuses to lie down." Perhaps they are referring to its continued popularity. They also mention that its sequels, "by Baum and other hands, are very uneven in quality, and have been variously regarded as a new kind of fairy-tale, or merely the best that could be achieved by mechanistic minds." They mention critics' neglect of *The Wonderful Wizard of Oz* and repeat as true the probably incorrect idea that Baum named Oz after letters on a file drawer.[7] They admit to the book's continued popularity, "much helped by the 1939 film and Harold Arlen's songs [...]," and mention that the Oz books were "sometimes not allowed on to library shelves because they were thought to be 'poorly written'" (241). Thus ends their discussion of the Oz books. Nodelman then praises Baum's invention while Hunt and his collaborators call it "pedestrian." And both Nodelman and Hunt and his collaborators seem more comfortable discussing Baum's books' flaws than their good points.

Another example of the lack of respect that critics have for Baum's Oz books involves one of the most prestigious collections of essays about children's literature — *Only Connect*, edited by Sheila Egoff and others. In its first and second editions, Brotman's excellent essay on the Oz books appears. By the third edition, not only is Brotman's essay no longer present, but also Baum's name is given incorrectly as Frank L. Baum both in the index (405) and in the text of one essay in which the name appears (280). In one other essay he is mentioned, but there his name appears simply as Frank Baum (385). Does this set of facts indicate that more people than just Hourihan still feel contempt for Baum? Does it indicate that in an attempt to gain respectability, serious studies of children's literature must not only jettison Baum but also rob him of his name?

Baum's books' being best sellers and Baum's having written his books to make money complicate matters further for serious critics. Although there is some controversy about how many copies of Baum's Oz books really have been sold, there is agreement that they sold and still sell very well.[8] His fourteen Oz books are all still in print in various hardback, paperback, and electronic editions. Baum was and is a popular author, and for many literary critics, popular authors, other than, say, Shakespeare and Mark Twain, are suspect. Thus, Baum has several counts against him from the start as far as serious literary critics are concerned.

Yet toward the end of the twentieth century serious essays about *The Wonderful Wizard of Oz* began appearing, and a few critics wrote book-length studies of him and his works. They show that he is worthy of serious study, even though some critics still consider Baum essentially the author of one decent book. David L. Russell, for example, admits that *The Wonderful Wizard of Oz*, for all of what he considers to be its faults, is "an American institution," but he adds that Baum's subsequent Oz books are "largely mediocre," written "on the demand of his youthful readers" (15–16). Thus, Russell possibly implies that works written at the request of children are, of necessity, mediocre.

I hope that the following book *shows* that Baum is worthy of serious study. Deborah Thacker writes, "The marginalisation of writing for children and its link with popular culture place it in a relationship with definitions of high culture that are constantly contested in postmodern formulations" ("Playful Subversion" 139). If Thacker is correct, then it seems high time to engage in serious reevaluation of Baum's Oz books, works that remain popular but are so often dismissed as *mere* children's books and *mere* popular entertainment, not worthy of being treated in the same ways that critics treat parts of what Thacker calls "high culture." But as boundaries between so-called high and low culture break down, perhaps readers can give Baum a fresh reading, possibly seeing the richness of his works, a richness many critics insist just is not there.

Another obstacle to any serious study of the Oz books is Baum's long-recognized inconsistency. Although his inconsistencies bother some adult readers, it seems that they did not bother him and do not bother his child readers.[9] Baum really does create many contradictions between books as well as within books. Michael O. Riley voices the frustration some critics feel confronting these contradictions when he writes about Baum's second Oz book, "in regard to the details of the imaginary world of Oz, *The Marvelous Land [of Oz]* is one of the more inconsistent books in the series, and the discrepancies make it difficult to sort out which alterations were the result of a change in his conception of Oz and which were the result of carelessness and hasty writing" (104).

Most of the contradictions probably do involve "carelessness and hasty writing." Some involve simple matters of plot. For example, in *The Marvelous Land of Oz* the wicked witch Mombi says, "The Wizard brought to me the girl Ozma who was no more than a baby, and begged me to conceal the child." Readers know that Mombi is truthful here since, when she says these words, Glinda's magic pearl does not turn black. Ozma, in the form of Tip, is present when Mombi says these words (256). In *The Patchwork Girl of Oz* Ozma tells the Shaggy Man, "when I was a baby girl, I was stolen by an old Witch named Mombi" (219). In *The Wonderful Wizard of Oz* the Wizard is a humbug; he has no real magic. In *The Marvelous Land of Oz* Mombi says that in exchange for hiding Ozma, the Wizard "taught me all the magic tricks he knew. Some were good tricks, and some were only frauds" (256–57), indicating that the Wizard when he first comes to Oz has real magic. Even Glinda's palace moves around: in most of the Oz books it is south of the Emerald City; in *The Emerald City of Oz* General Guph says it is "at the North of the Emerald City" (38), but since he is a Nome, he may not know the palace's location. In *Tik-Tok of Oz*, however, the *narrator* says that it "stands far north of the Emerald City" (16). Changes of this sort seem to reflect carelessness on Baum's part.

Other contradictions involve the entire conception of Oz. As Michael Patrick Hearn asserts, "The world of Oz described in *The Wizard of Oz* differs significantly from that described in later novels" (xcv). Most of Riley's book is dedicated to showing how Baum's conception of the kind of place Oz is, especially its size, seems to change as the series progresses. Some of the changes are basic. For example, in books like *The Marvelous Land of Oz*, *The Emerald City of Oz*, and especially *The Patchwork Girl of Oz*, there are clear references to children in Oz who apparently grow larger as they grow older and do so relatively recently or even in present time. In *The Tin Woodman of Oz* Baum writes that when Queen Lurline turned Oz into a fairyland, "Those who were old remained old; those who were young and strong did not change as the years passed them by; the children remained children always, and played and romped to their hearts' content, while all the babies lived in their cradles and were tenderly cared for and never grew up" (132). In some of Baum's Oz books characters die. In *The Wonderful Wizard of Oz*, for example, witches die, and even in *The Emerald City of Oz* Billina the hen says that one of her children has "died of the pip" (65). In *The Tin Woodman of Oz* Baum writes, however, that after Lurline performed her enchantment, "no one in Oz ever died" (132).

Although some critics try to reconcile many of Baum's contradictions, they are ultimately unsuccessful. As a result of contradictions of these kinds, any attempt to see Oz as, say, a consistent eutopia — and there have been several — is doomed to failure.[10] Incidentally, Baum seems to have not really thought of Oz as a eutopia at all, although he may have at times felt that was a better place than the United States in which he lived, especially considering that he lived through the Civil War, the Gilded Age, the Spanish-American War, and most of World War I. Actually, Baum's Oz is from first to last in many ways a very frightening place.

In the "Introduction" to *The Wonderful Wizard of Oz* Baum writes, "Modern education includes morality; therefore the modern child seeks only entertainment in its wonder-tales and gladly dispenses with all disagreeable incidents." Baum adds that his first Oz book "aspires to being a modernized fairy tale, in which the wonderment and joy are retained and the heartaches and nightmares are left out" (ix). Many critics use these words as a guide to their reading of Baum's books. Barry Bauska is fairly typical, writing, "In Oz itself there are no real horrors. Unlike the ogres that lurk in "Hansel and Gretel," *Struwwelpeter*, or even "Cinderella," the witches and meanies of the land of Oz are extremely vulnerable [...]" (23). Bauska adds, "if monsters do turn up in Oz, they surely do not prosper there" (24n7). In his introduction to Baum's *Animal Fairy Tales* (a book first published in the *Delineator* in 1905 and in book form in 1969), Russell P. MacFall claims that, except in a non-Oz story published in 1962 — years after Baum's death — "The Tiger's Eye," "that reveals dark depths," Baum is "the otherwise sunny storyteller of Oz" (7).[11]

The Oz I find in Baum's books is very different from that of Bauska and MacFall: it is full of "horrors" and hardly consistently "sunny." Baum was, several critics believe, a better creative writer than critic; David L. Greene and Dick Martin, for example, write about Baum,

"Fortunately he did not succeed in leaving out nightmares and heartaches [...]" (12). His books are full of the stuff of nightmare, the kind of stuff one would want to banish from a true eutopia. The darkness in Baum's Oz books — the nightmarish stuff — was one of their main attractions for me when I was a child and still helps make them enjoyable for me. Drawing on numerous psychological sources, Deborah O'Keefe argues that being frightened while reading is not just fun for children but also psychologically useful (44–46). At any rate, Baum was a master at scaring children — and some adults. The following chapters describe a darker Baum than most critics see or apparently even wish to see.

In spite of what Baum writes, his books also include lessons in morality. Baum's own statement about modern education may lead a critic like Nodelman to write that "[...] Baum's refusal (or maybe his inability, but who really cares?) to provide his imaginings with an underpinning of meaningfulness probably does him in [...]." And Nodelman concludes that Baum "rarely offers any messages at all" as far as specialists in children's literature are concerned (12). Exactly what Nodelman means by "messages" is unclear. Baum's Oz books are full of moral teachings, and perhaps those are the kinds of "messages" that Nodelman has in mind. At Baum's best, the messages grow subtly from his texts. Usually, they are implied, but often they become explicit before a work ends.

Another obstacle to producing a serious study of Baum's Oz books is what critics call Baum's weak plotting. Even some of his greatest defenders — such as Katharine M. Rogers — recognize that his "plots tend to be weak and episodic," but Rogers calls this fact "beside the point, since tightly constructed plots are not desirable in all novels, especially those written for children. Baum's usual aim was to present a series of wonderful experiences rather than to drive purposefully toward a climax" (242).[12] Actually, how one can demonstrate that either an episodic or a cumulative plot is necessarily better than the other, whether it occurs in literature for children or adults, is unclear. What matters is whether the plot form or lack thereof is appropriate to the material being treated. Rogers is certainly correct about what she calls "Baum's usual aim," as Baum himself announces in his essay, "Modern Fairy Tales" (1909). Still, his "aim" seems less important than his achievement. Some of his books seem tightly plotted, and in at least one its episodic plot is entirely appropriate. Although he was often careless as he wrote, he also was often very careful, especially in terms of his plotting.

One of the most controversial aspects of this present book is the argument that some of Baum's books show a great deal of knowledge of various literary traditions; that is, he is far from being "unliterary." Jerry Griswold goes so far as to say that Baum's essay, "Modern Fairy Tales," shows that he "was no amateur folklorist. He was intimately familiar with the history of his genre and with the techniques of Perrault, the Grimms, Lang, Andersen, and subsequent writers who set out to write fairy tales" (32). He was, in fact, a professional writer of books, especially fairy tales, for children, something that in itself would indicate that he was steeped in fairy tales and myths and the stories in which those myths are embodied. He also seems to have been intimately familiar with other kinds of literature, apparently drawing not only on fairy tales and myths but also on epic, picaresque, and utopian traditions, and often he subverts the very traditions he draws on. In other words, he seems to have been a far more sophisticated author than most critics believe.

Another of the most controversial aspects of the present study is the argument that some of Baum's Oz books have fairly tightly constructed plots that tend to develop organically and that in most of those works characterization, plot, and setting complement one another in important ways. In his beautiful centennial edition of *The Annotated Wizard of Oz* Michael Patrick Hearn recognizes that *The Wonderful Wizard of Oz* "is [...] well structured." He focuses on the dichotomies he finds in the book, including recognizing that "Far from being prosaically anticlimactic, the second half of the book reflects the first" (xcix). I have written elsewhere on the way the hero quest helps structure the first Oz book ("Dorothy's Timeless Quest"). Deborah O'Keefe notes the circular structure of the first Oz book but claims that "the later Oz books [...] contain unstructured journeys rather than neat, circular plots" (56–57), a statement that is true of only some of the later books. For O'Keefe, "The task faced by Oz people and Oz readers is not, as it is in many other fantasies, understanding the shape of an intricately designed plot, but rather following a linear pattern and coping with one piece at a time" (57), again a statement true of only some of Baum's Oz books. In this connection, O'Keefe also asserts, "While Oz people don't develop or grow, they care about being themselves, avoiding vanity, and tolerating all kinds of other creatures" (60). Here, she is essentially correct, with a few major exceptions. In the first Oz book Dorothy grows considerably, and in the second one Tip grows so that he eventually is able to be himself (really herself), Ozma, rightful ruler of the Emerald City. In the third, *Ozma of Oz*, both Dorothy and Ozma grow. There are also a few additional exceptions. However, most of the characters remain static, so plot, setting, and character *development* rarely go together, but plot, setting, and character often do.

In the popular magazine *New Yorker* in a mostly positive response to Hearn's centennial edition of *The Annotated* Wizard of Oz, John Updike, almost always a perceptive reader, argues with Hearn's assertion that the first Oz book is well structured. "As a writer, Baum rarely knew when to quit," Updike asserts, "unfurling marvel after marvel while the human content — a content shaped by nonmagical limitations — leaked away." Updike says that in the last section of *The Wonderful Wizard of Oz*, "[...] Baum's tale dillydallies through further complications on the way to the Good Witch of the South, with fresh humanoid gadgetry like Fighting Trees and armless Hammerheads and a mechanical plot dependency on the Golden Cap and its three-wish control of the Winged Monkeys." Of the later Oz books Updike claims, "It is hard to read Baum's later Oz books without feeling the exploitation in progress, by a writer who only dimly understands his own masterpiece" (86). Thus, the idea of Baum as careless plotter even in his first Oz book continues in spite of some of the best efforts of critics to destroy it, and the idea that Baum is essentially "unliterary" persists as does the idea that the later Oz books are of even less literary value than the first one. The present book tackles all three of these issues.

A number of Baum's Oz books after the first are also fairly well structured, including *The Marvelous Land of Oz*, *Ozma of Oz*, and *Dorothy and the Wizard in Oz*, which are the second through fourth Oz books, as well as, strangely enough, *The Tin Woodman of Oz* and *Glinda of Oz*, which are two of his last three Oz books. Often the shapes of these plots become visible only after placing them in the context of other groups of works by Baum himself and by other authors. However, none of Baum's Oz books could pass what Wayne C. Booth calls "[...] Aristotle's twin tests of transposability and expungability of the parts [...]" (126).[13] In each are episodes that can be omitted without damaging the work as a whole and episodes that can be reordered without damaging the work. Even in some of Baum's more tightly structured works, some episodes seem present simply for the sake of entertainment and excitement. No organic necessity seems to exist for all parts even of *The Wonderful Wizard of Oz*. The encounter with the fighting trees (187–89), for example, seems irrelevant to the rest of the story although the adventures in the China Country and the forest are relevant. At the same time, however, not many books written for an adult audience, even those considered masterpieces, could stand up to Aristotle's twin tests.

All of Baum's Oz books involve some kind of quest or quests. That fact should not be surprising; as Margery Hourihan points out, "The tale of the hero and his quest has been the master story of Western civilization, and it has been especially ubiquitous in children's literature" (233).[14] What is surprising is the number of variations and even subversions of the quest that appear in Baum's Oz books. Often, quests provide structure for the books.[15] At times the quests attain mythic proportions of the sort Joseph Campbell discusses in *The Hero with a Thousand Faces*.[16] Yet in works such as *The Road to Oz, The Patchwork Girl of Oz*, and *Tik-Tok of Oz*, although quests are central to the stories and help unify their plots, the quests hardly attain mythic levels: individual parts of the plots do not contribute in significant ways to the growth of protagonists within these books, and seldom do individual parts of the plots have any organic relationship to one another except for the fact that each gets the protagonists closer to fulfilling or not fulfilling their quests. Moreover, in some books, such as *Dorothy and the Wizard in Oz, The Patchwork Girl of Oz*, and *The Tin Woodman of Oz*, Baum carefully subverts the very quests he sends his characters on, ironically showing them to be unnecessary.

Another obstacle facing the serious Oz scholar is the lack of an authoritative edition of Baum's Oz books. No extended work has been done on establishing texts; on collating or even comparing changes Baum (or his publishers) made during his lifetime, except for brief discussions of changes in two titles that occurred[17]; or on publishing the results of such studies in a uniform format. This book arbitrarily uses the Ballantine paperback edition of the fourteen Oz books, mainly because the books are easy to obtain at a relatively inexpensive price. Even the first edition of each work would not necessarily be authoritative; considering early twentieth-century publication practices, especially involving books for children, they may be no more authoritative than any other editions published during Baum's lifetime.[18]

One of the pleasures at the start of the twenty-first century of doing serious work with L. Frank Baum's Oz books is being able to draw on the large amount of serious research and criticism that has been published about children's literature in general and about Baum in particular, especially about *The Wonderful Wizard of Oz*. As will become obvious, part of my critical method is to engage in dialogues with large amounts of this work. Suzanne Rahn provides excellent reviews of Baum criticism and scholarship,[19] noting the often diametrically opposed readings critics develop and pointing out that some critics consider Baum's first Oz book "the only one worth mentioning" (*Wizard* 78). Still, several excellent studies of some of Baum's other Oz books exist, including one by Rahn herself.[20]

As the following pages make clear, my debts to earlier explorers of children's literature and of Oz are great. Much of the recent work on children's literature and on Baum is well written, provocative, and even exciting. It carefully examines an area of literature often dismissed as not worth studying and shows that is it worth careful examination, and it takes an author often dismissed as less than third rate and demonstrates his importance in the history of American literature, American culture, and children's literature. It also shows the kinds of dividends one can produce by examining Baum carefully.

I consider myself privileged to follow the trails blazed in books by general students of children's literature and literary theory like Beverly Lyon Clark, Jerry Griswold, Margery Hourihan, Roger Sale, Deborah Thacker and Jean Webb, and Jack Zipes, all of whom, incidentally, treat Baum specifically; in books on Baum himself by Michael Patrick Hearn, Raylyn Moore, Suzanne Rahn, Michael O. Riley, Katherine M. Rogers, and Edward Wagenknecht; and in articles by authors like Jordan Brotman, Stuart Culver, Fred Erisman, Nancy Tystad Koupal, U. C. Knoepflmacher, and Douglas J. McReynolds and Barbara J. Lips. I hope that the present study will be considered worthy of these pioneers.

The focus in this book is Baum's fourteen Oz novels. Examinations of his non-Oz books and his other Oz works, such as *Little Wizard Stories of Oz* and *The Woggle-Bug Book*, occur only when doing so helps illuminate the Oz novels. What this book discovers is that Baum is in many ways a product of his time. In addition, often he bases the plots and shapes of his books on a number of myths, especially the hero quest myth, and that he in turn creates in his books a series of myths often contradictory to one another. Not all of Baum's Oz books are equally worthy of careful study, even in terms of their structure, but many of them are. Yet in even his weakest Oz books he creates interesting characters and exciting plots that tend to hold readers' interest. And in his strongest books his characters and plots are unified in ways that help make his books extremely powerful.

I do not expect all readers to agree with my interpretations of Baum's works or all of my conclusions. In fact, I hope that all will not agree, for the richness of some of Baum's Oz books allows for multiple interpretations. My overall objective in this book is to show that Baum's Oz books are worthy of careful study. I hope that I achieve that goal.

1

The Wonderful Wizard of Oz
Dorothy's Timeless Adventure

In the preface to *The Wonderful Wizard of Oz* L. Frank Baum calls his book "a modernized fairy tale, in which the wonderment and joy are retained and the heart-aches and nightmares are left out." He tried, he writes, to eliminate from it "the stereotyped genie, dwarf and fairy [...], together with all the horrible and blood-curdling incident devised by [...] authors" of European fairy stories "to point a fearsome moral to each tale" (ix). As many readers recognize, however, Baum is a better creator than critic.[1] In his book Dorothy and her companions face "monstrous" Kalidahs with "bodies like bears and heads like tigers" (62), a witch "so wicked that the blood in her had dried up many years before" (132), and "a most tremendous monster, like a giant spider" (202); so the work is certainly not devoid of "blood curdling incident." Also, even though *The Wonderful Wizard of Oz* is in many ways "modernized," especially in its depiction of Kansas as a modern kind of wasteland devoid of fertility and in Oz itself in its reliance on machines, Oz is, as Raylyn Moore points out, "constructed of the stuff of the primitive unconscious, the darkly glittering building materials of all myth and fairy tale" (123).[2] Part of the strength of *The Wonderful Wizard of Oz*, moreover, comes from Baum's use of one of the oldest and most prevalent patterns available to writers — that of the hero quest — which he blends with his intuitive knowledge of ageless aspects of the human psyche.

21

Baum did not have access to modern studies of the quest hero, such as *The Hero With a Thousand Faces* (1949) by Joseph Campbell and *Deconstructing the Hero* (1997) by Margery Hourihan, or to modern studies of the psychological aspects of fairy tales, such as *Once Upon a Time* (published in German as *Es war Einmal: vom Wesen des Volksmärchens* in 1962 and translated into English in 1970) by Max Luthi or *The Uses of Enchantment* (1976) by Bruno Bettelheim. But he did have access to hundreds of myths and fairy tales. Drawing on them in creating his masterpiece, he structured his story the way tales — such as those of Odysseus, Aeneas, Jack who climbs the beanstalk, and Snow White — have been structured for centuries. In fact, it is surprising how closely Baum's work follows the basic pattern. To see *The Wonderful Wizard of Oz* simply as Dorothy's quest for a way to return to Kansas is to miss many of the sources of the book's strength, for like most quest heroes, Dorothy achieves far more than simply finding a way home.

According to Campbell, what he calls the monomyth — that is, the one myth that he feels lies behind most other myths — in its most general terms involves a "*hero*" who

> *ventures forth from the world of common day into a region of supernatural wonder: fabulous forces are there encountered and a decisive victory is won: the hero comes back from this mysterious adventure with the power to bestow boons on his follow man* [*Hero* 30].[3]

The main phases of Dorothy's journey clearly fit this pattern, except perhaps for the idea of her having boons to bestow when she returns, since *The Wonderful Wizard of Oz* ends immediately after she gets back to Kansas, and in the book she gives boons only to residents of Oz. But, as will become apparent, even in Kansas she retains the power to bestow boons. As Campbell points out, although the hero of myth may save his entire culture, a fairy-tale hero usually "achieves a domestic, microcosmic triumph" (*Hero* 37–38). Dorothy's story is, as Baum notes, basically a fairy tale; still, in Oz she saves two cultures — the Munchkins and the Winkies — by killing witches that enslave them and possibly a third — that of the Emerald City — by getting rid of the humbug Wizard that rules it, but she brings back to Kansas the ability to achieve only a domestic triumph.

In Campbell's more detailed analysis of the monomyth, a hero, "setting forth from his commonday hut or castle, is lured, carried away, or else voluntarily proceeds, to the threshold of adventure" (*Hero* 245). Dorothy's story begins with her orphaned, living with her Aunt Em and Uncle Henry in the equivalent of a "commonday hut." In fact, the house in the 1939 movie based on the book is palatial compared with the one in the book, which has only one room with "a rusty looking cooking stove, a cupboard for the dishes, a table, three or four chairs, and the beds. Uncle Henry and Aunt Em had a big bed in one corner, and Dorothy a little bed in another corner." The house has "no garret at all, and no cellar — except a small hole, dug in the ground, called a cyclone cellar [...]" (1). Stuart Culver is exactly right when he points out that Dorothy "lives in abject, not genteel, poverty" ("What Manikins Want" 99).[4]

The land around the house is also bleak:

> When Dorothy stood in the doorway and looked around, she could see nothing but the great gray prairie on every side. Not a tree nor a house broke the broad sweep of flat country that reached the edge of the sky in all directions. The sun had baked the plowed land into a gray mass, with little cracks running through it. Even the grass was not green, for the sun had burned the tops of the long blades until they were the same gray color to be seen elsewhere. Once the house had been painted, but the sun blistered the paint and the rains washed it away, and now the house was as dull and gray as everything else [2].

Dorothy's family's poverty in this wasteland is so great that in a later Oz book, in spite of his hard work, Uncle Henry cannot pay his mortgage and faces the prospect of having to hire Dorothy out to do housework while he and Aunt Em hunt for work (*Emerald City* 14–16).

Dorothy does not voluntarily leave home. She is, to use Campbell's phrase, "carried away [...] to the threshold of adventure" by what Baum calls a "cyclone" (4). At the threshold, Campbell writes, the hero meets "a shadow presence" guarding the entrance. If the hero defeats "this power," he may "go alive into the kingdom of the dark (brother-battle, dragon-battle; offering, charm)" (*Hero* 245–46). Dorothy defeats the power: she unknowingly drops her house on the wicked Witch of the East (12) and is thus able to cross the boundary between the world of reality and fairyland unharmed.[5]

In the typical set of monomythic adventures as Campbell describes them, the hero meets "a protective figure (often a little old crone or old man) who provides the adventurer with amulets against the dragon forces he is about to pass" (*Hero* 69). Dorothy meets no such figure before her defeat of one of those forces: the wicked Witch of the East.

But immediately after killing the witch, Dorothy meets a "little woman" whose "face was covered with wrinkles, her hair was nearly white, and she walked rather stiffly." This is the good Witch of the North, who freely admits that she is not as strong as the witch Dorothy has just killed (12).

Still, this little woman has great power. When Dorothy asks the good Witch of the North to accompany her to the Emerald City, the woman replies, "No, I cannot do that, [...], but I will give you my kiss, and no one will dare injure a person who has been kissed by the Witch of the North." She then kisses Dorothy, and "Where her lips touched the girl they left a round, shining mark [...]" (17). This "amulet," to use Campbell's term, provides Dorothy with protection in her future journeys in Oz, especially during her encounter with the wicked Witch of the West. When the flying monkeys the witch sends to "destroy" Dorothy see the good witch's kiss, their leader says, "We dare not harm this little girl, [...] for she is protected by the Power of Good, and that is greater than the Power of Evil" (128), words which, incidentally, seem to contradict the good witch's assertion that she is not as strong as one of the wicked witches. Nonetheless, instead of destroying Dorothy, the monkeys carry her to the witch's castle. Even the witch herself fears the kiss: "The Wicked Witch was both surprised and worried when she saw the mark on Dorothy's forehead, for she knew well that neither the Winged Monkey [referring to the monkeys' leader] nor she, herself, dare hurt the girl in any way" (130).

Dorothy also has another amulet, the silver shoes that were worn by the wicked Witch of the East. Although the good witch does not exactly give Dorothy these shoes, she tells the girl that, because she is responsible for the wicked witch's death, the shoes belong to her, and she "shall have them to wear" (15). Later, seeing the shoes, the wicked Witch of the West trembles "with fear, for she knew what a powerful charm belonged to them" (130).

"Beyond the threshold," Campbell writes, the hero travels "through a world of unfamiliar yet strangely intimate forces, some of which severely threaten him (tests), some of which give magical aid (helpers)" (*Hero* 246). The Oz landscape is indeed unfamiliar to Dorothy. Whereas Kansas is gray, dry, and barren, most of Oz is colorful and fertile. In Oz Dorothy almost always finds abundant food and water. Yet readers often notice how intimate some of the unfamiliar forces are that threaten and help Dorothy, so much so that the makers of the

1939 movie treat her adventures as a dream, thus making her journey entirely internal; and one critic calls Oz Dorothy's "vision of what is possible *in* Kansas" (Hansen 101). In the book Baum allows readers no such easy escapes. He gives no indication that the story must not be taken literally or that Oz is not an objective place distinctly different from Kansas. Still, Dorothy's journey functions on at least two levels simultaneously, with, for example, the Scarecrow being an objectively real character and at the same time representing Dorothy's ability to think, the Tin Woodman her ability to love, and the Cowardly Lion her bravery. In addition, just as Max Luthi sees the battle with a dragon or other evil force in a folk fairy tale as "not only a symbol for the struggle with the dark side of our unconscious, what is evil or sinister within us" but also "a symbol for the struggle against evil in the world" (80–81), so one can easily see the threatening forces in Oz, such as the witches, as representing parts of Dorothy's psyche at the same time that they are objectively real.

Dorothy's adventures certainly involve the "tests" of which Campbell writes. Invariably, she passes them, sometimes through ratiocination, at times mixed with magic, but more often through blind luck. Her deciding to call the field mice to help her find the way back to the Emerald City after she kills the wicked Witch of the West (144) is an example of the former; her destruction of the wicked witches is an example of the latter. She does not even know of the existence of the wicked Witch of the East until after she kills her (12–13), and her throwing water at the wicked Witch of the West is not calculated to kill but results from a fit of anger when the witch steals one of Dorothy's silver shoes and vows to steal the other (133–34).

According to Campbell, arriving "at the nadir of the mythological round," the hero "undergoes a supreme ordeal and gains his reward" (*Hero* 246). Dorothy's supreme ordeal occurs when she is sent to "Kill the wicked Witch of the West" (109), a task she accomplishes only after becoming the witch's prisoner and kitchen slave (130). Her ultimate reward is to return home.

Campbell writes that if the powers remain friendly to the hero, his reward involves such things as "sexual union with the goddess-mother of the world (sacred marriage), his recognition by the father-creator (father atonement), his own divinization (apotheosis)" (*Hero* 246). Obviously, the rewards Campbell mentions do not apply literally to Dorothy. At one point she seems to achieve a kind of father atonement when the Wizard agrees to take her back to Kansas, but he breaks his promise when his balloon ascends without her aboard (175). As Moore recognizes, Dorothy discovers that he really is "no great, helping father at all" (135).

Dorothy's real reward involves a kind of mother atonement with Glinda the Good followed by a reunion with Aunt Em.[6] On a psychological level killing the two witches is Dorothy's way of working through the anger a child inevitably directs toward a mother who she feels has deserted her, in Dorothy's case by dying.[7] It also may involve her working through anger that she feels toward her surrogate mother, Aunt Em. In his brilliantly suggestive essay, U. C. Knoepflmacher sees Aunt Em as a "repressive figure" and sees Uncle Henry as Em's "equally grim and sullen mate" (49). That the two of them are unable to play with Dorothy or to nurture her because of the lack of joy and laughter in their lives is obvious. Thus, on a psychological level, in killing the witches, Dorothy may be avenging herself on two figures in the very real world, her dead mother and her living aunt. In fact, Knoepflmacher implies that Aunt Em's life on the prairie before Dorothy leaves may be a kind of life-in-death when he says that, like the wicked Witch of the West, Aunt Em also has blood that has dried up (50).

Since Dorothy does not destroy the first witch in a face-to-face encounter and since Dorothy's mother has apparently been dead and she has been with Aunt Em for a long time (2), thus giving her anger a chance to grow,[8] the mother atonement that results from this witch's death — namely, the good Witch of the North's blessing — is too easily achieved to produce the proper catharsis for the little girl. Consequently, Dorothy's subsequent killing of the wicked Witch of the West, her journey to Glinda's palace, and her loving reception by Glinda involve a kind of additional mother atonement that reconciles Dorothy to her mother's death, a necessary prelude to her return to Kansas and her reunion with Aunt Em.

On another, more obvious, level, Dorothy's killing of the wicked witches, especially the wicked Witch of the West, is a sign of her growth. In killing the wicked Witch of the West, she is killing something infantile in herself so that she can be reborn not as an adult but as a more mature, more responsible child. Baum indicates that the wicked Witch of the West has characteristics of a young child when he writes that she is afraid of the dark and afraid of water (133). Thus, when Dorothy kills the wicked Witch of the West, she may be psychologically working through her anger at her dead mother and her living aunt and simultaneously growing herself.

At any rate, after Dorothy kills the witch, she and her companions act much more assertively. When the friends return from successfully completing their assignment, the Wizard tries to delay seeing them. The Scarecrow then sends the message to the Wizard that "if he did not let them in to see him at once they would call the Winged Monkeys to help them, and find out whether he kept his promises or not." This threat frightens the Wizard into sending for them since "He had met the Winged Monkeys in the Land of the West, and he did not wish to meet them again" (153–54).[9] When she first meets the Wizard, Dorothy introduces herself as "Dorothy, the Small and Meek" (107). When she approaches him after she returns from the West, she says to the Wizard, "You must keep your promises to us" (154–55). Her use of the word "must" shows how assertive she now is. The Tin Man and the Lion are similarly assertive after their encounter with the witch. The Tin Man says "angrily" to the Wizard's attempt to delay, "You've had plenty of time already," and the Lion tries to frighten the Wizard with "a large, loud roar, which was so fierce and dreadful that Toto jumped away from him in alarm and tripped over the screen in a corner," thus revealing the "little, old man" the Wizard really is (155–56).

"The final work," Campbell writes, "is that of return"; if the powers bless the hero, he returns "under their protection" (*Hero* 246). The powers in the form of Glinda the Good Witch of the South bless Dorothy. Glinda explains to her about the silver shoes, Baum's version of seven-league boots found in fairy tales like Charles Perrault's "Le petit poucet," a title translated into English as "Hop o' My Thumb" or "Little Thumb"; the shoes can magically carry Dorothy back to Kansas. Then, Glinda sends the girl on her way (216–17).

According to Campbell, "the transcendental powers" cannot cross the "return threshold" (*Hero* 246). In *The Wonderful Wizard of Oz*, when Dorothy returns, she discovers that "the Silver Shoes had fallen off in her flight through the air, and were lost forever in the desert" that separates Oz from the rest of the world (218). Thus, Dorothy successfully completes her journey.

In the final phase of the monomyth, Campbell says that the hero returns with a "boon" that "restores the world (elixir)" (*Hero* 246). Dorothy, however, is involved in a fairy tale, so her boon need not restore the entire world. In fact, it does not explicitly restore anything

"Home Again" is the label on this illustration from *The New Wizard of Oz* (illus. W. W. Denslow; Indianapolis: Bobbs-Merrill, 1903), p. 149.

in this particular book, although she eventually (in *The Emerald City of Oz*) is able to take Aunt Em and Uncle Henry to Oz to live out their old age in happiness.

    The Wonderful Wizard of Oz ends immediately after Dorothy's return, when Dorothy has not yet received the power to return to Oz herself, much less take anyone else with her. As Aunt Em goes "to water the cabbages," Dorothy lands "on the broad Kansas prairie" in front of the new house Uncle Henry builds to replace the one destroyed by the tornado (217–19). As Aunt Em's activity indicates, Dorothy no longer is in a land of abundance and fertility: she returns to a place of poverty, drought, and unremitting, often unproductive labor.[10] Aunt Em embraces the little girl and asks, "where in the world did you come from?" But Dorothy has not been in the world, at least as her aunt understands the term. So Dorothy replies, "From the Land of Oz. [...] And here is Toto, too. And oh, Aunt Em! I'm so glad to be home again!" (219). Where then is the boon that Dorothy can bestow on others? Is it simply her presence? If so, the book is true to the ancient pattern in all important ways except this one.

Actually, Dorothy gains several things that can provide boons. On a wholly material level, she learns skills in Oz that will stand her in good stead in Kansas, including doing housework, which she does in the castle of the wicked Witch of the West (130–35), and sewing, which she does along with the Wizard when they put together his balloon (174). Her sweeping the remains of the wicked Witch of the West out of the kitchen after she melts the witch and then her cleaning the sugary mess off her silver slipper (135) show that Dorothy carries with her the Kansas virtue of cleanliness and has learned her lessons about housekeeping well.[11]

Yet Dorothy brings to Kansas a boon greater than being able to sew and clean and thus being able to help Aunt Em with the housework. As one would expect after seeing how closely the structure of Baum's book follows the pattern of the hero quest, Dorothy's voyage is in part one of self-discovery and growth. Moreover, if the story is viewed on a psychological level, Dorothy's growth should not be surprising, for, as Luthi points out, "nightmares involving evil spirits that come to carry off the dreamer often occur during important transitions" (113); although her adventures are not a dream, for Dorothy the tornado is the equivalent of Luthi's dream "evil spirits." In addition, if Dorothy's adventures in Oz involve working through her anger at feeling that her mother has deserted her and that Aunt Em does not provide satisfactory nurturing to take the place of the absent mother, then Dorothy should be more mature when she returns to Kansas.

One critic writes, "Selflessness and loving kindness constitute the very air of Oz" (Bewley 206). Although, as the existence of wicked witches indicates, this critic exaggerates, selfless love is one of the main attributes of the good characters in Oz. In eliminating the wicked witches, Dorothy allows the "selflessness and loving kindness" even greater sway over the magical country and its inhabitants. Baum, then, in a very real sense, resembles the creators of folk fairy tales who, Julius E. Heuscher says,

> penetrate behind the superficial appearance of things and discover a beautiful, significant, harmonious world. This harmony is frequently expressed even in the structure of the fairy tale, based usually on the number three. This number has always and everywhere been expressing spiritual entities [...] [16].

Threes abound in *The Wonderful Wizard of Oz*, ranging from the three members of Dorothy's family to her three most significant helpers in Oz. Her adventures in Oz are themselves structured around three separate quests, first for the Wizard, then for the death of the wicked Witch of the West, and finally for the palace of Glinda. Thus, it is fitting that Dorothy's larger quest be for something more than a mere physical place called home. And in the course of her adventures Dorothy finds something more: she finds within herself the ability to participate in the selfless love that characterizes most of the inhabitants of Oz. Once she finds this ability, she is ready to cross the threshold back to Kansas so that she can bring joy and love into the gray world of Aunt Em and Uncle Henry.

In Oz Dorothy receives numerous lessons in selfless love, especially from those most selfless of creatures, the Scarecrow and the Tin Woodman. According to Campbell, the monomythic hero must learn to have no regard for what the Hindu monk Shankaracharya calls "this corpse-like body" (*Hero* 123). Both of Dorothy's principal teachers have no regard for their "corpse-like bodies"; in fact, neither has a "corpse-like body," since neither has a body made of what Baum in his Oz books calls "meat," although at one time the Tin Woodman did.[12] Thus, it is fitting that he, rather than the Scarecrow, be Dorothy's foremost example of love, even though her actual achievement more closely approaches that of the Scarecrow.

A kind of love even led to the Woodman's abandonment of the body. He loved and wanted to marry a Munchkin girl who worked for an old woman opposed to the marriage.[13] The old woman went to the wicked Witch of the East, who enchanted the Woodman's axe so that it chopped off pieces of his body, which he had a tinsmith replace with tin. Finally, he became all tin, but he says, "alas! I had now no heart, so that I lost all my love for the Munchkin girl, and did not care whether I married her or not" (46–47). The Woodman thinks that without a heart he is incapable of love and compassion, but his actions repeatedly show that he is mistaken. Instead, what he has lost is the ability to lust, that is, to engage in love involving the appetites of the flesh. His love becomes entirely selfless and is directed toward all creatures, as the following episode demonstrates:

> Once, indeed, the Tin Woodman stepped upon a beetle that was crawling along the road, and killed the poor little thing. This made the Tin Woodman very unhappy, for he was always careful not to hurt any living creature; and as he walked along he wept several tears of sorrow and regret [55–56].

He begins to rust, so that he must be oiled. Consequently, he says, "This will serve me a lesson [...] to look where I step. For if I should kill another bug or beetle I should surely cry again, and crying rusts my jaw so that I cannot speak" (56).

Thus, his love is so selfless that he inflicts self-damage when he harms another creature. As the narrator comments, using irony that most adult readers should recognize, "The Tin Woodman knew very well he had no heart, and therefore he took great care never to be cruel or unkind to anything." As the Woodman himself says, "You people with hearts [...] have something to guide you, and need never do wrong; but I have no heart, and so I must be very careful" (56). Having achieved a stage of love that few mortal saints achieve, he becomes for Dorothy an example of a selflessness that she, of course, cannot attain. But what she does attain is great indeed.

Her achievement is closer to that of the Scarecrow. As one critic observes, "The important result of the Scarecrow's adventures with Dorothy was not that he got brains from the Wizard" but "that he developed his affections" (Sackett 219). The Scarecrow's ability from the first to solve problems shows that he has brains all along; his great concern toward the end of the book for Dorothy's happiness shows that he too can feel selfless affection. In fact, after the Wizard departs, the Scarecrow declares that only Dorothy's inability to "be contented to live in the Emerald City" keeps the friends from happiness and that he is so grateful to her for bringing him his "good luck" that he will "never leave her until she starts back to Kansas for good and all," even though staying with her involves leaving the Emerald City over which he now rules (179–83). Dorothy meets the Scarecrow before she encounters any of her other friends (25); she takes leave of him last (217). Thus, he has the most time to influence her, so it is not surprising that she attains a degree of selflessness similar to his.

When *The Wonderful Wizard of Oz* begins, Dorothy is a selfish little child, laughing and playing happily with Toto "all day long" and showing no concern for her aunt, who smiled when she first married Uncle Henry but "never smiled, now," or for her uncle, who "did not know what joy was" (2). When she first gets to Oz, her only concern is to return home. She tells the good Witch of the North, "I am anxious to get back to my Aunt and Uncle" (15–16). Thus, she shows that her real concern is for herself, as does her reaction when the good Witch of the North tells her, "you will have to live with us": she cries not for her aunt and uncle's sake but because "she felt so lonely among all these strange people" (16).

As Dorothy recognizes, she is "only an ordinary little girl who had come by the chance of a cyclone into a strange land" (24). Her very ordinariness endears her to readers. Also, it hints that she has within herself the possibility of considerable growth. That she is potentially capable of selfless love, for example, appears when she first encounters the Tin Man and asks him, "'What can I do for you?' [...] for she was moved by the sad voice in which the man spoke" (42). Before her journey ends, the potentiality becomes actuality.

Shortly after Dorothy finds and oils the Tin Man, he and the Scarecrow begin to discuss which is more important, a heart or brains. As Dorothy listens to this debate, she

> did not say anything, for she was puzzled to know which of her two friends was right, and she decided if she could only get back to Kansas and Aunt Em it did not matter so much whether the Woodman had no brains and the Scarecrow no heart, or each got what he wanted [48].

Here, Dorothy shows concern neither about this typical nineteenth-century-American head-heart debate nor, more significantly, about her friends' desires. In fact, she is so unconcerned about the Scarecrow and Tin Woodman that she confuses what each seeks. Thus, her attitude mirrors the self-centeredness she displays earlier in Kansas where she plays with Toto all day while her aunt and uncle toil ceaselessly.

As she travels through Oz, however, she becomes more concerned for her friends and for her aunt and uncle. When the field mice help pull the Cowardly Lion from the field of poppies, Dorothy "was glad he had been rescued" because "She had grown so fond of the big Lion" (87). When imprisoned in the castle of the wicked Witch of the West, she risks her own safety to sneak food to the Lion, whom the witch is trying to starve into submission so that he will pull her cart (131–32).[14] And after defeating the wicked witch, she is very concerned about rescuing the Tin Woodman and Scarecrow (137), the former of whom the monkeys drop on rocks and the latter of whom they unstuff and leave in a tree (127). The earlier Dorothy who just wants to go home would have returned immediately to the Emerald City to get her reward — her trip home — instead of spending precious time rescuing her friends.

When she first encounters the Wizard, Dorothy asks him to send her back to Kansas, "where my Aunt Em and Uncle Henry are," because, she says, "I don't like your country, although it is so beautiful. And I am sure Aunt Em will be worried over my being away so long" (107), words that indicate that she is becoming less self-centered than she is at the beginning of the book. Even after killing the witch and reuniting with her friends, however, Dorothy still has some distance to go before she learns to love selflessly, as Baum indicates when he writes about Dorothy and her friends:

> Now they were reunited, Dorothy and her friends spent a few happy days at the Yellow Castle, where they found everything they needed to make them comfortable. But one day the girl thought of Aunt Em, and said,
> "We must go back to Oz, and claim his promises" [140].

The idea of returning to the Wizard and thus to Aunt Em and Uncle Henry is clearly an after-thought.

After the Wizard proves unable to help Dorothy, she travels toward Glinda the Good's castle. On the way the companions travel through China Country, where Dorothy asks the china princess whether she would be willing to go home with Dorothy and "stand [...] on Aunt Em's mantle-shelf?" When the princess replies, "That would make me very unhappy," Dorothy responds, "I would not make you unhappy for all the world" (196–98), thus indicating a growing concern for others. When she arrives at Glinda's castle, the little girl tells the good witch that she wants to return to Kansas because "[...] Aunt Em will surely think something dreadful has happened to me, and that will make her put on mourning; and unless the crops are better this year than they were last I am sure Uncle Henry cannot afford it" (213). Her specificity here indicates that she is thinking seriously about the needs of others. The Scarecrow then reminds her that without her help, he would still be without a brain and standing in a field. The Tin Woodman tells her that without her, he would still be heartless and rusting in the forest. And the Cowardly Lion tells her that he would still be a coward. Then, the little girl, who earlier does not care whether her friends' wishes are granted, responds, "This is all true [...] and I am glad I was of use to these good friends. But now that each of them has had what he most desired, [...] I think I should like to go back to Kansas" (215–16). The sequence of events in this speech is important: Dorothy puts her friends' happiness ahead of her own. As should be expected with such a young girl, she cannot wholly dispense with concern for self; she is no Tin Woodman. But like the Scarecrow, she unhesitatingly puts others before self.

Dorothy is thus a true quest hero who achieves what Campbell calls "a domestic, microcosmic triumph," at least as far as the real world of Kansas is concerned, taking with her from Oz the potential for bringing joy into the world of two joyless people. Having worked through her own feelings of anger, she can truly be "glad to be home again." Her return then is fraught with the most important kinds of consequences for Aunt Em, Uncle Henry, and Dorothy herself, for even though she cannot bring the silver shoes with her, her adventures in Oz enable her to grow so that she can bring to Kansas a much more powerful source of magic, one of the most powerful sources in or out of fairyland — the ability to love selflessly. That the boon is not lost on Aunt Em is shown by the way she reacts when Dorothy returns: she becomes a nurturing, loving surrogate mother. Dorothy lands on the prairie and sees Aunt Em. Then, Baum writes, "'My darling child!' she [Aunt Em] cried, folding the little girl in her arms and covering her face with kisses [...]" (219). Here, for the first time in this book, Aunt Em reacts with joy and love, the kind of reaction that seems impossible for the woman described earlier as having no sparkle in her eye, never smiling, and pressing "her hand upon her heart whenever Dorothy's merry voice reached her ears [...]" (2). Hearn notes that "Aunt Em has changed remarkably in Dorothy's absence. She now knows how much Dorothy means to her and can finally express her deep love for her niece" (356). Perhaps Hearn is right; however, Baum tells readers nothing about what happens to Aunt Em when Dorothy is away. Aunt Em's change may occur not during Dorothy's absence but at the moment Dorothy returns. Perhaps Dorothy's ability to give selfless love enables Aunt Em to do the same.

Thus, Baum uses the timeless stuff of myth, fairy tale, and human psychology to structure *The Wonderful Wizard of Oz*. His "modernized fairy tale" has within it elements as old as the oldest oral literature with which scholars are familiar. By skillfully using these elements to structure his book and to provide some of its content, Baum makes Dorothy's quest universal and timeless and makes *The Wonderful Wizard of Oz* an object of enduring interest.

2

The Wonderful Wizard of Oz
THE WIZARD HIMSELF

Shortly after Dorothy arrives in Oz, the good Witch of the North tells her in a whisper: "Oz himself is the Great Wizard [...]. He is more powerful than all the rest of us together" (15). The whisper may indicate the awe in which she holds the Wizard. A few minutes later, when Dorothy asks about the Wizard, "Is he a good man?" the good Witch of the North replies, "He is a good Wizard. Whether he is a man or not I cannot tell, for I have never seen him" (17). The Wizard, of course, has her and the other inhabitants of the Land of Oz fooled, a fact that Dorothy discovers later in the book. When Dorothy, the Scarecrow, the Tin Man, the Cowardly Lion, and Toto expose the Wizard as a humbug, Dorothy says to him, "I think you are a very bad man," to which he replies, "Oh, no, my dear. I'm really a very good man; but I'm a very bad Wizard, I must admit" (162). As late as the *Emerald City of Oz* Dorothy echoes the Wizard's words and sentiments, saying, "You were always a good man [...] even when you were a bad wizard" (246).

That he is in the first Oz book a very bad Wizard is indisputable. He is certainly not the central character in the book — Dorothy is. But the book's title makes him prominent, to say the least.[1] The title of the book when it was first published, *The Wonderful Wizard of Oz*, is, it seems, ironic, for the Wizard is not wonderful in the usual way for a wizard. Still, that he is able to fool so many people over such a long period of time is wonderful. It would even be unbelievable if readers did not have in the example of the Tin Man, the Scarecrow, and the Lion proof of Baum's recognition that some people want to be fooled, demand to be fooled, even after the truth slaps them in their faces. However, whether the Wizard is a good man is a different question. That he is important in the book that bears his name is obvious, so it seems worthwhile to treat him in some detail.

When the Wizard first arrives in Oz riding in his balloon, the inhabitants greet him as "a great Wizard," an idea of which he does not disabuse them, he says, "because they were afraid of me, and promised to do anything I wished them to" (160–61). He apparently has no scruples about using their fear to enable him to become and remain their ruler. "Just to amuse myself, and keep the good people busy," the Wizard says, "I ordered them to build this City, and my palace; and they did it all willingly and well." He calls it the Emerald City because "the country was so green and beautiful," he tells Dorothy and her friends, "and to make the name fit better I put green spectacles on all the people, so that everything they saw was green" (161). Thus from the first, he does not hesitate to use their fear and his humbuggery to produce a kind of stability in his kingdom. Sarah Gilead finds in fantasy a link between "modern culture" and "the lost wholeness and stability of an imagined (and largely imaginary) past" (288). Having lived through the American Civil War and the corruption of the Gilded Age, Baum probably felt that political stability is important, an idea clearly reflected in his Oz books, four of which deal directly with attempts to overthrow the government of Oz.[2] Still, until Dorothy arrives in Oz, the wicked witches provide their subjects also with a kind of political stability that is clearly not praiseworthy. Even though the Wizard through fear forces his subjects to do things, they apparently do them gladly and even see some of them as gifts from him rather than things they do themselves; when the Wizard leaves Oz, for example, Baum writes:

> the people always remembered him lovingly, and said to one another, "Oz was always our friend. When he was here he built for us this beautiful Emerald City, and now he is gone he has left the Wise Scarecrow to rule over us" [177].

Thus, he is a better ruler than the wicked witches, whose people both hate and fear them, even though his rule is designed primarily to protect and serve the Wizard, not to protect and serve the people.

The Wizard admits that he hides from his people: "Usually," he says, "I will not see even my subjects, and so they believe I am something terrible" (158). Not even the soldier who guards the Palace has seen him (103). The Wizard also fears that Dorothy and her companions will reveal his true identity to his people. One of the reasons he is willing to try to take Dorothy back to Kansas by balloon is that he is tired of hiding from his people and afraid of exposure:

> [...] I am tired of being such a humbug. If I should go out of this Palace my people would soon discover I am not a Wizard, and then they would be vexed with me for having deceived them. So I have to stay shut up in these rooms all day, and it gets tiresome [173].

Thus, like most rulers who rule by fear, he in turn fears his subjects.

Yet he fears the wicked witches even more than he fears his people, "for," he explains, "while I had no magical powers at all I soon found out that the Witches were really able to do wonderful things." The Witches of the North and South are good, so he does not fear them, "but the Witches of the East and West were terribly wicked, and had they not thought I was more powerful than they themselves, they would surely have destroyed me. As it was, I lived in deadly fear of them for many years [...]" (161–62).

Does a good man deliberately intimidate people into doing what he wants done? Possibly, if he truly believes that the thing wanted done is for the good of all. And yes, the killing of the wicked Witch of the West is for the good of all, but especially for the good of the Wizard himself, who apparently dreads some kind of retribution for an unsuccessful attack he made on her kingdom. But does a good man terrify people the way the Wizard does a child, a straw man, a man made of tin, and a timorous lion?[3] When Dorothy first sees the Wizard, he appears to her as "an enormous Head, without body to support it or any arms or legs whatever. There was no hair upon his head, but it had eyes and nose and mouth and was much bigger than the head of the biggest giant" (106). That this form would be more appropriate for the Scarecrow who seeks a brain than for Dorothy who seeks home shows the Wizard's lack of sensitivity, but not necessarily his lack of goodness. That it causes Dorothy to stare "in wonder and fear" (106) may show lack of goodness. His saying to Dorothy, "In this country everyone must pay for everything he gets" (109), contradicts his own being made ruler of the Emerald City with no payment on his part, again showing lack of goodness. His asking Dorothy to "Kill the wicked

Witch of the West," and promising that "when you can tell me she is dead I will send you back to Kansas" (109), certainly does not show goodness. He asks her to do what he could not do himself, and he promises her what he cannot deliver. Moreover, he sends her to conquer an adversary of which he is terrified.

When he appears to the Scarecrow as "a most lovely Lady" "dressed in green silk gauze," wearing "upon flowing green locks a crown of jewels" and equipped with "wings, gorgeous in color" (109–10), he shows himself in a form more appropriate for the Tin Man, who seeks a heart, rather than the Scarecrow. Again, this may show lack of sensitivity rather than lack of goodness. Still, he makes the same demand of the Scarecrow — "kill for me the Wicked Witch of the West," and again makes a promise he cannot fulfill: "[...] I will bestow upon you a great many brains, and such good brains that you will be the wisest man in all the Land of Oz" (111).

When the Wizard appears to the Tin Woodman as "a terrible Beast" "nearly as big as an elephant" with "a head like that of a rhinoceros, only there were five eyes in its face. There were five long arms growing out of its body, and also it had five long, slim legs. Thick, wooly hair covered every part of it, and a more dreadful-looking monster could not be imagined" (114), he again shows his lack of sensitivity. The Lion, not the Tin Man, wants to be King of the Beasts. Still, he does not necessarily show lack of goodness. The Tin Man, without a heart, feels only "disappointed" but no fear upon seeing this beast (114). Yet the Wizard asks the Tin Man to "Help Dorothy kill the Wicked Witch of the West," and tells him, "When the Witch is dead, come to me, and I will then give you the biggest and kindest and most loving heart in all the Land of Oz" (115), again asking one to do what he himself fears to do and promising something in return that he cannot deliver.

When the Wizard appears to the Lion as "a Ball of Fire, so fierce and glowing that [the Lion] could scarcely bear to gaze upon it" and with heat "so intense that it singed his whiskers" (115–16), the Wizard again shows lack of sensitivity: Dorothy, not the Lion, seeks the sunscalded land of Kansas. But he does not necessarily show lack of goodness, except that he terrifies the Lion and says, "Bring me proof that the Wicked Witch is dead, and that moment I will give you courage" (116), again demanding what he cannot achieve himself and promising what he cannot give.

Does a good man send a little girl, a Scarecrow, a Tin Man, and a Cowardly Lion to confront and kill a wicked witch of whom he is terribly afraid? Does a good man promise things he knows he cannot deliver?

At any rate, after Dorothy kills the wicked Witch of the West, she and her companions act much more assertively. When the friends return from successfully completing their assignment, the Wizard tries to delay seeing them. When greeted with this delay, the Scarecrow sends the message to the Wizard that "if he did not let them in to see him at once they would call the Winged Monkeys to help them, and find out whether he kept his promises or not." This threat frightens the Wizard into sending for them since "He had met the Winged Monkeys in the Land of the West, and he did not wish to meet them again" (153–54).

Why did such a humbug go into the West? His statement to Dorothy, quoted earlier, that he "soon found out that the Witches were really able to do wonderful things" (161), implies that he at first guessed that the wicked Witch of the West was as big a humbug as he was and consequently thought, like a good American imperialist, that he could extend his reign into her country, an idea of which he apparently was quickly disabused when he encountered the flying monkeys.

When she first meets the Wizard, Dorothy introduces herself as "Dorothy, the Small and Meek" (107). When she approaches him after she returns from the West, she demands, "You must keep your promises to us!" (154–55). The Tin Man says "angrily" to the Wizard, "You've had plenty of time already," and the Lion tries to frighten the Wizard with "a large, loud roar, which was so fierce and dreadful that Toto jumped away from him in alarm and tripped over the screen in a corner," thus revealing the "little, old man" the Wizard really is (155–56). When unveiled, he reacts with fear, revealing himself for the coward he is, saying: "I am Oz, the Great and Terrible, [...] but don't strike me — please don't! — and I'll do anything you ask" (156). Instead of being a magnificent Wizard, he appears to be a clown.

Even though they discover that the Wizard has no magical powers, three of the four comrades demand that the Wizard fulfill his promises to them. The Wizard pretends to provide the Scarecrow with a brain in the form of pins and needles and bran (230); actually, he is fooling the Scarecrow into thinking he is getting something of value when he is not. He does the same with Dorothy's other two companions:

the Tin Man gets a heart made of silk and stuffed with sawdust (233); and in a joke many of Baum's adult readers especially appreciate, he provides the Lion with courage "out of a square green bottle" (234). The Lion thus drinks his courage, a clear indication that the Wizard provides him with nothing of value. Knowing these gifts are useless, the Wizard rationalizes his humbuggery by saying to himself, "How can I help being a humbug [...] when all these people make me do things that everybody knows can't be done?" (235). According to Zeese Papanikolas, "the Wizard has discovered, albeit a bit sadly, his subjects' incessant need to be fooled" (105). However, living in Oz, they know that they live in a land in which magic works, and they think their Wizard can work that magic. Unlike the comrades, the people do not know that he is a humbug. Moreover, the Wizard knows full well that each of Dorothy's three companions already has what he desires. The Wizard simply fools them into believing he gives them what they already have. His explanation that he cannot "help being a humbug," is clearly a rationalization. The Wizard uses it to enable him to fool himself into thinking that he can in good conscience continue his self-serving rule.

At the end of the first Oz book the Tin Man and Scarecrow replace the wicked Witch of the West and the Wizard, and the Cowardly Lion rules in the forest as King of the Beasts, introducing possibilities of benevolent rule to places hitherto governed by rulers either unconcerned with the well-being of their subjects or, in the case of the Wizard, who may have some concern for his subjects, unable to keep the peace except through humbuggery and afraid to interact with his subjects. Moreover, Glinda, who has true magical powers at her command, shows her lack of corruption and her commitment to good rule when she uses the magic powers of the golden cap for the last time to have the winged monkeys carry the Scarecrow, the Tin Man, and the Lion to their kingdoms.

Jack Zipes theorizes that Baum created Oz "to express his disenchantment with America, if not with the course of western civilization in general." According to Zipes, Baum felt that "The American dream had no chance against the real American world of finance" that caused "the chances for the realization of utopia in America" to be "cancelled [sic] and forfeited" (121, 130). Michael O. Riley more moderately and probably accurately writes that Baum's Oz books reflect Baum's concern "about some of the directions America was taking — directions

"Exactly so! I am a humbug."

"Exactly so! I am a humbug," says the Wizard in the caption for this illustration from *The New Wizard of Oz* (illus. W. W. Denslow; Indianapolis: Bobbs-Merrill, 1903), p. 149.

that decreased the wonder, beauty, and quality of life in the country" (194). That Baum had at least a mild interest in politics and political movements and that he worked his interest into his Oz books is well documented.[4]

Little evidence exists that Baum's use of politics in the Oz books refers to specific political episodes or that it is in any way consistent. In their biography of Baum, Baum's son, Frank Joslyn Baum, and Russell P. MacFall assert that "[...] Baum was a story teller, not a social critic" and that even though Baum marched, they write, for William Jennings Bryan, whom MacFall and F. J. Baum call "the spokesman of agrarian discontent," and even though Baum "had felt the bitter breath of failure and hard times in the Dakota territory" and "had suffered [...] long, lean years in Chicago," "he did not," they write, "turn to resentful social criticism" (124). Yet in spite of what F. J. Baum and MacFall write, there is even reason to believe that Baum, basically a Republican, never supported the Populists, the Democrats, or William Jennings Bryan.[5] So statements about his political discontent, especially ones as immoderate as Zipes', seem based more on wishful thinking than any kind of evidence. Baum's few explicit statements of social criticism in his Oz books may not represent Baum's own true beliefs. After all, it is important to remember that it is often very difficult to read one's beliefs from one's works of fiction.

Yet Baum fairly consistently shows in his Oz books that he feels that a ruler should provide political stability, but it is even more important that a ruler should be honest and forthright and that the ruler's greatest responsibility is to her or his people. In Oz book after Oz book, the mark of a good ruler is his or her ability to make his or her subjects content. In *The Marvelous Land of Oz,* when the Tin Woodman asks the Scarecrow, "Are your subjects happy and contented [...]" (119), he voices what seems to be Baum's main standard for a ruler in Oz. By this standard alone, the Wizard does not seem too bad, although the people are happy and contented because that happiness and contentment serves the Wizard's needs, not because the Wizard cares about them. And how complete can their contentment be since they fear the Wizard?

Thus, it is not so easy to evaluate the Wizard in terms of his being a purely good or bad man. It is easy to see that he is a very bad Wizard. It is easy to see that his rule over the Emerald City is selfish, designed primarily for his own protection. But his subjects do not resent that rule; they even seem to respect and love as well as fear him. On the other hand, Glinda's subjects seem to respect and love her without the fear. Does his being loved by his subjects make him into a good man of a sort? The answer probably depends on whether one believes that the end justifies the means. However, when viewed in relationship to the love and selflessness of Glinda, the Wizard is not a good ruler, much less "a very good man" (162), as he calls himself. He is a selfish tyrant whose own needs at times happen to coincide with those of his subjects, and whose subjects do not mind — and even enjoy — being fooled by him. He especially shows how tyrannical he is by sending Dorothy, the Scarecrow, the Tin Man, the Cowardly Lion, and Toto to kill the wicked Witch of the West.

Does the Wizard, who is clearly an imperialist, represent Baum's condemnation of American imperialism, an imperialism made so obvious during the Spanish-American War of 1898, two years before *The Wonderful Wizard of Oz* first appeared? Some critics see the book as anti-imperialistic or least as having anti-imperialistic themes in it.[6] It is nice to think so. Still, in a later book, *Dorothy and the Wizard in Oz*, Baum has Dorothy and the Wizard probably destroy a whole country; neither the two characters nor the author shows any regret concerning the destruction. That hardly seems an appropriate reaction for an anti-imperialist. In many of his books Baum shows a dislike of armies and a hatred of warfare. But whether the man himself condemned any particular war or even American imperialism is debatable. As David E. Stannard demonstrates, Baum did at least once "urge [...] the wholesale extermination of *all* America's native peoples" (126). Tom St. John goes so far as to assert, "The original popularity of *The Wonderful Wizard of Oz* was fired by the desperate public need of the white middle classes to put a happy face on terror, on the sordid land-grab for the land sacred to the Sioux" (351).[7] St. John clearly exaggerates: the original and continued popularity of *The Wonderful Wizard of Oz* is clearly "fired" mainly by its exciting story line, original setting, and intriguing characterization. As Martin Gardner notes, Dorothy is "an attractive heroine from Kansas with whom American children could identify" (Introduction, *Surprising Adventures* vii). The Wizard, too, is a character with whom children and adults seem fascinated. At any rate, Stannard, St. John, and Baum himself give compelling reasons for not viewing Baum as being anti-imperialistic.

That the personality of the Wizard is part of what makes Baum's book popular is undeniable. And the Wizard's personality is ultimately an enigma. Even though he is a humbug and a coward, readers, strangely enough, especially child readers, tend to find him a sympathetic figure. Even Baum may have found him sympathetic, for in later Oz books he rehabilitates the Wizard. Perhaps the Wizard's resemblance to the traditional Trickster figure helps explain the sympathy many readers feel for him. Although in the first Oz book he ultimately is not a Trickster since he lacks the supernatural element of the Trickster, he is nonetheless a kind of clown, a figure who in trying to impose order instead creates a kind of chaos, as indicated by his use of the green glasses to produce an impression of greater wealth than is really present. According to Campbell, "In the paleolithic sphere from which," he writes, the Trickster "derives, he was the archetype of the hero, the giver of all great boons — the fire bringer and the teacher of mankind" (*Masks of God* 274). The Wizard *pretends* to be this kind of hero and even fools people into believing he is.

But ultimately, the Wizard is a clown and a very unheroic one at that. Two Jungian theorists, Ann and Barry Ulanov, write, "The clown figure presents the direct opposite of the stereotyped heroic male, the opposite of the archetypal masculine principle as embodied in the image of a wise and effective king" (186). This description certainly fits the Wizard, especially as he really is and as readers really see him once he is unmasked. His having worked for a circus (160) thus makes sense as far as his role in *The Wonderful Wizard of Oz* is concerned. He is a parody of a good ruler, a parody of a hero, but nonetheless, like the clown, a lovable figure.

He really does embody some of the worst traits of late nineteenth-century America (and of twenty-first century America), including tendencies to put style before substance and appearance before reality as well as to rule through fear and intimidation. He also desires to extend the areas over which he rules, making him an imperialist. Baum depicts the Wizard as a bad Wizard. Baum also depicts him as a bad man who, in spite of themselves, readers find appealing.

The Marvelous Land of Oz
TIP'S PROGRESS

Baum's second Oz book, *The Marvelous Land of Oz*, has attracted some critical attention, but it still remains largely unexplored.[1] Yet it too is worthy of serious study. Much of the discussion about this second book deals with whether it has a good plot and with how sexist it is. As for plot, the book arouses diametrically opposed views. Raylyn Moore calls *The Marvelous Land of Oz* "a well conceived adventure" (168). Katharine Rogers asserts that it "is loosely plotted," with no "quest or other clear narrative aim" (122).[2] However, at the book's center lies a quest, and the book has a very serious, fairly clear narrative aim. The basis of the quest is established early in the book when, running away from Mombi, Tip says to himself that he never did like her and adds, "I wonder how I ever came to live with her" (24). The rest of the book in a sense answers this question. Through most of the book Tip does not realize that he is on a quest in which he is the central figure. That quest, moreover, turns out to be much more important than Tip can possibly imagine. Shortly after he wonders how he came to live with Mombi, the Pumpkinhead asks Tip where they are going. Tip replies, "You'll know as soon as I do" (24), words that turn out to be true in ways Tip does not expect since his ultimate goal is the throne from which he — once he is changed back into Ozma — will rule the Emerald City.

The discussion about the book's sexism seems slightly misguided. Katharine M. Rogers points out that "a few years" after Baum's marriage to Maud Gage, daughter of the pioneer feminist Matilda Gage, "he was committed to feminism [...]" (13). Although it is difficult to find a point on which Baum is consistent throughout his Oz books, he tends to be fairly consistent in his pro-feminist stance. In *The Marvelous Land of Oz* the central character is Tip, a girl whom the witch Mombi has magically changed into a boy. Eventually, he again becomes a girl, Ozma, who then rules the Emerald City. Central to the book is not Baum's feminism or lack thereof but Tip's education so that when he becomes Ozma, she will be a good ruler who, in part as a result of self-knowledge, will use her power for the benefit of her people.

Running through the book is a discussion of good rule and rightful rulers. At the beginning of the book the Scarecrow rules the Emerald City. General Jinjur leads an all-female Army of Revolt that deposes the Scarecrow. In Oz, however, the holder of greatest power is Glinda, the good Witch of the South. Her well trained army eventually helps her end Jinjur's rule over the Emerald City and put the rightful ruler on the throne.

After Jinjur revolts, the Scarecrow, Tip, Jack Pumpkinhead, the Saw-Horse, the Tin Woodman, and the Woggle-Bug join what they think is a quest to return the Scarecrow to what he initially feels is his rightful throne. In actuality, the companions all are part of Tip's quest: he unknowingly seeks two things that he must have for the sake of Oz's and his own future: self-knowledge and the throne of the Emerald City. Tip's innocent question about how he came to live with Mombi holds the key to the successful completion of both of these quests.

Early in their quest some of the companions go to the Emerald City, easily enter the Royal Palace, and seemingly conquer Jinjur, only to discover that they are themselves conquered. After the Scarecrow uses a trick (he releases some mice he has hidden in his straw) and scares Jinjur and her soldiers from the palace, the Scarecrow wonders whether he has more right to rule than Jinjur. "It seems to me," he says, "that the girl Jinjur is quite right in claiming to be Queen. And if she is right, then I am wrong, and we have no business to be occupying her palace." The Woggle-Bug, however, points out that the Scarecrow was "the King until she came, [...] so it appears to me that she is the interloper instead of you." Jack Pumpkinhead agrees and adds that the Woggle-Bug's words are especially true since "we have just conquered her and put her to flight." However, discovering that the Army of Revolt surrounds the palace, the Scarecrow realizes that Jinjur still rules the Emerald City and that he and his friends are captives, although it will take Jinjur several days to get into the palace again (169–71). The Scarecrow's thinking here resembles that of Jinjur, who declares, "The throne belongs to whoever is able to take it" (162). From this point of view, power alone makes one a rightful ruler. Yet in the context of *The Marvelous Land of Oz* this idea is wrong. In fact, a central question in the book is what makes a ruler legitimate.

When Jinjur later again captures the Scarecrow and his companions, she declares, "[...] I am more fit to rule the Emerald City than a Scarecrow" (164). But toward the end of the book, shortly after Glinda and her army try, unsuccessfully they think, to find Mombi in the city, the Scarecrow says that in spite of his dislike of being king, he is willing to rule temporarily until the rightful ruler, Ozma, is found, "for," he says, "I understand the business of ruling much better than Jinjur does" (245); and he is right.

Still, as Rogers indicates, both the Scarecrow and Jinjur are "undeserving and incompetent candidates" for the throne of the Emerald City (84). In *The Marvelous Land of Oz* the Scarecrow shows his incompetence through his silliness, especially in the chapter pompously entitled, "His Majesty the Scarecrow" (63–72), which is, incidentally, the only chapter in which Tip does not participate. In this chapter, since Tip is not present, he is not associated with this main example of the foolishness of the Scarecrow and Pumpkinhead, both males, whom the female Jellia Jamb easily outwits. The Scarecrow and Pumpkinhead continue being silly throughout the book. For example, the Scarecrow repeatedly argues with the Tin Man at inappropriate times about the relative value of brains and hearts. Also, in trying to find out what happened to Pastoria's daughter, the person who should be ruler of the Emerald City, Glinda discovers three suspicious actions of the Wizard: "He ate beans with a knife, made three secret visits to old Mombi, and limped slightly on his left foot"; of the three, the Pumpkinhead thinks the limp is most suspicious, and the Scarecrow thinks his eating beans with a knife is most suspicious (230). Glinda, of course, recognizes that the visits to Mombi are at least part of the key to the mystery of what has happened to Pastoria's daughter. Often the Woggle-Bug and the Tin Man join the Scarecrow and Pumpkinhead in their silliness, indicating that Baum pokes fun at both male and female characters in this work. His highest, unequivocal praise goes to two female characters, Glinda and Ozma, although much of the praise of the latter occurs when she is still transformed as Tip.

Even before Jinjur captures the Emerald City, she shows that she is not fit to rule. As Tip first approaches the city, he asks Jinjur why she wants "to conquer His Majesty the Scarecrow?" She replies:

> Because the Emerald City has been ruled by men long enough, for one reason [...]. Moreover, the City glitters with beautiful gems, which might far better be used for rings, bracelets and necklaces; and there is enough money in the King's treasury to buy every girl in our Army a dozen new gowns. So we intend to conquer the City and run the government to suit ourselves [78–79].

In these words and the scene involving the mice Baum seems a thorough misogynist.[3] Yet most of the book subverts the very misogyny that Baum seems to be voicing here. Actually, the problem with Jinjur is not that she is female — after all, Glinda and Ozma are also female — but that Jinjur's reasons for wanting to rule are frivolous and selfish; they do not involve the welfare of the people. As she tells her army, "We march to conquer the Emerald City — to dethrone the Scarecrow King — to acquire thousands of gorgeous gems — to rifle the royal treasury and to obtain power over our former oppressors!" (81). The Scarecrow himself recognizes Jinjur's avarice: when he and the other questers are in the jackdaws' nest, he remarks that since the nest is full of jewels, it "would be a picnic for Jinjur [...] for as nearly as I can make out she and her girls conquered me merely to rob my city of its emeralds" (220).

Jinjur repeatedly shows that she is unfit to rule. When the Tin Woodman asks the Scarecrow, "Are your subjects happy and contented [...]" (119), he voices what Tip as Ozma eventually recognizes is the standard for a legitimate ruler in Baum's Oz. Instead of caring for her subjects' happiness and contentment, Jinjur luxuriates in the palace, eating caramels (162) and green chocolates (268) while the "vain girls" in her army dislodge all the jewels from their settings in the "public streets and buildings" (270). To make things worse, after the Scarecrow first escapes from the Emerald City, Jinjur sends for "old Mombi, the witch" to "come to the assistance of the rebel army [sic]" (125). Any enterprise in which Mombi is willingly involved cannot be concerned with just rule. By the end of Jinjur's reign she becomes such a bad ruler that Mombi is Jinjur's "chief counsellor." Jinjur is even willing to see Jellia Jamb, one of her subjects, intimidated and transformed into Mombi's shape in order to protect Mombi from Glinda and thus perpetuate Jinjur's rule (238–40). Glinda demands that Jinjur surrender, but when Mombi suggests resistance, Jinjur agrees, for, she says, "it is so aristocratic to be a Queen that I do not wish to be obliged to return home again, to make beds and wash dishes for my mother" (238), again showing concern not for her subjects but herself. She has none of the compassion and concern a good ruler must have. Even the Queen of the Field Mice is more concerned with the welfare of her subjects than Jinjur is with hers.[4]

As her treatment of Jellia Jamb shows, Jinjur is also vicious. According to Tip, she wants "to make a rag carpet of" the Scarecrow's "outside and stuff their sofa-cushions with" his straw (99). When she captures the questers, Jinjur declares "gaily" to her captives:

> I bear you no ill will, I assure you; but lest you should prove troublesome to me in the future I shall order you all to be destroyed. That is, all except the boy, who belongs to old Mombi and must be restored to her keeping. The rest of you are not human, and therefore it will not be wicked to demolish you. The Saw-Horse and the Pumpkinhead's body I will have chopped up for kindling-wood; and the pumpkin shall be made into tarts. The Scarecrow will do nicely to start a bonfire, and the tin man [sic] can be cut into small pieces and fed to the goats. As for this immense Woggle-Bug —[...] I think I will ask the cook to make green-turtle soup of you [...].

Then, she "cruelly" adds, "Or, if that won't do, we might use you for a Hungarian goulash, stewed and highly spiced" (164–65). Her assertion that it is all right to destroy some of her enemies because they "are not human" shows the kind of sophistry of which she is capable. When the Woggle-Bug suggests that he could survive by eating Jack's head, the Tin Man exclaims, "How heartless! [...] Are we cannibals, let me ask? Or are we faithful friends?" (172).[5] He clearly recognizes the humanity of each member of the questing party. Even Jinjur's saying that she will not destroy Tip is sophistry, for she will give Tip to Mombi, and Tip initially flees Mombi when she is about to turn him "into a marble statue" (19). What the narrator calls Jinjur's "programme of extermination" (165) for her enemies indicates her heartlessness, so much so that the Woggle-Bug refers to her quite rightly as "this terrible Queen Jinjur" (171).

Jinjur's cruelty and indifference to her subjects make her markedly different from the two characters in the story who are unquestionably fit to rule: Glinda and Ozma. Glinda, a powerful sorceress, is loved by her subjects. Although in terms of our modern standards her riding on a palanquin carried by twelve of her servants (233) is horrible, there is no indication that this mode of conveyance is anything but respectable in Oz (or in Baum's eyes) or that the servants have any objections to carrying Glinda. A more important aspect of Glinda's fitness to rule is connected with Jinjur's assertion, "The throne belongs to whoever is able to take it" (162). Glinda, who is able to take the throne, disagrees: although she manages easily to conquer the Army of Revolt, she does so not for her own sake but for the good of the citizens of the city. She wants to put not herself but Ozma, whom Glinda considers the rightful ruler, on the throne and thus return good rule to the city.

In order to make Ozma the rightful ruler of the Emerald City, Baum creates a mythological background for the city different from the one given in *The Wonderful Wizard of Oz*. After the Scarecrow says that he got the throne from the Wizard and the Wizard "took it from Pastoria, the former King," Glinda responds, "Then, [...] the throne of the Emerald City belongs neither to you nor to Jinjur, but to this Pastoria from whom the Wizard usurped it."[6] When the Scarecrow points out that Pastoria is now dead, Glinda says, "Pastoria had a daughter, who is the rightful heir to the throne of the Emerald City." The Scarecrow agrees that if the daughter — Ozma — still lives, she should rule. Glinda calls Ozma "the real heir to the throne of the Emerald City" and Jinjur "the usurper." About Ozma, Glinda says, "if the people knew that she lived, they would quickly make her their Queen and restore her to her rightful position" (227–28, 231). Glinda's use of phrases like "rightful heir," "real heir" and "rightful position" and her statement, "they would quickly make her their Queen," indicate that for Glinda (and for Baum, at least in this book) one gets the initial right to rule legitimately not from power alone but from rightful succession and the will of the people.

Glinda eventually captures Mombi, and Mombi eventually says that Ozma was transformed into the boy Tip. Hearing these words, Tip cries "in amazement," "Why, I'm no Princess Ozma — I'm not a girl!" ironic words since his real identity is Princess Ozma, a girl. Tip adds, "Oh, let Jinjur be the Queen! [...] I want to stay a boy, and travel with the Scarecrow and the Tin Woodman, and the Woggle-Bug, and Jack — yes! and my friend the Saw-Horse — and the Gump! I don't want to be a girl!" (257–59). Unlike Jinjur, Tip has no desire to rule and certainly no selfish desire.

Tip's most explicit objections, however, are not to becoming ruler, although he does say, "Oh, let Jinjur be the Queen!" Instead, he objects mainly to becoming a girl. Yet neither he nor anyone else explicitly considers the possibility of his staying Tip and still ruling, although his desire to become Tip again if he does not "like being a girl" implies that he thinks that perhaps as Tip he can rule. Still, he is really she, and he must become what he really is. According to the logic that drives morality in *The Marvelous Land of Oz*, to be a good ruler, Tip must be what Glinda calls "honest" (260), and the only way he can be honest is to cease being the boy Tip.[7] He must be a female — that is his honest gender, and he must rule — that is his honest role in life.

After Tip becomes Ozma, Glinda easily conquers the Emerald City and captures Jinjur. Earlier, when Ozma is still Tip, he promises Mombi that the witch will be provided for "in her old age" (260–61). Ozma also releases Jinjur on promise of good behavior (283). Unlike Queen Jinjur (and incidentally, unlike the typical quest hero[8]), who wants to destroy her opponents, Tip/Ozma forgives her opponents, again indicating her fitness to rule. Baum asserts about Ozma, "although she was so young and inexperienced, she ruled her people with wisdom and justice" (270). Thus, she is indeed a good ruler as well as a legitimate one.

In the course of his adventures Tip learns many things a good ruler needs to know. He learns the truth of the Woggle-Bug's statement that "Appearances are deceitful" (192), especially from the reaction of the Queen of the Field Mice to the illusions that Mombi creates; the queen knows that they are illusions and ignores them (127–56). When Tip first discovers his true identity, he desires to remain Tip, something that involves a deceitful appearance on his part; yet after his transformation into Ozma, she shows no desire to assume a false identity again. In effect, like the typical quest hero, Ozma returns to her true home: being the female Ozma and ruling the Emerald City.

Tip learns, as the Scarecrow tells him, "In an emergency [...] it is always a good thing to pause and reflect" (92). He also learns to apologize when he is wrong (101). In addition, he shows an ability to command when he tells the Gump, "Come back at once, I command you," and the Gump obeys him (188). All of these things will stand Tip in good stead once he becomes a ruler.

In the jackdaws' nest that is full of money and jewels that the birds cannot possibly use, Tip learns the lack of value of worldly treasure

MOMBI POINTED HER LONG, BONY FINGER AT THE BOY. 271

"Mombi pointed her long, bony finger at the boy." From *The Land of Oz: A Sequel to The Wizard of Oz* (illus. John R. Neill; Chicago: Reilly & Lee, 1904), p. 271.

(210–11), a lesson Jinjur never learns and a lesson that points directly to Ozma's statement at the end of the book about the only riches worth having being "the riches of content" (273), an idea that is central to several of Baum's works. In the nest he also sees the Scarecrow willingly sacrifice his straw — his physical being — for the good of his companions (205), so Tip sees a model of selflessness involving one who recognizes the lack of importance of physical things. Tip suggests stuffing the Scarecrow "with money" once the jackdaws scatter the Scarecrow's straw (210), indicating that Tip also recognizes how unimportant material wealth is. Thus, unlike Jinjur, Tip as ruler will not desire to steal the Emerald City's jewels or raid the royal treasury to buy material objects. Like a true quest hero, then, Tip in many ways undergoes an expansion of consciousness. In fact, Tip learns in the course of his adventures, as Ozma tells the Scarecrow and Tin Man, that "the only riches worth having" are "the riches of content!" (273), words that echo the Tin Man's earlier question to the Scarecrow about his subjects' contentment and happiness.

The words about "the riches of content" also involve one of Baum's central themes both in and out of his Oz books: that contentment is more valuable than wealth. For example, in Baum's short story, "The Discontented Gopher," in *Animal Fairy Tales*—a work published in 1905, the year after *The Marvelous Land of Oz*—when the Gopher Fairies give Zikky the gopher a choice between riches or contentment, he disastrously chooses riches, ultimately exclaiming, "Contentment is best! Contentment is best! [...] Some day I shall seek out my mother and tell her I was wrong, and that riches do not bring Contentment" (64). In this short story, too, incidentally, Baum shows that his literary practice is often quite different from his literary theory: although he writes "Modern education includes morality; therefore the modern child seeks only entertainment in its wonder-tales and gladly dispenses with all disagreeable incidents" (*Wonderful Wizard* ix), he repeatedly teaches morality in both his Oz and non-Oz works. "The Discontented Gopher" is also full of gruesome material: Zikky experiences excruciating pain when he gets shot in the hip (60) and a boy cuts off his tail (63). Yet the story clearly exists for the sake of the moral, and the tale becomes preachy. In Baum's best Oz books, including *The Marvelous Land of Oz*, the moral lessons grow out of the stories, and often Baum arrives at them in fairly subtle ways. Still, Baum is sometimes even preachy in his later Oz books.

From Tip's interaction with his "child"—the Pumpkinhead—and with one of his other creations—the Saw-Horse, Tip learns the kind of nurturing attitude a good ruler needs. His desire not to leave Jack "to the tender mercies of old Mombi" (24), his concern for Jack when

Jack's head comes off in the river (101–03), his concern for the Saw-Horse's comfort when he has to pound a stake into the horse's back so that Jack can grasp it as he rides (48), and his "warm interest in both the Saw-Horse and his man Jack" (149), all show Tip's growing nurturing abilities that will stand him in good stead as ruler.[9] He shows solicitude for the Scarecrow after His Majesty gets soaked in the river (103–05). Also, when he sees the illusion that Mombi produces of sunflowers with girls' faces, which Tip believes to be "alive! They're girls!" (128), he shows that he learns concern that goes beyond his own creations, that is, beyond what could be considered his immediate family. That Tip would learn concern for others should, however, be no surprise, for through most of his adventures he is exposed to two excellent role models in that regard: the Scarecrow and the Tin Man.

Tip also learns about bad rule by observing Mombi and Jinjur. He sees Mombi use the power associated with magic irresponsibly to bring the Pumpkinhead to life so that she can test the Powder of Life and create a servant to replace Tip (13, 21); she intends to use magic to turn Tip into a statue (13, 19–20); and she uses magic to support Jinjur's vicious rule. At first, Tip himself uses magic capriciously, bringing to life the Saw-Horse and the Thing with the Gump's head that the questers construct to get themselves out of the palace. Still, both of these acts help others: the first provides something for the Pumpkinhead to ride, and the second enables the questers to escape from the palace and thus from Jinjur.

Tip sees examples of good rule in the Scarecrow, the Tin Man, the Queen of the Field Mice, and above all Glinda. From Glinda, Tip learns about handling power responsibly, especially in terms of not agreeing with Jinjur's idea that the throne belongs to whoever can take it. In fact, in Glinda, Tip sees an example of consistently selfless use of power. And as Ozma, Tip will follow the standard Glinda sets, ruling "with wisdom and justice" (270).

Thus, *The Marvelous Land of Oz* has, for the most part, an organic plot in which each chapter in which Tip is present (and he is present in all but one) contributes to his growth and to his eventually becoming an "honest" as well as a wise and just ruler. Even the one chapter in which Tip is not present contributes to the overall plot and meaning of the book by showing most clearly that males are as capable of being foolish as females and are quite capable of being fooled by females.

Like Tiresias in Greek myth, Ozma is at different times male and female. When Baum made Ozma become Tip and then become Ozma again, perhaps he had in mind teaching Ozma, like Tiresias, to understand and sympathize with her subjects of both sexes. At any rate, she obviously learns such sympathy somehow, for she becomes a truly benevolent ruler concerned primarily with her subjects' welfare.

Ozma's changes in gender may have even greater significance. Ann and Barry Ulanov provide a clue from Jungian psychology. "No woman," the Ulanovs write,

> is simply female; she also has, within her own psychology, dynamic impulses, symbolic images, and carriers of energy that reflect every sort of association with the masculine. The converse holds true for the male. No person of either sex knows who he or she is without conscious assimilation of these opposite sexual sides of himself or herself, however, [sic] formed — culturally, physiologically, whatever [9].[10]

Baum himself seems to have combined an entrepreneurial spirit with the kind of gentleness that enabled him to create sweet books like *Dot and Tot of Merryland* (1901) and *The Little Wizard Stories of Oz* (1914), tales aimed at very young children; thus, he seems to have been able to tap what in his day would be considered both masculine and feminine sides of his personality. Rogers carefully demonstrates that Baum's marriage "did not conform to [what were then considered] conventional gender roles [...]. Frank was the sweeter and more compliant partner" (14–16). From his own experiences, then, Baum may have recognized that Ozma's sex changes and her reactions to them give her true self-knowledge of the sort she needs if she is to rule others well. In the jackdaws' nest the Gump says that he would like to be introduced to himself as completely as he has been introduced to the other members of the Scarecrow's company. The Scarecrow replies, "That will come in time [...]. To 'Know Thyself' is considered quite an accomplishment, which it has taken us, who are your elders, months to perfect" (192). That the Scarecrow's statement is silly and whether the Scarecrow really has self-knowledge are beside the point here: what matters is that by the end of the book, Tip/Ozma is well on his/her way to having the kind of self-knowledge of which the Ulanovs write.

In the beginning of *The Marvelous Land of Oz* Baum writes of Tip, "he grew as strong and rugged as any boy" (2), giving him physical traits that Baum's contemporary readers would consider decidedly masculine. Also, Baum writes that Tip has "a love of mischief" (9), something Baum's contemporaries would have also considered masculine. However, Baum also calls Tip "small and rather delicate in appearance" (33), giving him physical traits that Baum's readers would also consider feminine. A later book by another author dealing with a character who changes from male to female — Virginia Woolf's *Orlando* (1928) — works in some similar ways.[11] Herbert Marder observes, "Orlando is androgynous from the beginning [...]"; his/her "change has had to do with externals, with accidents, not with essences" (114–15). In *Orlando* Woolf writes:

> Different though the sexes are, they intermix. In every human being a vacillation from one sex to the other takes place, and often it is only the clothes that keep the male or female likeness, while underneath the sex is the very opposite of what it is above. Of the complications and confusings which thus result every one has had experience [...] [188].

As Marder sees Woolf's novel, in the character Orlando "the two sexes" are "almost evenly balanced" (115). However, as psychologists recognize, not all people are aware of their intermixture of sexes, nor do all recognize the kinds of advantages they can gain from recognizing this intermixture.

Unlike Orlando, in several ways Tip is decidedly masculine, and Ozma is decidedly feminine. Yet when Tip becomes Ozma, Ozma draws on what Baum's contemporary readers would consider feminine characteristics that were present in Tip's personality, especially his nurturing abilities. Tip's first words as Ozma are, "I hope none of you will care the less for me than you did before. I'm just the same Tip, you know; only — only —" to which the Pumpkinhead responds, "Only you're different!" words considered "the wisest speech he had ever made" (263–64). As Ozma, Tip really is, as the Pumpkinhead recognizes, "different," but at least as important is her own recognition that she is "the same." Thus, at the end of *The Marvelous Land of Oz* Ozma can tap her masculine and feminine sides so that in a very real sense she is, at least in Jungian terms, in harmony with herself; in turn, her rule brings harmony to the Land of Oz.[12]

The general pettiness of the Army of Revolt and especially of General Jinjur, their desire for pretty dresses and jewels, and their fear of mice make it initially seem as though in *The Marvelous Land of Oz* Baum is supporting traditional turn-of-the-twentieth-century ideas of male superiority and patriarchal authority. Martin Gardner writes that Jinjur "is Baum's portrayal of a suffragette of the time" and "a typical

feminist, albeit prettier" (x), thus accusing Baum of harboring the typical masculine prejudices of his day.[13] Jinjur, however, seems typical of
nothing except male-created stereotypes, ones that Baum ultimately
subverts in this book. The rule of Glinda and the ascendancy of Ozma,
both of whom are decidedly not silly, and the silliness of the Pumpkinhead and especially the Scarecrow (a silliness best illustrated in the
one chapter in which Tip is not present), indicate that in this book
Baum subverts some of the very things he initially seems to support.
In Oz ideas of male superiority are ultimately inadequate, for it turns
out to be a country in which females rightfully rule. Learning many
things when she is Tip, but especially about her own identity and about
good and bad rule, and learning the traits she will need to be a good
ruler, Ozma becomes a considerate, compassionate, and beloved queen.

Baum's second Oz book then treats important topics, and although
the book is often humorous, it treats those topics in serious ways. It
introduces typical sexist ideas of Baum's day only to subvert those ideas.
Clearly, what matters in Baum's fairyland is not a ruler's gender but
the ruler's ability to rule well. And in Oz women can and should rule
and wield real power. According to Hourihan, "heroes are tradition-
ally male and the hero myth inscribes male dominance and the pri-
macy of male enterprises" (68). Yet the central quest in *The Marvelous
Land of Oz*, like that in *The Wonderful Wizard of Oz*, involves what
turns out to be a female hero. In turn, the quest leads to female dominance. The book involves a quest for the throne of the Emerald City.
Although through a large portion of the book the Scarecrow seems to
lie at the center of the quest, Baum ultimately subverts that idea and
shows that Tip is at the center of the quest. During it, he must learn
his true identity, a secret intimately connected to his early question
about how he came to be living with Mombi. And at the center of *The
Marvelous Land of Oz* and giving the book unity lies a tale of the appropriate education of Tip, who is really Ozma, rightful ruler of the Emerald City. As Tip learns during his quest, it is not might that makes a
ruler, much less an excellent ruler. Tip engages in no feats of arms, nor
does he lead any kind of army. Rather, the ruler's legitimate right to
rule, the people's desire to make the person the ruler, and especially
the ruler's desire and ability to wield power benevolently make an excellent ruler.

In Baum's Oz the good ruler is concerned not so much with him-
or herself as with the happiness and contentment of his or her subjects;

she uses her power to make her "subjects happy and contented," to use the Tin Woodman's phrase, or to give her subjects what Ozma calls "the riches of content." And she can do these things only if she herself is content, a state reached in this book through observing carefully and learning from the actions of others and having self-knowledge that results in large part from drawing on both masculine and feminine sides of oneself. Thus, the education of the good ruler is simultaneously the education of the good person, one who can experience and in turn share with others "the riches of content."

4

Ozma of Oz
THE FIRST UNDERGROUND JOURNEY

During the last forty or so years of the twentieth century, children's literature authors, publishers, and publicists prided themselves on opening up children's literature to the exploration of all kinds of previously tabooed subjects. In a book published in 1976, for example, Masha Kabakow Rudman writes, "until fairly recently, books for young children attempted to shield their audience from problems, dissension, and dilemmas of social import" (3–4). By "young children" Rudman means under age twelve.

But claims that "until fairly recently" children's literature did not treat "problems, dissension, and dilemmas of social import" — problems like broken families, child abuse, racism, religious hypocrisy, and alcoholism — are destroyed by examining a pair of works from the nineteenth century often classified as children's books and sometimes used in the elementary grades, *The Adventures of Tom Sawyer* (1876) and *Adventures of Huckleberry Finn* (1884) by Mark Twain. In addition, many of the fairy tales, relegated to the nursery during the Victorian era, are horribly violent. "The Juniper Tree," for example, treats mutilation, murder, and child abuse; and "Aschenputtel," the German version of "Cinderella," treats self-mutilation performed at the instigation of the two mutilators' mother: one of Aschenputtel's step-sisters cuts off her heel and the other her toe so that their feet can fit into the slipper.

Lewis Carroll's *Alice's Adventures in Wonderland* (1865), with its destruction of so much that above-grounders take for granted, including the idea of a fairly consistent personal identity, and with its repeated threats of extinction for Alice, also treats the darker side of life. Even a story as seemingly innocuous as *The Tale of Peter Rabbit* (first published privately in 1901) by Beatrix Potter involves what people now euphemistically call a broken family and the death of a parent, the father. Moreover, the violent cause of his death — Mrs. McGregor put him into a pie — is central to Peter's own adventures, since he faces the exact same possibility.

L. Frank Baum claims to have found the idea of writing books that disturb and frighten children especially unpleasant: in the Introduction to *The Wonderful Wizard of Oz* he writes:

> the old-time fairy tale, having served for generations, may now be classed as "historical" in the children's library; for the time has come for a series of newer "wonder tales" in which the stereotyped genie, dwarf and fairy are eliminated, together with all the horrible and blood-curdling incidents devised by their authors to point a fearsome moral to each tale. Modern education includes morality; therefore the modern child seeks only entertainment in its wonder-tales and gladly dispenses with all disagreeable incidents [ix].

As generations of children have recognized and as literary critics are just now learning, Baum was not true to his words. One of the reasons readers love *The Wonderful Wizard of Oz* is that it contains "horrible and blood-curdling incidents."

In addition, Baum's first Oz book has some dark, disturbing aspects that are, perhaps, neither "horrible" nor "blood-curdling" in the usual sense, especially the idea of the Wizard's sending a straw man, a tin man, a fear-filled lion, and a little child on a mission that he himself is afraid to undertake, a mission that by all rights should result in the child's death. The Wizard also promises the four adventurers, if they successfully complete their mission, rewards he knows he cannot deliver. This kind of darkness is not confined to Baum's masterpiece, *The Wonderful Wizard of Oz*. It is even more obviously present in several other Oz books, including *Ozma of Oz*, third in the series, a book which, along with the second Oz book, *The Marvelous Land of Oz*, became the basis of a decidedly dark movie, *Return to Oz*, released in 1985. Yet *Ozma of Oz* rarely draws serious critical attention. One of the best essays on it, "Beneath the Surface of *Ozma of Oz*" by Suzanne Rahn, argues that Roquat, the Nome King, is "a distinctly American kind of monarch — the industrial capitalist whose power resides in the monopoly he controls": Rahn compares Roquat to figures like Andrew Carnegie, J. P. Morgan, and John D. Rockefeller (29). In support of Rahn's idea, it is interesting to note that in one of Baum's later books, *Rinkitink in Oz*, Kaliko, who is in that book the Nome King, says to Queen Cor and King Gos, "as a matter of business policy we powerful Kings must stand together and trample the weaker ones under our feet" (203), making him certainly sound like the stereotypical capitalist of Baum's day. Although Rahn's ideas are highly speculative, she is undoubtedly right when she insists that *Ozma of Oz* "exposes various abuses of wealth and power" (30). It is thus like *The Marvelous Land of Oz*, especially in the jackdaws' nest episode in which the Scarecrow gets stuffed with money and in the episodes involving Jinjur's abuse of her power as queen of the Emerald City.

In *Ozma of Oz*, traveling by boat toward Australia with her Uncle Henry, Dorothy washes overboard clinging to a chicken coop. Along with a hen, Billina, Dorothy floats to the Land of Ev, just across the deadly desert from Oz. After a series of adventures Dorothy and Billina end up in Oz, and Dorothy eventually joins Uncle Henry in Australia. From the moment Dorothy in a terrible storm mistakenly thinks she sees Uncle Henry on the deck of the ship they are taking to Australia until the time the Nome King's enchantment of the Tin Woodman is undone, a sense of uneasiness and dread pervades the book. Central to the uneasiness is the discrepancy between appearance and reality. Things are not the way they seem, and they usually appear to be far less sinister than they really are.

In *The Wonderful Wizard of Oz*, when Dorothy first reaches Oz, the good Witch of the North explains to Dorothy that while Kansas is "a civilized country," "the Land of Oz has never been civilized" (14). Dorothy herself may be regarded as a civilizing force in Oz, at the very least bringing good rule to several parts of the land that are earlier ruled by wicked witches. When Dorothy and Billina first reach Ev and see writing in the sand that reads, "BEWARE THE WHEELERS," Billina suggests the Wheelers may be automobiles, which she calls "dangerous things." She explains, "Several of my friends have been run over by them." Dorothy reassures the hen that where they now are, she does not have to worry about being run over by an automobile: "The people here haven't been discovered yet, I'm sure; that is, if there *are* any people. So I don't b'lieve," Dorothy says, "there *can* be any automobiles

[...]" (25). In this passage Dorothy assumes a great deal: she assumes that she knows where she is (or at least is not), and she assumes that she knows what *discovery* is. It is true that Ev has not been discovered by European-Americans, which seems to be the definition of *discovery* that Dorothy has in mind. But it has inhabitants and a civilization of its own. Moreover, the inhabitants of Oz know about Ev and its inhabitants. So Ev turns out to be anything but an undiscovered kingdom waiting to be discovered and conquered, as the Europeans tended to view the Americas. In fact, rather than conquering Ev, Billina and Dorothy have a difficult time surviving their adventures there and in the realm of the Nome King. Moreover, as Ozma's attempt to return the rightful ruling family to Ev shows, it is a country that in its own right deserves respect and preservation.

An early important example of the discrepancy between appearance and reality is also ironic when viewed in the context of the entire book. It too involves the Wheelers, who turn out to be harmless creatures with wheels instead of hands and feet. They write their warning in the sand to try to keep people from hurting them. Pretending to be dangerous, vicious creatures, the Wheelers scare Dorothy and Billina. Yet when Tiktok, the mechanical man Dorothy finds in a cave, recognizes their harmlessness, the leader of the Wheelers begins to cry and says, "Now I and my people are ruined forever," for "our only hope is to make people afraid of us, by pretending we are very fierce and terrible [...]. Until now we have frightened everyone, but since you have discovered our weakness our enemies will fall upon us and make us very miserable and unhappy." Like the Wizard in the first Oz book, the Wheelers, then, are humbugs. Dorothy agrees to keep the Wheelers' secret, "Only," she adds, "you must promise not to try to frighten children any more, if they come near you." The Wheeler leader promises (65–67), but Baum has no intention of keeping such a promise himself.

In the next episode in the book Dorothy meets the beautiful Princess Langwidere, who rules in the absence of the rest of the Royal Family of Ev. Langwidere shows her interior ugliness when she demands that Dorothy trade her head for one of the princess's thirty heads (she has one for each day of the month) (87) and when she complains about having to spend "at least ten minutes every day" dealing with "affairs of state" (96). When the princess demands that Dorothy exchange her head for the princess's head, Tiktok's clockwork runs down, so he is unable to protect Dorothy. As a result, the princess locks Billina in the castle chicken coop and locks Dorothy in one of the castle's towers until she will agree to exchange her head, sight-unseen, for the princess's twenty-sixth head. Dorothy still refuses, for "she was not used to" the princess's head, and it "might not fit her at all" (87). Princess Ozma of Oz, along with the Scarecrow, Tin Woodman, Cowardly Lion, Hungry Tiger, Sawhorse, and Royal Army of Oz, rescues Dorothy when Ozma and her party come to Ev on a mission to rescue the Royal Family of Ev from the Nome King.

The Royal Family of Ev's being prisoners of the Nome King involves the complete breakdown of family relations and the disruption of an entire kingdom. Ozma comes to Ev determined to make war on the Nome King for enslaving the wife and ten children of Evoldo, the former King of Ev. Her concern for political stability and right rule becomes obvious when she declares to the Nome King that "the Kingdom of Ev is in great need of its royal family to govern it" (149).

When Tiktok hears of Ozma's plans to make war on the Nome King, he says, "Why should you fight the Nome King? [...] He has done no wrong." Earlier, Tiktok tells Dorothy that Evoldo "used to beat all his servants until they died" and sold his family "in a fit of anger [...] to the Nome King, who by means of his magic arts changed them all into oth-er forms and put them in his un-der-ground pal-ace to orna-ment the rooms" (45–46). To Ozma he explains that the former King of Ev sold his family to the Nome King and then adds, "It was the King of Ev who did wrong, and when he re-al-ized what he had done he jumped in-to the sea and drowned himself" (113). Langwidere points out, "My uncle Evoldo was a very wicked man. [...] If he had drowned himself before he sold his family, no one would have cared. But he sold them to the powerful Nome King in exchange for a long life, and afterward destroyed the life by jumping into the sea" (113–14). Hearing these words, Ozma hopes to get the royal family back peacefully, since Evoldo did not get the long life he bargained for. Dorothy, Billina, and Tiktok join Ozma in her quest to liberate the Royal Family of Ev.

For all of his valor Tiktok misleads Dorothy and the members of Ozma's party. Wrong as it was for Evoldo to sell his family, it was also wrong for the Nome King to buy them. As they are about to enter the Nome King's domain, Tiktok misleads them further when he assures them, "The Nome King is hon-est and good natured. [...] You can trust him to do what is right" (144).

When Ozma's party enter the underground kingdom, they find themselves even more misled by appearances. Baum writes of the Nome King:

> This important monarch of the Underground World was a little fat man clothed in gray-brown garments that were the exact color of the rock throne in which he was seated. His bushy hair and flowing beard were also colored like the rocks, and so was his face. He wore no crown of any sort, and his only ornament was a broad, jewel-studded belt that encircled his fat little body. As for his features, they seemed kindly and good humored, and his eyes were turned merrily upon his visitors [...] [145].

When Dorothy and Ozma look at the Nome King, they are reminded of another famous character, so they are convinced that Tiktok is right and that the king must be "hon-est and good natured":

> "Why, he looks just like Santa Claus — only he isn't the same color!" whispered Dorothy to her friend; but the Nome King heard the speech, and it made him laugh aloud.
> "'He had a red face and a round little belly
> That shook when he laughed like a bowl full of jelly!'"
> quoth the monarch, in a pleasant voice; and they could all see that he really did shake like jelly when he laughed [145].

When the Nome King lights his pipe, he looks "even more like Santa Claus." Dorothy and Ozma find themselves "relieved to find the Nome King so jolly" (146). Suzanne Rahn calls this part of the book "an excellent lesson for children in the dangers of taking people at face value" ("Beneath the Surface" 28). It also ultimately becomes an excellent lesson for Ozma and Dorothy to look beneath appearances to reality. After she is freed from the Nome King's enchantment, Ozma comments, "The King has not treated us honestly, for under the mask of fairness and good nature he entrapped us all [...]" (202). Thus, learning to discern between appearance and reality is central to the book: the Wheelers appear much more ferocious than they are, and the Nome King appears much nicer than he is.

Roger Sale and Katharine M. Rogers make what seem to be some strange statements about the Nome King. In "L. Frank Baum, and Oz" Sale says that, because of Baum's desire to write American rather than European fairy tales, "all his 'wicked' creatures [are based] on the image of the naughty or spoiled child rather than the image of evil stepmothers," and he calls the Nome King "Baum's best villain [...] whose power is never really useful to him or threatening to others and whose folly and tantrums are much more childish than really malevolent" ("L. Frank Baum" 585–86).[1] However, some of Baum's monsters seem at least partially based on the monsters of European fairy tales, such as his wicked witches and his evil giants. Even Baum's Nomes seem to have European ancestry, based on the gnomes of European folklore.[2] Also, when the army of Nomes appears to Dorothy and her friends (*Ozma* 151) and when the Nome King transforms members of Ozma's party, he certainly seems both powerful and threatening. Actually, the Nome King's being "childish" may be more sinister than Sale imagines. Following Sale, Rogers insists that the Nome King is not a terrible villain: "Even the wickedest Nomes are periodically reduced to naughty children, and children know that naughty children cannot seriously hurt them, while the traditional fairy-tale villains, ogres and evil stepmothers (bad fathers and mothers), can" (172). It is unclear what children Rogers is writing about; considering all that psychologists, sociologists, and educators know about bullying, it is clear that most children are fully aware that "naughty children" can and often do hurt them considerably.[3]

The attempt to free the Royal Family of Ev would have resulted in the permanent transformation of Ozma and her party into bric-a-brac had it not been for a series of accidents involving Billina the hen and the Nomes' great fear of eggs. When Ozma explains that Roquat should free the Royal Family of Ev because Evoldo did wrong to sell them, the Nome King replies, "According to the laws of Ev, the king can do no wrong" (146). This kind of sophistry tinges all of the Nome King's arguments. When Ozma says that the royal family should be freed because Evoldo did not get the long life he bargained for, the king says that he is not to blame for Evoldo's suicide. When Ozma threatens to take the royal family away by force, Roquat shows her his army, one far superior to Ozma's puny army. When the Cowardly Lion threatens to spring on the Nome King "and tear him in pieces," he finds that, because of Roquat's magic, he can only jump straight up in the air and land exactly where he begins (151–52).

Roquat nonetheless offers Ozma and her followers an opportunity to rescue the royal family and take them from his palace. Because the Nome King appears so benign, Ozma and her followers accept (156–57). Each of the members of Ozma's party, except for the Cowardly Lion, Hungry Tiger, and Sawhorse, is to have a chance to identify the members of the Royal Family of Ev, who have become ornaments or pieces of bric-a-brac in the Nome King's palace. If any of them identifies a member of the royal family, then that person or creature will retain his or her proper form, and the member of the royal family will be restored to his or her form. If any does not make at least one correct guess, then that person also becomes part of Roquat's collection. Ozma begins with eleven guesses (154–55). Each subsequent person gets one additional guess so that in theory all may be freed (161). To Ozma the task initially appears fairly easy. But she quickly discovers how many ornaments the Nome King has and how difficult her task really is. She then recognizes that the Nome King "laughed good naturedly with his visitors, when he knew how easily they might be entrapped" (158). Ozma shortly becomes a part of the king's collection (157–62), as do most of her followers (163–80). Before Dorothy tries to make her guesses, she recognizes Roquat's sophistry, telling him, "It seems to me [...] that you are not so honest as you pretend to be" (177). Because of her recognition of the truth, it seems appropriate that she manages to guess one of the family members' identity and thus escapes enchantment (182).

Billina falls asleep beneath the Nome King's throne and, as a result, hears the secret of using the colors of objects to identify the transformed people. Winning the right to try to guess, she frees from their transformations all members of the Royal Family of Ev and of Ozma's party except for the Tin Woodman, whom Billina later frees from his transformation when she recognizes that he is a green-tinted tin whistle shaped like a pig that Evring, a prince of Ev, has taken from the palace (196–203, 225–27).

When they are back in their own forms, Ozma and her followers understand the Nome King. Ozma declares, "The King has not treated us honestly, for under the mask of fairness and good nature he entrapped us all, and we would have been forever enchanted had not our wise and clever friend, the yellow hen, found a way to save us." The Scarecrow calls the King "a villain," and the one private in Ozma's army says of the king, "His laugh is worse than another man's frown." Even Tiktok admits, "I thought he was hon-est, but I was mis-tak-en" (202). Remaining true to his sophistical ways, the Nome King points out that he said that if their transformations are broken, the royal family and Ozma's party could "leave the palace in safety," but he will not let them leave his kingdom. Instead, he says he will "hurl you all into my underground dungeons, where the volcanic fires glow and the molten lava flows in every direction, and the air is hotter than blue blazes" (208). In spite of the humor of the king's last phrase in this quotation, Dorothy, Ozma, and their friends again face the threat of very real danger.

When faced with danger, Ozma's officers prove to be cowards. Only the private attempts to conquer the Nome King, and the private is easily defeated (200). But the Scarecrow saves the day by hurling one of Billina's eggs at Roquat. Since Nomes are terrified of eggs, the other Nomes flee in horror, and at the urging of Billina, Dorothy grabs the Nome King's magic belt, rendering him harmless (212–13). When the king realizes that his belt is gone, Baum forcefully reminds his readers of the Nome King's non-whiteness through the absence of his usual color: "The Nome King clapped his hand to his waist, and his rock colored face turned white as chalk" (214).

No one has ever explained entirely satisfactorily why eggs terrify Baum's Nomes. Still, two commentators give at least plausible explanations. Rogers writes that since eggs symbolize "new life," they are appropriately "poisonous to Nomes, whose kingdom is lifeless." They also are "the quintessential female product." The Nomes Ozma's party meets are all males, "and the values of their kingdom — accumulation of wealth and militarism — are associated with the lack of female influence" (160). Like Rogers, Sally Roesch Wagner sees political implications in *Ozma of Oz*, as well as several other Oz books, writing, "The enemy of peace is the militaristic and regimented Nome Kingdom, whose king represents the force and violence that ensures power over others in the patriarchal system" (12). Although Wagner oversimplifies here — there are other enemies to peace in Oz, she is quite right in associating the Nomes with a patriarchal system. Wagner argues that "the egg is the symbol of the matriarchy" (12), an idea that corresponds nicely to Rahn's connecting the Nomes with accumulation of wealth and with militarism. In a sense, the Nomes' underground kingdom is lifeless; its location aligns it with hell. In *Ozma of Oz* it also involves the horror of a kind of living death for people once they become objects in Roquat's collection. Also, readers see no female Nomes, whereas the driving forces in Oz itself are female. However, arguments that militarism and the accumulation of wealth are, even for Baum, necessarily "associated with lack of female influence" are not entirely convincing: Baum's Army of Revolt in *The Marvelous Land of Oz* is, after all, entirely female, and in the same book Glinda has an excellent all-female army. The Nomes' fear of eggs may at least in part be a comic

The Nomes and the eggs, as shown in *Ozma of Oz* (illus. John R. Neill; Chicago: Reilly & Lee, 1907), p. 232.

touch Baum invented, perhaps with no particular significance, to liven up an otherwise grim atmosphere in his book. Many children feel that throwing eggs can be fun.

As Ozma's party leaves, Roquat's army attacks. Dorothy then uses the magic belt to change the foremost warriors into eggs, which roll around in the cavern and cause the rest of the army to flee in panic (211–20). Ozma, Dorothy, and her friends then escape to the earth's surface, reinstate the Royal Family of Ev as rulers of their land, and travel to Oz. For most readers the book ends happily when Dorothy returns to the real world and reunites with her Uncle Henry, even though Billina, who remains in Oz, sensibly tells Dorothy that she is "very foolish to go back into that stupid, humdrum world again" (245).

But does the book really end happily? For some readers in the early twenty-first century perhaps it does not. Some critics argue that *The Wonderful Wizard of Oz* reflects racist attitudes that not only did not bother but even may have pleased most of Baum's early readers. Tom St. John goes so far as to assert, "The original popularity of *The Wonderful Wizard of Oz* was fired by the desperate public need of the white middle classes to put a happy face on terror, on the sordid land-grab for the land sacred to the Sioux" (351). As has been noted, St. John exaggerates. As Rogers points out, Baum had the ability to "create a wonderful world," that he was then able to make "believable" (241). Still, St. John argues, not entirely convincingly, that Baum incorporates racism aimed at African Americans, Orientals, and especially American Indians into his masterpiece (351–58), and Baum at one time did advocate "the wholesale extermination of *all* America's native peoples" (Stannard 126). Baum does so in an editorial on 20 December 1890 in the *Aberdeen Saturday Pioneer*, an editorial Rogers calls "truly shocking," in which Baum calls the Indians "curs" who should be exterminated (259n27). Thus, it is no surprise that St. John is able to find racist attitudes in Baum's first Oz book.[4]

In *Father Goose, His Book* (1899) Baum has a poem entitled "Little Nigger Boy," accompanied by a scurrilous illustration by W. W. Denslow, who also was Baum's illustrator for *The Wonderful Wizard of Oz*. The stanza that Denslow illustrates reads:

> There was a little nigger boy
> Hadn't any coat;
> So he tried to borrow one
> From a nanny goat.

The third stanza reads:

> There was a little nigger boy
> Hadn't any collar;
> And when the copper collared him
> Nigger boy did holler. (n. pag.)

In his introduction to a reprint edition of *The Woggle-Bug Book* (1905), published two years before *Ozma of Oz*, Douglas G. Greene points out, "Many of the characters in *The Woggle-Bug Book* are ethnic stereotypes," including a black washerwoman and "Irish, Swedish, Chinese, and Arab characters" (xv). The book, Greene feels, "is dominated by the kind of humor that Baum thought the public wanted," including ethnic jokes (xvi-xvii). In the book itself Baum uses what most readers today consider outrageous dialect to characterize his minorities and goes so far as to call a "Chinaman" a "Chink" (26). Actually, as the examples just given show, Baum seems to have accepted unquestioningly the prevalent racism of his day. In *Mary Louise and the Liberty Girls*, for example, he apparently sees nothing wrong with

There was a little nigger boy
Hadn't any coat:
So he tried to borrow one
From a nanny goat.

Illustration to "Little Nigger Boy," from Baum's *Father Goose, His Book* (illus. W. W. Denslow; Chicago: Geo. M. Hill, 1899), n. pag.

writing of an "old black mammy, Aunt Sally" (20). Calling her a "mammy" and "Aunt" seems matter of course for him. Later in the same book her writes "of an aged pair of negroes named 'Aunt Sally' and 'Uncle Eben,' who considered themselves family possessions and were devoted to 'de old mar'se an' young missy'" (64). Baum's use of quotation marks really doesn't excuse the demeaning use of "Aunt" and "Uncle" or the outrageous, gratuitous use of dialect. Also, his writing that the two people "considered themselves family *possessions*" (emphasis added) may even imply an acceptance of slavery on the part of the characters in the book and of Baum himself. The old lie that slaves were happy under slavery thus apparently surfaces in one of Baum's books.

In *Ozma of Oz* readers can also see Baum's racism at work. It is important to remember that in *Ozma of Oz* Baum emphasizes the color of the Nomes and the Nome King, and he does so in a way he does not in his later Oz books involving Nomes. Dorothy's assertion that the Nome King "looks just like Santa Claus — only he isn't the same color" (145) becomes important in this context. Sale's assertion that the Nome King is like a "naughty or spoiled child" fits the racist idea that non-whites are like children. However, part of the explicit prejudice of nineteenth- and early twentieth-century America includes the idea that beneath their childlike exterior non-white males are barbaric creatures (look at what happens when the "copper" collars Baum's "nigger boy," and why does he need to be collared?) who lust to "possess" white females. According to Joane Nagel, "Early-twentieth-century concerns about white men's waning social autonomy, personal power, and sexual virility were heightened by biological theories of race popular at the time that supported black men as 'hyperpotent'" (115).[5] The non-white Nome King lusts to literally possess Ozma and Dorothy. The Nome King, however, hardly seems "hyperpotent." In fact, Baum manages to play against the idea of hyperpotency in several ways. First, he has the Nome King turn the people into actual objects — ornaments and pieces of bric-a-brac — thus excluding the possibility of having sexual relations with them. Second, the king himself in the end turns out to be relatively impotent, raging without effect, a characteristic Roquat also displays in several later Oz books. He also is unable to keep his transformed prisoners or his prisoners once they are changed back into their original forms. Finally, his fear of eggs, which are, at the very least, connected with and perhaps symbols of reproduction, ironically underscores the king's and all of the Nomes' lack of potency. The Nomes then represent the racial other and in some ways at the same time are a parody of the racial other, especially the racial other's supposed sexual lust for white women and their supposed hyperpotency.

Incidentally, in *The Emerald City of Oz* Baum still has Roquat lusting after white women and desiring to transform them into objects that he can possess. In that book he is called Roquat the Red (10), perhaps another reference to his skin's not being white. He plans to conquer Oz with the help of a number of terrible allies, but insists to his general that he claims

> Ozma and Dorothy as my own prisoners. They are rather nice girls, and I do not intend to let any of those dreadful creatures hurt them, or make them their slaves. When I have captured them I will bring them here [to his kingdom] and transform them into china ornaments to stand on my mantle [143].

In a later Oz book by Baum, *Tik-Tok of Oz*, Baum does not treat the Nome King's color, as he does in *Ozma of Oz* and perhaps does in *The Emerald City of Oz*. Still, in that later book, the king wants to keep Polychrome, who is the Rainbow's Daughter, with him "always" as his queen or daughter or wife or aunt or grandmother (170–71).[6] In spite of the king's ridiculous list, the point is that in *Tik-Tok of Oz* he desires another female, a fair maiden, who dwells above ground, thus continuing his desire to possess non-Nome, apparently white women.

Ozma, Dorothy, and Baum himself seem agreed that it is absolutely wrong for Roquat to change the members of the Royal Family of Ev and of Ozma's party into ornaments. In fact, throughout Baum's Oz books transformations are the most horrible forms of magic one can perform, so much so that in the second book in the series, *The Marvelous Land of Oz*, Glinda the Good declares, "I never deal in transformations, for they are not honest, and no respectable sorceress likes to make things appear what they are not" (259–60). Transformations involve substitution of appearance for reality that robs an individual, human or non-human, of his or her very essence.

But what about the Nomes that Dorothy transforms into eggs? Apparently, they are never changed back into their original forms. Brian Attebery recognizes the wrongness of transformation in the Oz books, except when it is done to return a character to his or her original form, but he blithely dismisses Dorothy's transformation of the Nomes as "a matter of self-defense. The Nomes do not have the Western respect for the individual that Oz shares with America, anyway" (106). Attebery's argument seems strange: he implies that only individuals who respect others as individuals need be respected as individuals. It is regrettable that Baum probably agreed. Baum might, however, defend Dorothy's actions on additional grounds. Again, when she first sees Roquat, she says, "he looks just like Santa Claus — only he isn't the same color!" In fact, Nomes are "the color of rocks" (139). Roquat himself is "grayish-brown" (150). Nomes are thus, from Baum's point of view, non-whites and therefore members of an inferior race, so he feels (and most of his early readers felt) that they do not deserve fair treatment. For Baum, Roquat's absolute viciousness beneath his pleasant exterior apparently typifies the behavior Baum attributes to the darker races. (Remember that the boy in the poem has to be collared.) Roquat is depicted as the racial other who appears to be happy and childlike — even like Santa Claus — but just beneath the surface is a raging monster who wants what the dominant group has, especially its women.

Since Baum is at times inconsistent, it is always dangerous to use later (or even earlier!) books to explain things that appear in a particular book. Still, some of his later writings help readers recognize and understand his racism in *Ozma of Oz*. In connection with the Nomes representing the racial other, it is interesting to note that in *The Emerald City of Oz* and *The Magic of Oz* the Nome King tries to conquer Oz, and in *Tik-Tok of Oz* Baum writes that the Nome King wants all the wealth "mortals" have (81). In *Rinkitink in Oz* Baum writes:

> The word "nome" means "one who knows," and these people are so called because they know where all the gold and silver and precious stones are hidden in the earth — a knowledge that no other living creatures share with them. The nomes are busy people, constantly digging up gold in one place and taking it to another place, where they secretly bury it, and perhaps this is the reason they alone know where to find it [199].

The Nomes' keeping the knowledge of the location of the riches in the earth to themselves and their activity of burying and reburying their gold indicate a kind of obsession on their part; Baum here describes them as being like misers, wanting the gold and other riches not for any use they may have but simply to have them. In *Ozma of Oz* Roquat even seems to desire the women of Oz and Ev along with other people from those two countries just for the sake of having them, since Baum writes of no one other than the questers entering Roquat's chambers where he keeps his bric-a-brac and ornaments. So the Nomes ultimately fit the stereotype of the racial other in that they are greedy creatures, wanting the dominant group's women, power, and wealth, things for which they ultimately have no use other than to possess them.

Baum's racism and the apparently justified assumption that his contemporary adult readers shared his racism, then, provide present-day adult readers what may be the most horrifying experience of all when reading *Ozma of Oz*, for they give readers insight into real people who read and wrote in America during the earlier part of the twentieth century. But is this book unusual among children's books because it is racist? Hardly, as so many children's classics, from Heinrich Hoffman's *Struwwelpeter* (1845) to P. L. Travers' unrevised *Mary Poppins* (1934), so amply demonstrate. At any rate, Baum's Oz books do not usually make their racism as explicit as so many other children's books do, yet in at least two of them — *The Patchwork Girl of Oz* and *Rinkitink in Oz*— the racism is pretty explicit. Interestingly, Jane Yolen writes, "A child who can love the oddities of a fantasy book cannot possibly be xenophobic as an adult" and asks, "What is a different color, a different culture, a different tongue for a child" exposed to the diverse cultures that one finds in works of fantasy (54). The world, however, does not appear to work the way Yolen here suggests it does. If Baum — obviously nurtured on fairy tales, myths, and fantasies and the creator of so many fantasies himself— can apparently accept so much of the racism of his day, then children nurtured on similar tales in our day can probably still be racist. Nonetheless, it seems that children can read the Oz books without being aware of or negatively affected by the racist attitudes in some of them.[7]

Certainly, in *Ozma of Oz* Baum achieves his effects on his readers not by dispensing "with all disagreeable incident," as he promises he will do in the Introduction to *The Wonderful Wizard of Oz*, but by structuring his work around disagreeable incident. Remove the threats to Dorothy — and vicariously to the little children who read his books, agree "not to try to frighten children," and one cannot write books as powerful — and incidentally as lucrative — as the Oz books. Baum knew full well the same secret that Lewis Carroll, Mark Twain, and even Beatrix Potter knew: if children's books are to be really successful, horror must lie somewhere near their centers. But he also incorporated into his books what was one of America's dirty little secrets, namely, that racism lay at the heart of a great part of the American vision before and around the turn of the twentieth century and allowed the nation to destroy ruthlessly the indigenous people and exploit ruthlessly other people considered non-white. Thus, he worked carefully into his narrative of Dorothy's encounter with the Nomes his own and his contemporaries' feelings of what they thought to be the superiority of the white race as well as numerous things, including near-drowning, possibilities of mutilation and death, and transformation, deliberately designed "to frighten children."

Accordingly, *Ozma of Oz* is an extremely dark, extremely unsettling book. Rahn correctly writes, "The stifling underground realm, with its crowds of Nomes endlessly toiling at the furnaces, and huge, deserted palace rooms, becomes the dark backdrop for the sunlit Emerald City, whose wealth, leisure, and beauty are for all its citizens to enjoy" ("Beneath the Surface" 30). Like the underground realms in *Dorothy and the Wizard in Oz*, the domain of the Nome King is, as has been mentioned, a kind of hell.[8] *Ozma of Oz* ends with Ozma's quest successful since the Royal Family of Ev is free; Dorothy, Ozma, and their friends are triumphant; Ozma and her friends are back in the Emerald City; and Dorothy is in Australia with Uncle Henry. Dorothy acts decisively when she refuses to change heads with Langwidere. She also willingly goes on Ozma's quest and again acts decisively to enable that quest to end successfully. She and Ozma also grow in that both learn to look beneath appearance to reality.

Nonetheless, at the end of *Ozma of Oz* the Kingdom of the Nomes remains intact. True, Roquat no longer has his magic belt, but he still can do great harm. And in future Oz books he tries to do just that. Moreover, some readers may wonder about all the Nomes that Dorothy transforms into eggs. Their obedience to their ruler results in their becoming just as immobilized and much more fragile than the Royal Family of Ev and the members of Ozma's party are when they are ornaments in Roquat's apartments. But for the Nomes there seems no chance that the transformation will ever be reversed.

5

Dorothy and the Wizard in Oz
BAUM'S *INFERNO*

In *Dorothy and the Wizard in Oz* (fourth book in the series) Dorothy's adventures are nightmarish. The book resembles in several ways Lewis Carroll's *Alice's Adventures in Wonderland*. Both books involve underground journeys. Alice falls down a rabbit hole and journeys through a bewildering series of adventures in the underground world she finds there. During an earthquake Dorothy falls into a crack in the earth and, like Alice, has extremely unpleasant experiences beneath the ground. Just as the setting and actions of Carroll's book in some ways resemble those of Dante's *Inferno* (especially the chapter entitled, "A Mad Tea-Party," in which characters travel endlessly in a circle [58]), so do the setting and actions in Baum's. Alice has some very unpleasant experiences underground, including almost "shrinking away altogether" when a fan she holds makes her small (17) and losing her own identity: when the Caterpillar asks her, "Who are *you*," she replies, "I — I hardly know, Sir, just at present [...]" (35). Dorothy too faces possible death underground.

According to Ray Bradbury, "We float and fly through Oz on grand winds that make us beautiful kites. We trudge and fight our way through Wonderland, amazed that we survive at all" (xiv). Yet readers hardly "float and fly" through the landscape of *Dorothy and the Wizard in Oz*, even the parts of the book set in Oz itself. Bradbury continues that "in Oz [...] reside amiable villains who are really not villains at all." He then indicates that the words, "in Oz," refer not only to the Land of Oz but also to the other magical kingdoms in the books when he supports his assertion by calling the Nome King, who lives outside the boundaries of Oz, "a fraud and a sham, for all his shouts and leaping about and uttering curses. Whereas Wonderland's Queen of Hearts really *does* chop off heads and children are beaten if they sneeze" (xiv). Actually, in the course of Carroll's book the queen chops off no heads, although she genuinely desires to do so. The Duchess's baby, however, does get abused: it gets violently shaken, tossed up and down, and flung at Alice (49). More importantly, even though Roquat is in some ways "a fraud and a sham," he does indeed turn some people, including Ozma, into bric-a-brac, and his threats genuinely scare Dorothy. And in Baum's fourth Oz book the truly horrible villains really desire to kill Dorothy.

David L. Greene and Dick Martin call *Dorothy and the Wizard in Oz* a "tale of gloom, bravery and frustration" (28). Angelica Shirley Carpenter and Jean Shirley call it "the gloomiest of the series" (95). Raylyn Moore recognizes that it represents "the turning of the tide" in terms of Baum's conception of the Oz books. Up to this book the enemies Dorothy and the people of Oz face are not "really 'bad,'" Moore claims. But in *Dorothy and the Wizard in Oz* Dorothy meets "enemies" who apparently desire "to destroy the protagonal party utterly." Moreover, Moore recognizes that the "number of absolutely vicious enemies in this book" and "the underground, gloomy mise-en-scene [sic]," produce "an over-all effect of oppressiveness and lowering evil" (165–66), just the kind of effect Bradbury detects in the Alice books but *not* in the Oz books.

In 1909, in his essay entitled "Modern Fairy Tales," Baum writes, "The Secret of Alice's success lay in the fact that she was a real child, and any normal child could sympathize with her all through her adventures." Although *Alice's Adventures in Wonderland* "may often bewilder the little one," Baum adds, Alice herself "is doing something every moment, and doing something strange and marvelous, too; so the child follows her with rapturous delight" (138). Richard Kelly calls Alice "'our' representative in a world of disorder, contradiction, violence, arbitrariness, cruelty, rudeness, frustration, and amorality" (82). Morton M. Cohen writes, "The reader feels along with Alice throughout her wanderings, and those feelings are the most important part of the journey" (148). Baum's words in his essay about the child's being bewildered but nonetheless following Alice "with rapturous delight" imply that he sees Alice in basically the same way Kelly and Cohen do. Moreover, like Alice as Baum sees her, Dorothy is clearly intended to be "a real child" with whom "any normal child could sympathize."

Thus, it is not surprising that in *Dorothy and the Wizard in Oz* Baum repeatedly indicates to his child readers that Dorothy will survive her adventures. In his prefatory note, entitled "To My Readers," for example, he writes that in this book Dorothy, "as sweet and gentle and innocent as ever," is "the heroine of another strange adventure" (ix). Dorothy really does not act heroically in the book. Still, the word "heroine" implies that the book will end happily for her. In the same note Baum also tells his readers, "Princess Ozma [...] is again introduced in this story, and so are several of our old friends of Oz" (ix), reassuring readers that until Ozma appears, the story will not end. Since the adventures that involve serious danger to Dorothy occur before Ozma enters the story, the readers are assured of Dorothy's survival.

In *Dorothy and the Wizard in Oz* an earthquake swallows Dorothy, her second cousin Zeb, Jim the Cab-horse, and Dorothy's cat Eureka. Shortly after they float down to the Land of the Mangaboos, who are heartless vegetable people, an earthquake also swallows the Wizard, who has eight miniature piglets with him and who joins Dorothy and her companions. They then go on a quest for the surface of the earth. They wander through a glass mountain that becomes granite as they travel to the Valley of Voe, where invisible bears almost devour them, and then through Pyramid Mountain to the Land of Naught, where they fight the vicious Gargoyles. Then, once more inside a mountain, they pass through the Den of the Dragonettes in an attempt to reach the earth's surface, but instead, Dorothy and her companions arrive at a dead end inside the mountain. They cannot go back because of a revolving rock that stops revolving when their buggy dislodges a stone that falls under it, thus blocking their escape route (146). Only through a magic trick can they escape. And the trick itself that could have taken them to the Land of Oz any time during their adventures in effect makes absurd and unnecessary all the very real dangers they face.

As Moore points out about descents into the underground, of which those into the Nome King's realm are examples, they are "classic mythic" devices that in Jungian psychology represent what Moore calls "the retreat into the unconscious during sleep" (167). On one level, then, *Dorothy and the Wizard in Oz* represents Baum's nightmare journey into the inferno of his own mind. In the first Oz book, *The Wonderful Wizard of Oz*, Dorothy becomes a genuine quest hero who grows considerably as she rids the Land of Oz of the wicked Witch of the East and the wicked Witch of the West. In the third Oz book, *Ozma of Oz*, she again grows and acts heroically, refusing to give Princess Langwidere her head and capturing the Nome King's magic belt, thus depriving him of most of his magic and enabling Ozma to complete her quest to free the imprisoned and enchanted Royal Family of Ev. In *Dorothy and the Wizard in Oz*, however, Dorothy is not heroic in any way. And only through trickery does Baum enable Dorothy to survive and return to the real world as it exists in the book.

Hourihan argues convincingly that the Alice stories involve "deconstruction of the conventional hero story [...]" (209). Similarly, in *Dorothy and the Wizard in Oz* Baum actually subverts the idea of Dorothy as hero that he establishes in *The Wonderful Wizard of Oz* and *Ozma of Oz* and that he refers to in "To My Readers" in *Dorothy and the Wizard in Oz*. In *Dorothy and the Wizard in Oz* Dorothy is for the most part a passive little girl who relies on others, especially the Wizard, for guidance and decisive action. Baum makes it most clear that he is subverting the idea of Dorothy as hero in the chapter ironically titled, "Dorothy Picks the Princess." The title implies heroic and decisive action on Dorothy's part. Yet in the chapter the Wizard, not Dorothy, formulates the plan to pick the princess, and Dorothy merely helps him do the actual picking. The closest she comes to being in charge of this action is when, after each of them seizes one of the princess's hands, Dorothy says, "Pull!" (48–49).

The book is replete with horrors. The first is the series of earthquakes that swallow Dorothy and her friends. When they fall into a crack in the ground a quake produces, "Blackness engulfed them on every side, and in breathless silence they waited for the fall to end and crush them against jagged rocks or for the earth to close in on them again and bury them forever in its dreadful depths" (7). Although Baum writes that Dorothy has experienced adventures before, "The horrible sensation of falling, the darkness and the terrifying noises, proved more than Dorothy could endure and for a few moments the little girl lost consciousness" (7–8). Baum here creates a scene worthy of the pen of Edgar Allan Poe about a little girl who experiences premature burial.

Her losing consciousness implies that even for this girl who has experienced so much, this episode is extremely terrifying.

As indicated earlier, in several ways Dorothy's adventures resemble the underground adventures of Lewis Carroll's Alice. Like Alice, Dorothy plunges toward the earth's center, except that Alice's plunge occurs in what is for her a dream. Baum, however, does not allow his readers to think that Dorothy's adventure is a dream, although a psychological critic would probably connect her descent with Baum's own nightmares.[1] Moreover, Dorothy's fall, like Alice's, becomes extremely slow, but Dorothy and Zeb still feel, as Baum writes, "terror of reaching the bottom of this great crack in the earth, and the natural fear that sudden death was about to overtake them at any moment" (9), a fear Alice does not share as she falls. As Dorothy and her friends fall, rocks pelt "the buggy top, and Jim screamed almost like a human being when a stone overtook him and struck his boney [sic] body" (9), a passage that foreshadows Jim's being able to talk. Still, Jim "was more frightened than injured" (9). Also, Alice journeys to and through Wonderland alone. Dorothy has the comfort of companions from her own world. Alice, by sheer willpower, finally asserts her own superiority to the creatures in Wonderland when she recognizes that the royal figures that threaten her are only parts of a deck of playing cards and that the other creatures are only small animals, and she wakes up (Carroll 97–98). Dorothy too ultimately escapes from underground through a gimmick, but her adventures are for her not a dream, so she cannot simply awaken from them.

Dorothy's first set of adventures involves the heartless vegetable Mangaboos. The Mangaboo prince decides that since Dorothy and her companions do not belong in his kingdom, all except the Wizard will be destroyed immediately and not planted again; the Wizard will be kept as the prince's sorcerer until another wizard is ripe (46). When a Mangaboo dies or begins to spoil, it gets planted and then begins to grow again (44). That kind of relief, too, the heartless Mangaboos will deny Dorothy and her friends, although it could, of course, do them no good. After hearing the prince's words, Dorothy and the Wizard pick the princess who has been ripe for a week. The newly plucked

Opposite: "Horse, buggy and all fell slowly," reads the caption for this illustration from *Dorothy and the Wizard in Oz* (illus. John R. Neill; Chicago: Reilly & Lee, 1908), p. 24.

HORSE, BUGGY AND ALL FELL SLOWLY.

princess replaces the prince, but lacking a heart, she too decides to destroy the travelers: the people, she says, will be thrown "into the Garden of Twining Vines, [...] and they will soon crush you and devour your bodies to make themselves grow bigger. The animals [...] we will drive to the mountains and put into the Black Pit" (61). Bauska claims that "the nasty Mangaboos turn out to be only potatoes and can always be mashed or baked" (23). However, neither Dorothy nor her companions seem able to mash or bake them all. When the Mangaboos drive the animals into the Pit, the vegetable people force Dorothy, Zeb, and the Wizard in after them; and the Mangaboos wall them all in (66–68). Again, Dorothy and her companions face premature burial.

The Pit proves to be a tunnel going through the mountain. At the tunnel's end is the beautiful Valley of Voe. When the Wizard first sees it, he says, "It wouldn't be so bad [...] if we were obliged to live here always. We couldn't find a prettier place, I'm sure," but as becomes clear in *Ozma of Oz*, in Baum's books appearances are often deceiving. The absence of any visible inhabitants in the Valley of Voe puzzles even the Wizard, who thinks that the place looks so inviting (78). Soon, the travelers find out from a family living in the valley that the people and animals in the Valley of Voe are invisible from eating the delicious dama-fruit. For the people the invisibility is a blessing, for it protects them from the ferocious bears that roam through the valley. Thus, the Valley of Voe is not such a pleasant place, especially for Zeb, the Wizard, and Dorothy, who do not wish to become invisible. Instead, they simply want to get home (84–87). Their only hope is to enter Pyramid Mountain before the bears devour them. They succeed in getting into Pyramid Mountain by using a plant that enables them to walk on water and their buggy's wheels to stay on the water's surface. But before they get onto the water, bears attack them. The Wizard kills one, and the bears wound Jim, who fights bravely to help everyone escape (95–98).

In the Valley of Voe the invisible family the travelers visit tell them about the Land of Naught and the horrible Gargoyles. Dorothy says, "If the only way to get home is to meet the Gurgles, then we've got to meet 'em. They can't be worse than the Wicked Witch or the Nome King" (91), recalling her heroic deeds in earlier books. Her confusing

Opposite: "**Through the black pit**" in *Dorothy and the Wizard in Oz* (illus. John R. Neill; Chicago: Reilly & Lee, 1908), p. 81.

THROUGH THE BLACK PIT.

gargoyles with *gurgles*, however, makes her into a slightly comic figure. On the way to the Land of Naught, the travelers meet the Braided Man of Pyramid Mountain, who, living all alone, manufactures flutters and rustles. He gives a box of rustles to Dorothy and a box of flutters to the Wizard. The braided man tells the travelers how, on the earth's surface, he made post-holes and, after stacking them end-to-end until he ran out of room, put them one on top of the other. Then, he fell into the deep hole he had thus created and ended up in the mountain (107). After hearing this story, "the Wizard tapped his forehead significantly, to indicate that he thought the poor man was crazy" (108). The braided man's harmless insanity nicely counterpoints the insane, irrational viciousness of so many of the other inhabitants of the underground world, such as the Mangaboos, the invisible bears, and the Gargoyles, thus making that viciousness appear all the more terrible. In fact, Baum often uses humor in the midst of his nightmarish episodes to produce a kind of counterpoint or even chiaroscuro effect.

As counterpoint, the braided man episode provides a breather for the reader, a change in pace, a rest from the horrors of the rest of the underground journey. Chiaroscuro is a little more complicated. In a book that was published in 1869, long before Baum wrote his Oz books, H. P. Robinson points out that the word *chiaroscuro* literally means "light-dark," but the literal meaning is inadequate to express its true meaning (116). The juxtaposition of light and dark makes the dark appear darker and the light lighter. Robinson quotes the painter Fuseli as writing, "The exclusive power of chiaroscuro is to give substance to form, place to figure, and to create space" (115).[2] A more recent art critic, Robert S. Huddleston, writes that chiaroscuro "accentuates the illusion of depth, giving the objects depicted a greater sense of mass and weight while simultaneously heightening their three-dimensionality [...]" (18). Baum's verbal chiaroscuro works in similar ways. The braided man episode helps create a feeling of space in the midst of the claustrophobic passages involving the journey inside the mountains. It also gives substance, paradoxically, to the whole of the underground realm, most of which is so different from, so much more threatening than the braided man and the place where he dwells. The episode involving the braided man lightens the journey through the underground realm, but, paradoxically, it hardly seems enough to lighten a work as dark as *Dorothy and the Wizard in Oz*. In fact, like the later episode involving the dragonettes, the braided man episode functions to make the surrounding episodes even darker.

After their visit with the braided man, the travelers continue up the inside of the mountain until they get to the Land of Naught. When Jim first sees it, he decides he would rather face the invisible bears in the Valley of Voe (112), even though he was wounded by them. The Land of Naught is made entirely of wood, including the animals; and the Gargoyles themselves are "evil" looking flying creatures that quickly and without provocation attack the travelers, using their wooden arms as clubs. The Wizard soon realizes that the companions have no chance of defeating the Gargoyles, so Dorothy wonders, "why fight at all?" to which the Wizard responds, "So I may die with a clear conscience" (116). Again, the Wizard is the one who advises heroic action, and again, a little girl faces death.

The travelers discover that they cannot hurt the Gargoyles but can, as people in the Valley of Voe tell them, scare the Gargoyles by making noises. Soon, however, the Gargoyles manage to wrap their arms around the travelers and thus capture them. The Gargoyles then decide to rest before destroying their captives, giving the travelers an opportunity to steal some of the Gargoyle's wings and escape by flying to the base of the mountain on the other side of the Land of Naught. There, the Wizard uses the stolen wings to light a fire to stop the Gargoyles who pursue them. He says, "Perhaps the flames will set fire to all that miserable wooden country, and if it does the loss will be very small and the Gargoyles never will be missed" (135), words that echo Baum's idea in the *Aberdeen Saturday Pioneer* for 20 December 1890 about exterminating Native Americans. Here, the Wizard hopes to exterminate the natives of the Land of Naught, and Baum in no way indicates that he finds any problems with what the Wizard hopes to do.

Unlike the other two mountains, the mountain the travelers enter from the Land of Naught has no regular stairs through it; instead, the book becomes extremely claustrophobic as the companions travel through a crack in the earth. After their comic encounter with the dragonettes, baby dragons who would love to eat the travelers but cannot because their mother tied their tails to the rocks to keep them out of mischief (141), the travelers take a path that they hope will lead to the earth's surface. They also hope not to meet the mother dragon coming back from hunting on the surface, for if they do, she will catch them and feed them to her babies. They then pass through the part of the tunnel with the turning rock, which gets stuck behind them, so they cannot go back. Finally, they get to a large cave through the top of which they can see genuine sunlight. But the cave has no outlet (146–48).

Jim the valiant Cab-horse gives up hope: "Folks don't fall into the middle of the earth," he says, "and then get back to tell of their adventures — not in real life. And the whole thing has been unnatural because the cat and I are both able to talk your language, and to understand the words you say," to which Dorothy responds, "don't you lose heart, Jim, for I'm sure this isn't the end of our story, by any means" (148–49). Incidentally, these words along with Baum's subversion of the hero quest may make Baum a practitioner of metafiction, an idea that should not be very surprising since, according to Thacker, children's fiction from the nineteenth century on foreshadows many aspects of metafiction.[3] The Wizard speaks of them all being "starved together" and their bones being "scattered over the floor of this lonely cave" (150). Thus, in metaphoric terms the travelers' underground journey is a circle: they end up just as they began — facing premature burial; thus also their journey resembles those of the inhabitants of the upper circles of Dante's hell who travel endlessly in circles and of the participants in the Mad Hatter's tea-party doomed to travel endlessly around the table. All of the hard work of Dorothy and her companions to reach the earth's surface leads them ironically to a place where they can see sunlight but must starve below ground. Then Dorothy remembers that every afternoon at four o'clock Ozma looks at Dorothy through her magic picture, and if Dorothy makes a certain motion, Ozma will transport her to Oz (152).[4] Four o'clock comes, Dorothy disappears with Eureka in her arms, and soon the others follow (156).

Through the intervention of Beatrice, Dante is able to travel safely through hell and purgatory and heaven, a trip he needs to take to overcome the state of doubt and depression he is in at the beginning of *The Divine Comedy*. It would probably be stretching things to compare Ozma to Beatrice since readers have no indication that she watches over Dorothy at any time during her trip underground or that she is in any way responsible for that trip. Nor do readers see Dorothy undergoing any significant growth or healing of the sort Dante does. When thus placed in the context of Dante's *Inferno, Dorothy and the Wizard in Oz* becomes all the more horrifying since the trip below ground apparently serves no purpose and since no benevolent force watches and protects Baum's travelers.

Moreover, Baum shows that the whole underground journey is unnecessary: a means of escape is present all along. Dorothy just conveniently forgets about her ability to go to Oz. One could argue that during her first journey in Oz, Dorothy also has with her all along the ability to return home; after all, she gets the silver shoes early in the course of her adventures, and they enable her to go back to Kansas. However, in *The Wonderful Wizard of Oz* Dorothy has no idea about the kinds of powers the silver shoes have. Only after Glinda tells her that the shoes can get her home and explains how to use them, does Dorothy know some of their powers. In the meantime, the little girl grows considerably. On the other hand, in *Dorothy and the Wizard in Oz* Dorothy knows about the way to get to Oz before the book begins. She does not grow in any way during the course of her journey. She just conveniently forgets the means of getting to Oz until she is trapped underground with no possibility of escape.

Even the Land of Oz provides no end to the unpleasant adventures. During the travelers' journey underground, Jim the Cab-horse works harder than all the others, pulling the buggy through passages inside the mountains and fighting valiantly against the Mangaboos, the invisible bears (he is the only one wounded in that fight), and the Gargoyles. He does these things without complaint even though he is old and bony. Before he reaches Oz, however, he brags that he can outrun any wooden horse (155), and when he reaches Oz, he becomes more egotistical, saying how superior he is to the Sawhorse. When the Scarecrow suggests a race, Jim accepts, but the Sawhorse tries to discourage Jim, for he recognizes how unfair the competition is since the wooden horse never tires. Zeb reminds Jim that although he may have been a racehorse once and he does come from Kentucky, he is now very old (193). When Jim loses the race, he angrily kicks the Sawhorse. Immediately, the Hungry Tiger attacks Jim and sends him "rolling over and over." When Jim recovers, he apologizes (196). But the harm has been done. Jim recognizes that "to be just an ordinary horse in a fairy country is to be of no account whatever," and he says to Zeb about Oz, "It's no place for us [...]" (197). The valiant old cab-horse seems to deserve better.

Even less pleasant is what happens after Ozma accuses Eureka of eating one of the Wizard's miniature piglets. Throughout the book Eureka's relationship to the pigs is complex. Earlier, in the land of the Mangaboos, Eureka plays with and even protects them (65–67). Yet when she gets hungry, as she does on the journey through Pyramid Mountain, she asks whether she can eat one, even though they point out that they were once her "good friends." When Jim says to her that if she injures a piglet, he will chew her up "instantly," she responds that she fears Jim's few remaining teeth, "So the piglets will be perfectly safe, hereafter, as far as I am concerned" (109–11). Nonetheless, Eureka has a trial that is every bit as ridiculous as the one in *Alice's Adventures in Wonderland*, where the queen says, "Sentence first — verdict afterwards" (Carroll 96). Before Eureka's trial Ozma herself declares the kitten guilty: Eureka has, after all, repeatedly threatened to eat the piglets, and she was spotted coming out of the room where the missing piglet was last seen (201–03).

Considered guilty before her trial, Eureka refuses to act in her own defense, even though she faces the death penalty (204, 212). The trial includes the presentation of no evidence. The Tin Woodman, acting as defense attorney, tries to convince the jury that Eureka is too sweet to eat a piglet, but Eureka will not tolerate such a defense, demanding that the Tin Man tell the jury "it would be foolish for me to eat the piglet, because I had sense enough to know it would raise a row if I did. But don't try to make out I'm too innocent to eat a fat piglet if I could do it and not be found out. I imagine it would taste mighty good." After only "a few minutes," the jury finds her guilty, since, they say, "Kittens have no consciences, so they eat whatever pleases them" (213–14), words that show that the trial itself means nothing to the members of the jury since their decision is based solely on preconceptions they have about cats and not on anything they hear during the proceedings.

To save Eureka's life, the Tin Woodman lies, saying that he has found the missing piglet and showing the jury another piglet the Wizard gives him for that purpose (214). But Eureka demands that all eight piglets be produced (215), something that the Wizard cannot do. Only then does Eureka say that the missing piglet is alive; when Eureka grabbed it to eat it, the piglet refused to cooperate: "Instead of keeping still," Eureka says, "so I could eat him comfortably, he trembled so with fear that he fell off the table into a big vase that was standing on the floor." At first, the piglet did not get entirely through the neck of the vase, so Eureka thought she still might get him, "but he wriggled himself through and fell down into the deep bottom part — and I suppose he's there yet" (216). After the trial, even though the piglet is safe,

Eureka is in disgrace, since she did desire to eat the piglet and only an accident kept her from doing so. She is confined in Dorothy's room. As a result, she wants to return home (218). But strangely enough, the people of Oz never recognize that the kitten's trial shows that their justice system does not arrive at the truth. Nor do they show any remorse for having decided to put the kitten to death for a crime she did not commit. They even show no remorse for the trial's and verdict's effect on Dorothy, who suffers when she thinks that her kitten will be executed (204).

From beginning to end, then, *Dorothy and the Wizard in Oz*, like *Alice's Adventures in Wonderland*, is full of unpleasant adventures, most of which have potentially tragic consequences. Even after the escape from underground, happiness does not come to Baum's travelers, for the Land of Oz itself proves unpleasant. Thus, Eureka, Dorothy, Zeb, and Jim are all glad to return to the United States. Only the Wizard remains in Oz.

In the beginning of *Dorothy and the Wizard in Oz*, in his introductory note entitled "To My Readers," Baum writes, "It's no use; no use at all. The children won't let me stop telling tales of the Land of Oz" (ix). Perhaps these words indicate that by the time he was writing *Dorothy and the Wizard in Oz* Baum was already tired of writing Oz books. After all, in the introductory note he explicitly adds, "I know lots of other stories, and I hope to tell them, some time or another; but just now my loving tyrants won't allow me" (ix). Perhaps by writing a book with so many unpleasant episodes, he hoped to get his "loving tyrants" to leave him alone so that he could tell his "other stories." If so, his strategy did not work. The book proved to be exciting even if unpleasant.

At any rate, in *Dorothy and the Wizard in Oz*, although Baum reassures his readers that Dorothy will survive, he creates a series of decidedly unpleasant, even nightmarish underground kingdoms that rival Lewis Carroll's Wonderland in terms of nastiness. And the unpleasantness carries over into the Land of Oz itself. In fact, Oz is so unpleasant that the characters from the real world — except the Wizard, an old humbug — are glad to escape from it. And that the Wizard remains seems fitting, for in this book the Land of Oz itself is a kind of humbug that hardly proves a happy place of escape and refuge for Zeb, Jim, Eureka, and even Dorothy.

Thus, this fourth Oz book involves a subversion of the traditional quest. It includes a nightmarish journey that involves numerous attempts to destroy Dorothy. The little girl again travels through a kind of hell, just as she does in *Ozma of Oz*. But she performs no heroic feats to escape that hell. When she reaches Oz, however, the nightmare continues. Only her return to the so-called real world produces an end to the nightmare. And the nightmare itself is not a dream but a series of episodes having objective reality in the world Baum creates in *Dorothy and the Wizard in Oz*.

6

The Road to Oz
BAUM'S PICARESQUE

In the note "To My Readers" that prefaces the fifth Oz book, *The Road to Oz*, Baum reminds readers that in the preface to his fourth Oz book, he expresses a desire "to write some stories that were not 'Oz' stories, because I thought I had written about Oz long enough; but," he adds, "since that volume was published I have been fairly deluged with letters from children imploring me to 'write more about Dorothy,' and 'more about Oz,' and since I write only to please the children I shall try to respect their wishes" (n. pag.). Baum, of course, was not wholly honest here: he also wrote to please adults and to make money. Still, he really does seem to have been growing tired of writing Oz books; and in his sixth Oz book, *The Emerald City of Oz*, he announces the end of the Oz series.

Critics do not usually put *The Road to Oz* among the best of Baum's books. Fairly typical is Katharine M. Rogers, who complains about the way Baum states the book's themes explicitly rather than letting them grow out of the tale (166). On the other hand, in his essay on Oz, Roger Sale writes that *The Road to Oz* is "perhaps the most enchanting of the magic journeys" ("L. Frank Baum" 582). Sale supports this assertion with several quotations from the book, especially centering around the first meeting of Dorothy and Button Bright. He quotes a long passage of dialogue between Dorothy and Button Bright that occurs when they first meet (dialogue occurring on 17–18 of *The Road to Oz*), and then comments, "This is wonderful, and wonderful for showing why Baum is best on the magic journeys to magic countries" ("L. Frank Baum" 583).

In his book Sale praises this passage even more highly, saying it is "perfect, one of my favorite moments in all children's literature" (236).[1] Then he explains just why he thinks the meeting between the two characters is so appropriate, not only for what is said but also for the time it occurs in the course of Baum's book. He also rightly points out that in contrast with the Wizard of Oz in the first Oz book, Johnny Doit in *The Road to Oz* is a real "American wizard" ("L. Frank Baum" 576). Most importantly, Sale recognizes in *The Road to Oz,* "The journey forces careful timing, if only of an instinctive sort, on Baum, and the events need not be arranged causally for their sequential relations to be important" (*Fairy Tales* 236). He then goes on to say that what happens in the passage he quotes from *The Road to Oz* also occurs "with other characters met early on in his [Baum's] best magic journeys [...]," and mentions the meeting with Billina in *Ozma of Oz*, with the Scarecrow in *The Wonderful Wizard of Oz*, with Jack Pumpkinhead in *The Marvelous Land of Oz,* and "to a lesser extent" with the Patchwork Girl in *The Patchwork Girl of Oz* and the Ork in *The Scarecrow of Oz* (*Fairy Tales* 236). Thus, he praises elements of Baum's plotting here, but at the same time, interestingly, he withholds judgment that those elements may be deliberate on Baum's part: the timing may be "only of an instinctive sort," even though it occurs so frequently. Thus, he is apparently not willing to go so far as to admit that Baum is a conscious artist, even though Baum creates at least one "perfect" episode, according to Sale, and creates similar episodes in book after book.

The plot of *The Road to Oz* is episodic, with no overall character growth or organic relationship between parts: as Sale notes, the episodes in the book are not related "causally." The journey is, as Sale points out, "enchanting," but it does not involve the kinds of episodes that the earlier books contain, episodes that for the most part help illuminate character or that work together to produce some kind of unified effect — unless a series of haphazardly arranged episodes can be said to be unified through their very haphazardness. In *The Road to Oz* it is at least possible that just such a unity may be at work.

That Baum had grown tired of writing Oz books shows in *The Road to Oz*. It is the first of his Oz books to show no real concern for plot *development*. Riley writes that the plot of *The Road to Oz* is among Baum's "weakest." He adds that just one adventure in the book is suspenseful, but he does not say which one. Other weaknesses, he writes, involve the reader's knowing early in the story about the upcoming celebration of Ozma's birthday, and he considers "Ozma's explanation" of confusing the crossroads to get Dorothy to Oz "unsatisfactory" (152). What Riley calls the only suspenseful episode is probably the one involving the Scoodlers, who want to make Dorothy and her companions into soup (99) and who throw their heads at the travelers (101).[2] The Shaggy Man in turn ultimately tricks the Scoodlers so that he can throw the heads into a "black gulf" (113). Even that episode, however, involves no real danger for Dorothy, the reader discovers, when Ozma tells her, "I've watched you in my Magic Picture all the way here, [...] and twice I thought I should have to use the Magic Belt to save you and transport you to the Emerald City. Once was when the Scoodlers caught you, and again when you reached the Deadly Desert" (197). Actually, readers probably are aware that Ozma is in control of Dorothy's journey long before Ozma says so, since when the travelers leave Foxville, King Dox asks Dorothy to get him an invitation to Ozma's birthday party (45), and when they get to Dunkiton, King Kick-a-Bray makes the same request (73).

In spite of *The Road to Oz* having, according to Riley, little suspense, on the whole he praises the book, saying, among other things, that it is "pastoral" and "sunny" so that it becomes a "perfect foil for the darkness and danger of *Dorothy and the Wizard in Oz*," and it provides "breathing space" before "the serious and ominous story" that Baum tells in the next Oz book, *The Emerald City of Oz* (152). When *The Road to Oz* is viewed in the context of these other two books, Riley is right: even the leisurely, episodic plot structure can be seen as providing a kind of "breathing space." Yet when the book is read by itself, the strengths Riley mentions apparently become weaknesses. Riley adds that the book's "lack of a strong plot" allows "Baum to concentrate more fully on the nature of Oz itself" (152), a statement that would be very difficult to support adequately, especially since about half the book is set outside Oz. Riley concludes that *The Road to Oz* is "a tour de force of place" and adds that the work is one of Baum's "most exhilarating and satisfying" fantasy books (159).

According to Rogers, it is "beside the point" to argue "that Baum's plots tend to be loose and episodic," for "tightly constructed plots are

. SHAGGY MAN CAUGHT THE HEADS AND TOSSED THEM INTO THE GULF
BELOW

not desirable in all novels, especially those written for children" (442). She adds that Baum usually tried to create "a series of wonderful experiences rather that to drive purposefully toward a climax" (442). Still, until *The Road to Oz* Baum's books do have fairly tight plot structures that "drive purposefully toward a climax." Even in his sixth Oz book, *The Emerald City of Oz*, in which he experiments with dual plot structure, the episodes in the Nome King plot point toward a definite climax. And in several of his later Oz books — including *The Patchwork Girl of Oz*, *The Lost Princess of Oz*, *The Tin Woodman of Oz*, and *Glinda of Oz*—the plot structure, if not organic, is definitely not just episodic since a genuine climax occurs in each.

The Road to Oz consists of a series of sometimes unrelated adventures involving Dorothy; Toto; the Shaggy Man, who comes to Dorothy's family's farm; Button Bright, whom the travelers meet shortly into their journey; and Polychrome, the Rainbow's Daughter, who slides down the rainbow to the ground and gets left behind when the rainbow rises (52–53). In fact, the only relationship between all the episodes is that they get the travelers closer to Oz and to Ozma's birthday party. Without distorting things too much — in fact, possibly without distorting them at all — the book can be labeled a picaresque tale, a kind of rogue's progress, with the Shaggy Man as the picaro or rogue at its center. Riley writes that to call the Shaggy Man a "bum" or "hobo" is to mislabel him since Baum in no way implies that "circumstances or any deficiencies within" Shaggy forced him to become the kind of character he is (153). But O'Keefe point blank labels him a "hobo" (60). Nothing in the definitions of *hobo* seems to indicate that one must be "forced" into being one. Some people apparently choose to be hoboes.[3] The Shaggy Man certainly seems to be a hobo, one who deliberately chooses a life of wandering, a choice that does not change substantially even after he reaches Oz.

Riley also notes that the Shaggy Man and the Wizard might be called "misfits of society" and that in his Oz books most of Baum's positive male characters usually are either such misfits or are non-human. From this fact Riley theorizes that Baum lacked "faith or confidence in the aggressive American male" who was trying to civilize America (154).

Opposite: "**The Shaggy Man caught the heads and tossed them into the gulf below.**" From *The Road to Oz* (illus. **John R. Neill; Chicago: Reilly & Britton, 1909**), p. 121.

In the first Oz book, the Wizard at least tries to be an "aggressive American male" when he leads an army into the Land of the Winkies, but he is badly defeated, and he certainly tries to be one (and apparently succeeds) in the land of the Gargoyles in *Dorothy and the Wizard in Oz*. And Baum himself—with his many get-rich-quick schemes—tried to fulfill that role with little success. Riley, then, seems for the most part correct about Baum's attitude toward "the aggressive American male": in his Oz books (unlike in some of his other books, like those in the Aunt Jane's Nieces series) his male characters tend to be misfits like the Wizard, the Shaggy Man, and even Uncle Henry, who cannot earn a living on his farm.

According to Graham Allen, modern theorists view texts, both literary and non-literary, "as lacking in any kind of independent meaning. They are what theorists now call intertextual," so "Reading [...] becomes a process of moving between texts" (1). Allen's statements, especially the one about reading becoming a process of moving between texts, seem extreme, but they are useful in understanding individual pieces of literature because they demand that they be placed in contexts. Placing *The Wonderful Wizard of Oz* and other works by Baum in contexts that go beyond Baum's own works is useful. For example, the hero quest helps explain many otherwise puzzling things about them. Also, placing *Dorothy and the Wizard in Oz* in the contexts of Baum's other books and of Dante's *Inferno* and Lewis Carroll's *Alice's Adventures in Wonderland* helps readers better understand Baum's individual book. Placing the works in larger contexts also helps readers understand other Baum books, especially *The Road to Oz* and *The Tin Woodman of Oz*. Theories of intertextuality help explain why placing *The Road to Oz* in the context of picaresque novels may even allow readers to justify its having an episodic plot rather than the kind of cumulative plot that Baum's earlier works have.

Critics recognize how difficult it is to define the term *picaresque*. Richard Bjornson explains about the term "picaresque novel," "In broad general terms, it is usually employed to describe episodic, open-ended narratives in which lower-class protagonists sustain themselves by means of their cleverness and adaptability during an extended journey through space, time, and variously predominantly corrupt social milieux" (4). Although Bjornson uses most of his book to show how greatly oversimplified this usual description is, he admits that in novel after novel that he studies, "a characteristic pattern of experience—

ambiguous links with the past, departure from home, initiation, repeated contacts with a dehumanizing society and its pressures to conform — recurred with striking regularity" (7).[4]

When discussing American literature before Baum's time, critics often point to two of Mark Twain's novels, *The Adventures of Tom Sawyer* and *Adventures of Huckleberry Finn*, as picaresques. For example, Frederick Monteser writes, "The American picaro really made his first appearance in Mark Twain's works [...]," and then goes on to discuss the two aforementioned novels, the latter of which, Monteser writes, "appears to have been a conscious effort to write an American picaresque novel" (81–84). Most critics, however, qualify their labeling of *Adventures of Huckleberry Finn* as a picaresque novel. Alexander Blackburn, for example, calls Huck "an *apparent* picaro" (178; my emphasis). What distinguishes Huck from the usual picaro is Huck's moral growth in the course of the novel. As Henry Nash Smith argues about Huck's "growth in moral insight," "It is as if the writer himself were discovering unsuspected meanings in what he had thought of as a story of picaresque adventure" (199); as James M. Cox argues, "Huck's relation to and involvement in Jim's freedom lift him out of the childhood world and lift his lies from what we might call the world of low picaresque into what we want to see as the realm of higher humanity" (394). These two eminent Twain scholars are correct. Thus, Huck through his internal growth makes a powerful contrast with the usual picaro and with the Shaggy Man. Still, like the usual picaro, Huck goes on a journey during which he has ample opportunity to see and judge the inhumanity of humankind.

Baum's novel nicely fits the pattern of the picaresque, except that the Shaggy Man gets to see aspects of the inhumanity of the inhabitants of Foxville and Dunkiton — foxes and donkeys respectively — and of the Scoodlers, who, although they more closely resemble humans than foxes and donkeys do, have detachable heads with two faces on each one, one white and one black, so they are decidedly non-human. The Shaggy Man is a rogue. He is a thief: before the action begins, he steals the love magnet (200), and he steals apples; he even puts Toto in his pocket and carries the dog off with him (2). In a twist on the usual pattern, the Shaggy Man comes across societies that are truly dehumanizing, societies that give Button-Bright a fox's head (36) and the Shaggy Man himself a donkey's head (71). Unlike Huck, who learns compassion in part through his encounters with dehumanizing societies, the Shaggy Man, more in keeping with the tradition of the picaro, seems to learn no great lessons during his adventures in *The Road to Oz*, at least until he gets to Oz and bathes in the Truth Pond.

Robert Alter points out that the picaresque hero usually "travels alone and struggles alone" (10), which seems to be exactly what the Shaggy Man does before he meets Dorothy and begins his magical journey to Oz. The Shaggy Man definitely seems to "feel at home in the picaresque tradition of hardship and adventure" (79), words Alter uses to describe the picaresque hero as he appears in works written in and after the latter half of the eighteenth century. As for the central character of a picaresque novel, the picaro, he is, Alter writes, "a man who does not belong, a man on the move, and a man who takes things into his own hands" (107). These words also apply to the Shaggy Man, who prefers to wander even after he gets to Oz. In *The Patchwork Girl of Oz* the Shaggy Man says, "I've been a rover all my life, and although Ozma has given me a suite of beautiful rooms in her palace I still get the wandering fever once in a while and start out to roam the country over" (126). As for "taking things into his own hands," he literally takes Toto into his hands and his pocket, and he serves as leader of the small group traveling toward Oz, saving them from the Scoodlers and calling on Johnny Do it when the travelers' journey seems to come to an end at the edge of the Deadly Desert. According to Alter, "In the traditional picaresque novel, [...] the hero already is what he is; sometimes splendidly, sometimes ignominiously, but always confidently, he is himself" (124). These words too apply to the Shaggy Man. Wherever he is, he remains the Shaggy Man. In Oz, where he has access to all that magic and wealth can provide, he prefers to wear shags. Even with a donkey's head, he still remains the Shaggy Man.

Stuart Miller defends the episodic plot of the picaresque novel, for it may, he writes, "reveal a chaotic lack of order in the world and in ourselves and thus be more philosophic than the causal plot." Miller uses the word *philosophic*, he writes, "in the sense of true." In the picaresque plot, Miller explains,

> The discrete fragments into which its events are broken express anything but order. The infinite possibilities of the picaresque plot express total openness. Since there are no limitations of probability, the door is left open to the fantastic, the improbable, and even the weird. The picaresque plot expresses an intuition that the world is without order, is chaotic [9–10].

As Baum's earlier writings — and those of many other writers of fantasy — show, what Miller calls the "causal" (9) as opposed to the episodic plot also can include "the fantastic, the improbable, and even the weird." Nonetheless, in *The Road to Oz* the episodic structure does seem to work. The whole book is a leisurely journey led by a rogue to what is, for most of the journey, at least to the travelers, an unknown destination. If he were not such a rogue, Dorothy and especially Toto would not be on the trip. Nor would he need to receive the kind of love that the love magnet that he carries with him generates. Perhaps it is pushing Baum's book too much, but its very lack of a causal plot may mirror the chaos of what Baum considered the real world, the world in which he lived. And thus the book may have a kind of unity consisting of a disunity that appropriately expresses the kind of world of which the Shaggy Man is representative.

At first, the trip itself seems to have no destination. The Shaggy Man asks Dorothy to show him the way to Butterfield "so I shouldn't go there by mistake." When Dorothy asks him where he wants to go, he replies, "I'm not particular, miss" (5). When they finally must pick a road to travel, they follow the Shaggy Man's advice to "take the seventh road [...]. Seven is a lucky number for little girls named Dorothy." When Dorothy asks, "The seventh from where?" he replies, "From where you begin to count" (14). Only as the book unfolds do the adventurers begin to get hints that they are on the road to Oz. But they seem to understand those hints more slowly than the reader does. But of course, the reader knows the book's title; the characters in the book do not.

Even though at the end of *The Road to Oz* the Shaggy Man tells the truth that he stole the love magnet, he tells it not because of any organic, internal growth but because, he says, "having bathed in the Truth Pond, I must tell nothing but the truth" (201). As it does in *The Marvelous Land of Oz*, in *The Road to Oz* transformation produces that which is untrue: a boy with a fox's head and a man with a donkey's head. The Shaggy Man and Button-Bright both bathe in the pond in order to restore their heads to their natural forms. As an added bonus, the pond makes them both have to tell the truth. That the Shaggy Man, however, remains basically unchanged is demonstrated in *The Road to Oz* by his saying that he is not sad he stole the love magnet (201). But he gives the love magnet to Ozma to hang over the gates of the Emerald City (203), possibly as a ploy to be allowed to stay in Oz and possibly because he is convinced that Ozma is right when she says, "in Oz we are loved for ourselves alone [...]" (201). He also takes pride in his individualism and respects the individualism of others (as long as that individualism does not infringe on his individualism), so in a very real sense he belongs in Oz as Baum embodies it in most of his books.

In "Modern Fairy Tales," first published in 1909, Baum writes that what children "want is action —'something doing every minute'— exciting adventures, unexpected difficulties to be overcome, and marvelous escapes" (140). *The Road to Oz*, which not coincidentally appeared the same year as the essay, follows this formula. So do at least portions of most of the Oz books that Baum wrote after the fifth one. Nonetheless, when viewed in the context of the picaresque tradition, *The Road to Oz* takes on new dimensions. Outside Oz is chaos; inside Oz is order. Thus, the Shaggy Man's adventure fittingly ends in the beautiful Emerald City at Ozma's well ordered birthday celebration.

It might again be stretching the book too far to say that the Shaggy Man's staying in Oz represents Baum's recognition that, even in the midst of order, some chaos is both necessary and desirable, even enjoyable. At any rate, the Shaggy Man's becoming a resident of Oz does make Oz more *true* (to use Miller's term), that is, more like life as most readers know it.

7

The Emerald City of Oz
Goodbye to Kansas, Goodbye to Oz

In his note "To My Readers" in *The Road to Oz* Baum writes that he has another Oz story to tell and adds, "perhaps that book will be the last story that will ever be told about the Land of Oz" (n. pag.). He here refers to what became *The Emerald City of Oz*, a book in which Baum indicates that he hoped to be writing his last Oz book. At the end of the book, because of danger of invasion from abroad and because of the invention of the airplane, Glinda makes Oz "invisible" to the rest of the world, including the magical kingdoms around Oz (296–97). In a final section of the book entitled, "How the Story of Oz Came to an End," Baum quotes a message from Dorothy written on a stork's wing:

> *You will never hear anything more about Oz, because we are now cut off forever from all the rest of the world. But Toto and I will always love you and all the other children who love us* [298].

Baum then adds, "we have no right to feel grieved, for we have had enough of the history of the Land of Oz to fill six story books, and from its quaint people and their strange adventures we have been able to learn many useful and amusing things" (299).

That Baum wanted to stop writing Oz books is clear. Why he wanted to do so is a matter of debate. The usual (and most sensible) explanation is one based on Baum's own statements: he was tired of

writing Oz stories and wanted to tell other tales. In the prefatory section of *Dorothy and the Wizard in Oz*, entitled, "To My Readers," Baum
writes, "It's no use at all. The children won't let me stop telling tales
of the Land of Oz. I know lots of other stories, and I hope to tell them,
some time or another; but just now my loving tyrants won't allow me"
(ix). He writes a similar thing in the preface to *The Road to Oz*. After
The Emerald City of Oz he wrote two major non-Oz books — *The Sea
Fairies* (1911) and *Sky Island* (1912) — neither of which sold as well as he
would have liked (Rogers 191–93). He then returned to writing Oz
books because of pressure from children, from his publisher, and from
his purse: he needed the money Oz books brought him.

By the end of *The Emerald City of Oz* Baum had Dorothy leave
Kansas, never to return. Jack Zipes wonders whether the American
frontier's closing "and the limitations of American society" made Baum
decide to have Dorothy live permanently in Oz. Zipes asks what "Baum
saw in the American 'civilizing process' which forced him to make Oz
invisible to the outside world" (122). As his mentioning of "the American 'civilizing process'" and his use of "forced" indicate, Zipes here
loads his argument. Perhaps Baum saw nothing that *forced* him to make
Oz invisible; perhaps he was not forced but simply made a choice. It
is thus not surprising when Zipes concludes that Ozma's decision to
make Oz invisible results from her feeling that outsiders "mean tragedy
for utopia" (130). Following the lead of many other critics, Zipes obviously feels that Baum created in his Oz books an American eutopia.[1]
Zipes continues that Baum felt that "capitalist entrepreneurs" using
technology would "doom" "utopian developments like Oz," and that
in making Oz invisible Baum indicated that he felt that any chance of
creating an American "utopia" was "cancelled and forfeited." According to Zipes, for Baum "the real American world of finance" destroyed
the American dream (130). Again, Zipes seems to exaggerate here. Actually, very little is known about Baum's politics, except that scholars are
now reasonably sure that he was not a supporter of William Jennings
Bryan, as several biographers and critics claim he was, and that he was
a life-long Republican who was not very concerned about politics once
he stopped writing newspaper editorials.[2] In other words, Baum apparently was not nearly as discontent with America and American politics
as some literary critics try to make him seem.

Many critics read *The Emerald City of Oz* as the book in which
Baum introduces the idea of Oz as a utopia (probably meaning

"eutopia" or "good place" in terms of its more modern meaning). They base this idea on the beginning of Chapter 3, where Baum gives a description of Oz that points in the direction of its being a place where everyone is "happy and prosperous," no one gets sick, "no one ever died unless he met with an accident that prevented him from living," there is no money, everything belongs to the ruler, each person works half the time and plays half the time, and all share with their neighbors (21–23). So many critics see Oz as a kind of eutopia that Richard Flynn, who does not consider Oz a eutopia, labels this idea "a tradition of wishful thinking" (121). Once the kind of Eden these critics see in Oz is shut off from the outside world, real adventure would have to cease to exist.

Oz is not a "highly eclectic eden," as Raylyn Moore calls it (147); it is not "an ideal country," as S. J. Sackett calls it (207); it is not "the Kansas of our hearts, [...] that home we are always searching for, that green, good place" (107), as Zeese Papanikolas calls it. Instead, it is fairly easy to see it as a totalitarian state ruled by a kind of marriage of technology and magic that Orwell's Big Brother would have envied. With her magic picture and with her servant Glinda's great book of records, Princess Ozma of Oz is able to spy on every action of her subjects, and with her monopoly on magic, she is able to exert total control. In *The Emerald City of Oz* Baum even declares that "[...] Ozma was accustomed to having her own way" (47), an idea that could easily lead to totalitarian rule. Fortunately, in Baum's Oz books Ozma is a benevolent ruler who places her subjects' contentment above everything else.

Several fiction writers recognize the tyrannical, dystopic possibilities in Baum's Oz. For example, Gregory Maguire in his extremely popular book *Wicked* (1995) makes the Wizard a tyrant who deposes and perhaps puts to death Ozma and runs what looks like a twentieth-century police state involving a group significantly called the Gale Force that "march [...] all over the poor and the weak. They terrify households at three in the morning and drag away dissenters — and break up printing presses with their axes — and hold mock trials for treason at midnight and executions at dawn," Elphaba, the protagonist of the novel, declares. In addition, she says, "It's government by terror" (187).[3] In *Paradox in Oz* (1999) Edward Einhorn recognizes the potential for harm that a monopoly on magic and technology has: Einhorn creates an alternate Oz in which the Wizard tells Ozma, "[...] I'm a very bad man. But I'm a very good wizard" (76), and uses the magic picture "to monitor the actions of everyone throughout Oz. The Picture shows them [the Wizard's assistants] anything they want to see, so that I can wipe out any hint of treason before it begins" (90–91). Perhaps these fiction writers have at least as clear a view of what is implicit in Baum's Oz as the critics do who claim that it is a utopia or, more properly, a eutopia.

When one considers dystopic possibilities inherent in the marriage of technology and magic in Oz, that Ozma is a benevolent ruler is perhaps beside the point since, as *The Lost Princess of Oz, The Magic of Oz,* and *Glinda of Oz* indicate, there are other residents of Oz who are desirous of taking her rule from her and who apparently would not hesitate to impose tyrannical rule on Oz. The often inconsistent Baum apparently had no intention of making Oz into his idea of a kind of Eden, although in *The Emerald City of Oz* and again in *The Tin Woodman of Oz* he describes it in terms some of which are Edenic.[4]

Some of the adventures Dorothy has in *The Emerald City of Oz* itself belie the idea that everyone is happy. In Utensia, for example, when Dorothy asks the army of spoons what would happen if she "set" Toto on them, a spoon replies that they will kill Toto with their muskets. Billina warns Dorothy, "Don't risk it [...]. Remember this is a fairy country, yet none of us three happens to be a fairy." A spoon also threatens to cut off some of Dorothy's toes (165–66). The kitchen utensils bicker with one another and even threaten to chop Dorothy to bits (167–77). Although Dorothy feels that the source of these threats makes them rather funny, they still indicate that some of the inhabitants of Oz are quite discontent. In Bunnybury, moreover, the king spends most of his time "blubbering and wailing" because he does not, he claims, want to be king (205–06), until his interaction with Dorothy convinces him otherwise (224–25). These episodes show that even in lands supposedly under Glinda's control not everyone is happy.[5]

Just as *Ozma of Oz* has as its villain the Nome King, so does *The Emerald City of Oz.* Rogers writes about the Nomes that "the wickedest" of them "are periodically reduced to naughty children, and children know that naughty children cannot seriously hurt them, while the traditional fairy-tale villains, ogres and evil stepmothers (bad fathers and mothers), can" (172). Again, if Rogers is right about the Nome King's being a "naughty" child, then the residents of Oz have as much reason to fear him as children have to fear bullies. In *The Emerald City of Oz* the Nome King desires to and tries to conquer Oz, presenting a genuine threat to the inhabitants of Baum's fairyland.

The Emerald City of Oz has a double plot. In the first, the Nome King plans to dig and digs a tunnel beneath the Deadly Desert in the hopes of conquering Oz, and General Guph finds him an especially vicious assortment of allies to help the king achieve his goal, one of whom, the First and Foremost, states explicitly, "When we get through with Oz it will be a desert wilderness. Ozma shall be my slave." The Grand Gallipoot also claims Ozma as his slave, to which Roquat replies, "We'll decide that by and by" (269). Through most of the book the residents of Oz do not suspect what is happening, and as Baum writes, "An unsuspected enemy is doubly dangerous" (11). The allies that General Guph collects, of course, all desire rewards for helping the Nome King, for, as Baum writes, "People often do a good deed without hope of reward, but for an evil deed they always demand payment" (57). Actually, as the armies march through the tunnel Roquat digs beneath the Deadly Desert, readers discover that each of the bands of allies intends to betray the others and have the conquered Oz all to themselves, just as Roquat intends to betray all of them (277–79). The Growleywogs plan to take from Oz all the gold and silver they want as well as the magic belt, and their Grand Gallipoot wants to make Roquat his own slave, while other Growleywogs claim as slaves the Scarecrow, Tiktok, and the Tin Woodman (78–79).[6] The Phanfasms intend to "use King Roquat's tunnel to conquer the Land of Oz. Then," their leader says, "we will destroy the Whimsies, the Growleywogs and the Nomes, and afterward go out to ravage and annoy and grieve the whole world" (123). Even General Guph, Roquat's own general, hopes to betray his leader. Guph says to himself that he wants to "throw him [Roquat] away and be King of the Nomes myself" (81). This kind of treachery stands in marked contrast to the behavior of the residents of Oz, who intend to remain with their ruler and faithful to her even when they think defeat is inevitable (271–72).

Unlike the Nome King and his evil allies, Dorothy is the kind of person who does a *good* deed without hope of reward, and the inhabitants of Oz display love for one another. Dorothy accomplishes "wonders," Baum writes, "not because she was a fairy or had any magical powers whatever, but because she was a simple, sweet and true little girl who was honest to herself and to all whom she met." Baum then adds, "In this world in which we live simplicity and kindness are the only magic wands that work wonders, and in the Land of Oz Dorothy found these same qualities had won for her the love and admiration of the people" (43). Thus, Baum again preaches morality, in spite of what he writes in the Introduction to *The Wonderful Wizard of Oz*.

In the second plot, Aunt Em and Uncle Henry move to Oz. In Kansas they face eviction since Uncle Henry cannot meet the payments on the mortgage he takes when he rebuilds his house after the cyclone. They say that they will try to find work, but they know that to do so will be difficult at their age. They hope they will be able to continue to send Dorothy to school, but probably she will have to work as a maid or nursemaid (14–16). It is interesting that by the time of this book, Dorothy helps Aunt Em with the housework (13), showing that some of the lessons she learned during her journey in Oz as recounted in *The Wonderful Wizard of Oz* have come in handy: among other things, she learns to do housework when she is held prisoner in the castle of the wicked Witch of the West. However, Aunt Em and Uncle Henry need not seek jobs, and Dorothy need not work as a nursemaid or maid. Instead, Dorothy gets Ozma to agree to allow her aunt and uncle to come to Oz to live (27–28). Home thus becomes for Dorothy the Emerald City, and her journeys in this and future Oz books begin and end there. Whereas the enemies of Oz regard each other with suspicion and intend to betray one another, the inhabitants of Oz, unlike their enemies, greet Dorothy and her aunt and uncle with love and consideration. This plot involving Dorothy's family's move to Oz continues with a tour Aunt Em, Uncle Henry, the Wizard, Dorothy, the Shaggy Man, and Omby Amby, Captain General of Ozma's army, as well as Billina and Toto, take of some of the stranger parts of Oz.

The two plots of *The Emerald City of Oz* are thus ironically related: as Aunt Em and Uncle Henry become accustomed to Oz and at home there, the Nome King, his armies, and his allies set in motion plans intended to destroy Oz. As the tour of Oz proceeds, the Nome King prepares to conquer Oz and enslave all of its inhabitants, including those on the tour. When Ozma finds out about the coming invasion, she lets her trusted counselors know. The two plots come together when Dorothy and her companions reach the Land of the Winkies, where the Tin Man tells the tourists about the invasion. They all then travel to the Emerald City, where Ozma tells them that she cannot fight the Nomes and their allies.

Unlike the Ozma of *Ozma of Oz*, who sets out to make war on the Nome King, in *The Emerald City of Oz* she displays what seems to be total pacifism, declaring, "No one has the right to destroy any living creatures, however evil they may be, or to hurt them or make them unhappy" (270). She offers Aunt Em, Uncle Henry, and Dorothy the opportunity to return to Kansas rather than face slavery, but they refuse (271). Earlier in the book Henry sensibly remarks, "I like Oz better than Kansas, even [...]" (87). When offered a chance to return to Kansas and thus escape slavery in Oz, Aunt Em declares, "I've been a slave all my life [...] and so has Henry. I guess we won't go back to Kansas, anyway. I'd rather take my chances with the rest of you" (271–72), reminding readers of the grinding poverty and unremitting hard work that Kansas represents to her and Henry. In these words that Aunt Em speaks, Baum clearly engages in social criticism of the sort that some critics see him engaging in often. Em and Henry are among the dispossessed, the ones who struggle hard throughout their lives without achieving even a modicum of worldly success. For them, the American dream has become a hollow promise, and life in America has become a dead end. But what is true for them is not necessarily true for everyone in America as Baum sees the nation.

The Tin Woodman fears "that those who are not fairies, such as the Wizard, and Dorothy, and her uncle and aunt, as well as Toto and Billina, will be speedily put to death by the conquerors" (255). When Dorothy asks him what can be done about it, he replies, "Nothing can be done! [...] But since Ozma refuses my army I will go myself to the Emerald City. The least I may do is to perish beside my beloved Ruler" (255–56). Thus, the invasion of the Nome King and his allies cannot be dismissed as a childish prank with no possible bad consequences. At one point in the novel the invasion at least seems to have very serious potential consequences for all of the inhabitants of Oz, especially for the one with whom readers most identify themselves — Dorothy. When things in the novel seem most bleak, however, when conquest by the Nomes and their allies seems inevitable, the Scarecrow figures out how to keep Oz free without hurting anyone (274).

Ozma's pacifism in *The Emerald City of Oz* echoes a theme that runs through many of Baum's Oz books and many of his non-Oz books. He fairly consistently ridicules armies, especially officers, and shows the absurdity of war, sometimes making it ridiculous, as he does in *The Patchwork Girl of Oz* (278–96). According to Rogers, "evil powers" are in the Oz books the only ones with "effective armies," for, she asserts, "Baum advocated pacifism" (160). However, in *The Marvelous Land of Oz* Glinda has an effective army. And in *Ozma of Oz* Ozma intends to use her army to conquer the Nome King, although her army is certainly not effective. Also, what Rogers calls the "evil powers" have armies that are not, it seems, all that effective since they always ultimately get defeated. Moreover, Baum dedicates his thirteenth Oz book, *The Magic of Oz*, "to the Children of our Soldiers, the Americans and their Allies, with unmeasured Pride and Affection" (vii), so he may not have been entirely consistent even in his pacifism. After all, one of his sons, Frank Joslyn Baum, had a military career, serving in the Philippines as well as in the American Expeditionary Force in Europe in World War I.[7] However, America did not get involved in World War I until years after *The Emerald City of Oz* appeared. Even in the dedication to *The Magic of Oz*, however, Baum is ambiguous: supporting the children may not be the same as supporting the soldiers themselves, and supporting the soldiers, of which his son was one, may not be the same as supporting the war.

In his non-Oz books Baum is even more ambiguous about war than he is in his Oz books. As Angelica Shirley Carpenter and Jean Shirley show by examining different editions of *Aunt Jane's Nieces in the Red Cross* (which Baum wrote under the pseudonym Edith Van Dyne), Baum's antiwar sentiment became more explicit as World War I progressed. In the 1915 edition "war was a noble idea," Carpenter and Shirley write. In the 1915 edition, they write, the battle scenes are mild; in the 1918 edition the battle scenes are much starker (118–19).

Most of the revisions in the 1918 edition of *Aunt Jane's Nieces in the Red Cross* are aimed toward showing Baum's antiwar sentiments. In fact, in the Foreword he writes explicitly:

> I wish I might have depicted more gently the scenes in hospital and on battlefield, but it is well that my girl readers should realize something of the horrors of war, that they may unite with heart and soul in earnest appeal for universal, lasting Peace and the future abolition of all deadly strife [5].

The novel does not really depict very graphically the horrors of war — at least, not by twenty-first century standards, but with its deaths and mutilations, it is much more graphic than the 1915 edition. The 1918 edition of the novel begins with the nurses and their supporters speaking of neutrality (12) and a desire to aid all wounded (115), no matter what side they are on, since the nieces consider "the wounded and dying" to be "innocent sufferers" (12). It ends with a determination on the part of the nieces' uncle, who financed and led the nurses' expedition to Europe, to do all he can to defeat "the Central Powers" (270).

Still, early in the book one of the nieces states what seems to be Baum's central idea about the war: "It is merely wholesale murder by a band of selfish diplomats" (12).

In a book first published in 1918, also under the pseudonym Edith Van Dyne, *Mary Louise and the Liberty Girls*, Baum at least appears to support the war effort and to laud patriotism, even though he does, as Rogers points out, bravely defend German-Americans. Rogers, moreover, points out Baum's own German heritage (222). Still, Mary Louise and her friends actively support the war effort and hunt for and bitterly condemn any hint of treasonous activity, even though their guesses about such activity are usually wrong. At the end of *Mary Louise and the Liberty Girls* Mary Louise declares to the Liberty Girls, "We're a real part of the war, [...] and I'm sure that in the final day of glorious victory our girls will be found to have played no unimportant part" (255).

It is difficult to reconcile Ozma's statements in *The Emerald City of Oz* with those of Mary Louise in *Mary Louise and the Liberty Girls*. One problem here involves trying to determine a person's philosophy solely on the basis of what that person writes in pieces of fiction. A good writer, it seems, is especially able to keep his own ideas separate from the ones he uses in his works, and Baum seems to have been a good writer. In addition, Baum seems to have been unconcerned with being consistent from book to book (or at times even within books). The best one can do is say that Baum usually voices pacifistic sentiments in his works of fiction. However, as times change, his position in those works changes. And there is always the possibility that his position in real life is different from the one he espouses in the works of fiction.

At any rate, once Aunt Em and Uncle Henry reach Oz, the plot involving them becomes disjointed as they travel from one adventure to another, each involving bizarre creatures. However, except for when Dorothy wanders from the party, there is little conflict, and there is no real connection between episodes except that they all involve unusual, bizarre parts of Oz. General Guph, on the other hand, deals with more and more dangerous groups in his attempt to get allies. He knows that if he fails, Roquat will put him to death; however, Baum writes that Guph "was not at all anxious or worried. He hated every one who was good and longed to make all who were happy unhappy" (53), so he looks forward with delight to invading Oz and is willing to endure hardship to accomplish that end. When he finds himself in danger with the various groups he seeks as allies, he nonetheless seems quite courageous. The extremely strong Growleywogs toss him in the air and let him fall on the ground, but that does not deter the general from getting them involved in the attempt to conquer Oz. Incidentally, after describing the Growleywogs' muscles, Baum writes, "It seems unfortunate that strong people are usually so disagreeable and overbearing that no one cares for them. In fact, to be different from your fellow creatures is always a misfortune" (75), words that make them indeed look like bullies.[8] The Phanfasms take Guph prisoner, and the First and Foremost threatens to kill him, but Guph wins them as his allies. The quest in this book, then, is one involving vicious people and vicious goals. It is an inverse version of the quest in *The Wonderful Wizard of Oz* that involves an innocent little girl who produces benevolent results.

Although Ozma decides that she cannot defend her country, the invasion fails when the Scarecrow comes up with the idea of filling the Nomes' tunnel with dust so that when the invaders arrive at the Emerald City, they are very thirsty. When they leave the tunnel, the first thing they see is the Forbidden Fountain that contains the Water of Oblivion. Because of their thirst, they drink from the fountain and forget everything, including why they came to Oz. Then, Ozma uses the magic belt to send them back to their original countries. Thus, Baum has Ozma find a way to defeat her enemies without fighting them.

Before the invasion occurs, the Wizard and Dorothy discuss airships. The Wizard hates them. Dorothy says that they are not all bad and soon will be flying "all over the world, and perhaps bring people even to the Land of Oz." The Wizard feels that that would be a bad thing, saying, "I must speak to Ozma about that [...]. It wouldn't do at all, you know, for the Emerald City to become a way-station on an airship line," and Dorothy agrees but does not know what can be done about it. The Wizard hopes to fix things so that airships will never go where people want them to go, hoping that that will "keep them from flying to the Land of Oz" (230–31). After the invasion fails, Glinda separates Oz from the rest of the world so that no future invasion can occur and, incidentally, so that no airships from our world can get to Oz. Thus, Baum's farewell to Oz does grow organically out of parts of the plot even though many parts of the plot themselves have little in the way of organic relationship to one another.

Growleywogs, as pictured in *The Emerald City of Oz* (illus. John R. Neill; Chicago: Reilly & Lee, 1910), p. 259.

The loosely knit structures of *The Road to Oz* and of the travelogue parts of *The Emerald City of Oz* foreshadow the kinds of plots Baum uses in many of his later works, plots characterized by the "exciting adventures, unexpected difficulties to be overcome, and marvelous escapes" that Baum in his essay on "Modern Fairy Tales" says children want. Even though, like *The Patchwork Girl of Oz* and *The Lost Princess of Oz,* these books may involve particular quests, the quests take the characters from one unrelated adventure to another until they are completed, usually in unexpected ways. Thus, Aunt Em and Uncle Henry's sightseeing journey in *The Emerald City of Oz*— something quite possibly intended to be a farewell tour of Oz for Baum's readers — foreshadows the kinds of plots of a number of the Oz books Baum was yet to write.

8

The Patchwork Girl of Oz
SAVING UNC NUNKIE

A quest is central to *The Patchwork Girl of Oz*, but it turns out to be unnecessary: the solution to Ojo's problems comes not as a result of his quest but as a result of Glinda's intervention. According to David L. Greene and Dick Martin, "*The Patchwork Girl of Oz* is the first really excellent book after *Ozma of Oz*." The book, they say, "tells how Ojo matures. He learns about honesty and punishment — and ultimately that nothing, not even restoring his uncle, justifies cruelty to a living creature" (35–37). Ojo hears these things, but it is doubtful that he learns any of them, especially the lesson about cruelty. True, the Tin Woodman tells him, "To tear a wing from a butterfly would cause it exquisite torture and it would soon die in great agony," and the narrator says that Dorothy "knew in her heart that the Tin Woodman was right," but after the Tin Woodman speaks, Ojo says "sadly," "The yellow country of the Winkies [...] is the only place in Oz where a yellow butterfly can be found," showing that he still wants a butterfly's wing to save his uncle. He even adds "miserably," "Unless I get the wing — just one left wing —[...] I can't save Unc Nunkie" (332–33), words, especially "just one left wing," that clearly indicate that he is still willing to cause a butterfly agony for the sake of saving his uncle.

Peter Glassman claims that *The Patchwork Girl of Oz* "begins to show Baum's improving ability to plot his Oz stories," and adds, "*The*

Patchwork Girl of Oz is a classic quest. Ojo, Scraps, and their companions have an urgent reason for their journey, and the story reaches its
conclusion when their mission to save Unc Nunkie is accomplished"
(344). Glassman's definition of "classic quest" certainly does not seem
to match Campbell's definition. Ojo does not achieve any real inner
growth, and the Wizard (acting under Glinda's directions), not Ojo,
restores Unc Nunkie and Margolotte. Nonetheless, the book does have
a definite climax with the restoration of Unc Nunkie and Margolotte
and the renaming of Ojo from Ojo the Unlucky to Ojo the Lucky. But
most of the episodes in the book have little to do with producing the
actual climax.

In *The Patchwork Girl of Oz*, Baum carefully subverts Ojo's quest:
it is ultimately a waste of time. He gains nothing of value from it. The
restoration of his uncle is in no way the result of anything Ojo does.
The hero of a true quest does not just seek and perhaps find something; that hero experiences internal exploration and an expansion of
consciousness as a result of his or her journey and causes significant
changes in the external world. In a fairy tale those changes may benefit
only the quester's family; in a myth they may have universal
significance. Yet any changes that may occur in Ojo are superficial and
imposed from without rather than from within, and Ojo causes no
changes in the external world other than to give the Patchwork Girl
more in the way of brains than Dame Margolotte intended for her to
have (23–25). That act, however, occurs before he begins his quest for
the items that will reanimate his uncle.

In *Dorothy and the Wizard in Oz* Dorothy and her companions
experience a series of terrifying adventures. They finally escape from
their predicament through a kind of gimmickry: Dorothy remembers
that she can return to Oz simply by making a particular motion at a
particular time. But Dorothy does not purposely allow the adventures
to continue; she seems genuinely to forget about Ozma's promise to
watch her at a certain time. In *The Patchwork Girl of Oz* Ozma
announces that Glinda knows from the start about Ojo's quest, and
Ozma says, "Glinda also knew that Ojo would fail to find all the things
he sought." Glinda also knows all along how to break the enchantment
that Margolotte and Unc Nunkie are under. She sends for the Wizard
and tells him how to break it (338–39). Why she does not intervene
at once is never explained, nor does anyone ask. Perhaps she desires to
give Ojo a chance to grow and gain self-confidence, but his lamenta-

tion about not being able to get a butterfly wing indicates that he does neither of these things.

Michael O. Riley also considers *The Patchwork Girl of Oz* a "success," in part because it resembles *The Wonderful Wizard of Oz,* a work Riley writes is "the only other book thus far in which Baum had utilized the quest motif inside Oz" (178). Baum also uses the quest motif inside Oz in *The Marvelous Land of Oz;* however, Riley is probably right that the use of the quest helped and helps make *The Patchwork Girl of Oz* a success, at least financially.[1] Riley adds that another reason for the book's success is that in *The Patchwork Girl of Oz,* as in *The Wonderful Wizard of Oz,* just as the quest is about to be concluded successfully, "the characters are balked." The Wizard does not take Dorothy to Kansas; Ojo cannot get the final ingredient he seeks (178). But Dorothy's quest has a third segment to it in which she succeeds, and she also grows considerably. Ojo returns to the Emerald City, where all his efforts become irrelevant when the Wizard performs the magic that Ojo's quest is supposed to make possible. Still, Riley admits that in *The Patchwork Girl of Oz* at times Baum goes "beyond the bounds of the story," introducing "exotic locales and quaint characters for their own sakes [...]" (179). Examples of these kinds of things abound in *The Patchwork Girl of Oz.* Some of the obstacles Ojo and his companions meet on the Yellow Brick Road seem to be pure gimmickry, such as Chiss the giant porcupine that throws its quills (145), the gate that is not there (154–57), and the trick river that flows alternately in different directions, an episode that, incidentally, involves exploitation of a giant fish (316–17). One character that at first seems pretty central to the early part of the book — the phonograph — simply disappears. None of the characters regret its disappearance, and its terrible annoying of the characters seems irrelevant to the rest of the book.

Yet Baum was not wholly careless about the plot of *The Patchwork Girl of Oz,* as his use of foreshadowing shows. For example, Dr. Pipt says that he can work magic only for his "own amusement" because "Too many people were working magic in the Land of Oz, and so our lovely Princess Ozma put a stop to it" (27). It turns out that in stopping the practice of magic, she outlawed the picking of six-leafed clovers because witches and magicians used them in their charms. Ojo breaks the law, since Dr. Pipt needs a six-leafed clover to reanimate Dr. Pipt's wife, Dame Margolotte, and Unc Nunkie, who are petrified in an accident.

As Ojo seeks the things that Dr. Pipt says he needs to reanimate Unc Nunkie and Margolotte, he meets a Munchkin woodcutter who tells him that Dr. Pipt will "get in trouble" for animating the Glass Cat and the Patchwork Girl since "it's against the law for anyone to work magic except Glinda the Good and the royal Wizard of Oz" (62). At the end of the book Dr. Pipt is forbidden from making any more "Powder of Life," the mixture that brings Jack Pumpkinhead and the Sawhorse to life in *The Marvelous Land of Oz* and the Patchwork Girl, the Glass Cat, and the phonograph to life in *The Patchwork Girl of Oz*. The same woodchopper mentions to Ojo that he has a friend, another woodchopper, who is made of tin (63), providing Ojo with the answer to his earlier question to Dr. Pipt, "is there ever any oil in a man's body?" He asks the question because one of the things he must get is "a drop of oil from a live man's body" (49). Unfortunately, Ojo does not recognize that the woodchopper's statement about his tin friend answers Ojo's question much better than the answer Dr. Pipt gives, who tells Ojo that "there must be oil somewhere in a live man's body or the book wouldn't ask for it" (49). Foreshadowing of this sort indicates that Baum had some concern about plot. Nonetheless, he did not create the sort of tight plot he created in his first Oz book.

The Patchwork Girl of Oz involves a quest in which Ojo has to get a list of ingredients for a magic potion that will enable the Crooked Magician to undo the work of the Liquid of Petrifaction that spills on Margolotte and Unc Nunkie. Ojo manages to find each of the items until he has only one left, "the left wing of a yellow butterfly" (48). Without the ingredients, Ojo thinks, he will have to wait six years for Unc Nunkie's and Margolotte's restoration since it will take the Crooked Magician that long to make a new batch of the Powder of Life to restore them (46). However, the items Ojo has to find have no logical connection to his own growth. Even the last item, the butterfly's wing, is not connected to his growth since he does not on his own recognize that removing the wing would cause the butterfly pain and never acknowledges how terrible it would be to remove the wing.

Throughout his quest he thinks of himself as "Ojo the Unlucky," a label that Margolotte tells him is his (9). Whenever things go wrong, he says it is because he is Ojo the Unlucky. When Ozma calls him Ojo the Lucky, he corrects her, after which she says that he is lucky at that moment because he has been pardoned of his crime — picking a six-leafed clover (230). Only at the book's end, when Unc Nunkie and

Margolotte are restored, does Ojo say, "Yes, and it is true!" when the Tin Man says, "Didn't I say you were Ojo the Lucky?" (347). Thus, his feeling that he is now lucky is imposed from without rather than growing from within. Rogers calls Ojo the first "boy hero" that Baum put into a work of fantasy but says that he has "a negative attitude" that "nourishes itself." Still, by the end of the book, she says, Ojo "manages to rid himself of his 'Un,' and [...] is persuaded that he is Ojo the Lucky" (195–97). Whether Ojo is really a "hero" rather than simply a protagonist seems doubtful. Still, Rogers is right: he is *persuaded* that he is lucky; he does not discover it on his own. His feeling of being lucky does not grow from his adventures but rather comes from the Wizard's transforming Unc Nunkie and Margolotte so that they are no longer statues.

At one point Ojo and his companions make an underground journey to get water from a dark well, one of the ingredients Ojo needs to bring Unc Nunkie and Margolotte back to life. The trip involves going to the lands of the Horners and Hoppers and stopping a war that the inhabitants declare on one another. Although the episode gives Baum another opportunity to show his dislike of war, it involves none of the terror of the underground journeys in *Ozma of Oz* and *Dorothy and the Wizard in Oz*.

The most frightening episode of *The Patchwork Girl of Oz*, the one that draws most obviously on the stuff of nightmare, occurs right before the underground journey, when the companions travel through a rift in a canyon that itself is claustrophobic: it is so narrow "that they were able to touch both walls at the same time by stretching out their arms" (259). This rift leads directly to the barred-over cavern of a human-eating giant named Mr. Yoop. To get past him in such a place involves putting oneself in his reach. The Scarecrow devises a plan that works: he goes first, Mr. Yoop grabs him, and while Mr. Yoop is discovering that the Scarecrow is stuffed with straw, Ojo, Dorothy, and Toto are able to run beyond the cavern. Mr. Yoop then throws the straw man out of the cavern and grabs the Patchwork Girl, who goes last and whom Mr. Yoop in turn discovers is stuffed with cotton and throws from his cavern (264–65). Had he captured Dorothy, Ojo, or Toto, he would have eaten them. His literary ancestors are the devouring ogres of fairy tales, such as the one in "Jack and the Beanstalk," and the human-eating giants of myth, such as the ones Ulysses encounters in *The Odyssey*, including the human-eating Laestragonians and especially the cavern-dwelling Cyclops. The Mr. Yoop episode echoes the Scoodler-soup episode in *The Road to Oz*, except that Mr. Yoop is far more human in appearance than the Scoodlers; he even has the human title, *Mr*. Accordingly, the idea of his eating human beings is far more terrifying since it more directly conjures up fear of cannibalism. Like his predecessors in the use of human-eating monsters who have human forms, Baum in *The Patchwork Girl of Oz* draws on what Joseph Campbell in *The Masks of God* calls "six hundred thousand years of human experience" during which cannibals "were grim and gruesome, ever present realities" (68); thus, Baum adds an exquisite touch of horror to his work.

The humor involved in the Mr. Yoop episode makes it even more horrible. For example, above his cavern is a sign warning people away from Mr. Yoop. One line of the sign says, *"Age 400 Years 'and Up'* (as they say in the Department Store advertisements)" (261), thus reducing cannibalism to a commodity for sale in Baum's world.[2] The words, *"P.S.—Don't feed the Giant yourself"* (261), with its horrible pun, contain perhaps the most gruesome joke of all, with its combination of cannibalism and suicide and its echo of signs in zoos saying not to feed the animals.

Two more important points remain to be made about *The Patchwork Girl of Oz*: in it is further evidence of Baum's racism, and in it Baum continues the fiction created in *The Emerald City of Oz* that he is a character in his own story. Early in the book Baum has the phonograph sing part of what may have been a variation on a popular song from 1900, with words by Andrew B. Sterling, entitled "Ain't You My Lulu." The phonograph calls the song, "My Lulu." The first line the phonograph sings is, "Ah wants mah Lulu, mah coal-black Lulu" (130).[3] Baum apparently thought that his audience would not find the song offensive but would find it humorous. Again, Baum reflects the racism of his day.

Later in the book, while Ojo and his companions are on their quest for a dark well, before encountering Mr. Yoop, the travelers encounter the Tottenhots. Baum describes them as having "dusky skins and their hair stood straight up, like wires, and was brilliant scarlet in color. Their bodies were bare except for skins fastened around their waists and they wore bracelets on their ankles and wrists, and necklaces, and great pendant earrings" (244). Baum calls them "imps" (246). They play all night and sleep all day. At one point, they grab the Scarecrow and the

Mr. Yoop, from *The Patchwork Girl of Oz* (illus. John R. Neill; Chicago: Reilly & Lee, 1913), p. 259.

Patchwork girl and start tossing them around. Then, Dorothy "rushed among the Tottenhots and began slapping and pushing them until she had rescued the Scarecrow and the Patchwork Girl" (246). She succeeds so easily in rescuing her friends because Toto helps her, "barking and snapping at the bare legs of the imps until they were glad to flee from his attack." Some of them try to toss Ojo, but he proves too heavy. Some of the "little brown folks" who are slapped the hardest begin to cry, and they all disappear in their houses (246). Then, the travelers work out a compromise whereby the Tottenhots play outdoors all night while the travelers stay in one of the houses, which are really just holes in the ground (249–52).

In creating the Tottenhots, Baum draws on stereotypes of African-Americans and Africans and aligns them with what are often called Hottentots, a pejorative term for the Khoikhoin, a group of people living in Southern Africa. Still, Baum describes them not to appear like Khoikhoin but in part like stereotypical African Americans, with their dusky skin, their wire-like hair, and their desire to spend all of their waking hours playing. Apparently, he felt that his racial stereotyping here would simply amuse his white audience, and it is a shame that he was probably right.

Baum also depicts himself as a character in his book. In prefaces in the earlier Oz books he speaks directly to his readers. In the final chapter of *The Emerald City of Oz* he writes of receiving a message from Dorothy saying that no more will be told about Oz (298–99). In *The Patchwork Girl of Oz* he writes that he learns wireless telegraphy. Glinda finds out what he is doing. The Shaggy Man then communicates with Baum so that the children can have more Oz stories. Baum becomes Historian of Oz, and the series thus continues (ix-xi).

Although *The Patchwork Girl of Oz* has a definite climax — when Unc Nunkie and Margolotte are restored, it follows Baum's formula from his essay, "Modern Fairy Tales," of a series of adventures and narrow escapes tied together loosely by a narrative thread, here involving Ojo's search for ingredients to make a magic potion. Ojo ultimately fails in his search, but Glinda — working through the Wizard — intervenes to produce a happy ending. Thus, the book does not have the tight, organic unity of Baum's first three Oz books or even the unity of his fourth Oz book, a story involving another unnecessary, ultimately subverted quest.

Tik-Tok of Oz, The Scarecrow of Oz, Rinkitink in Oz

"Exciting Adventures," "Unexpected Difficulties," "Marvelous Escapes"

Tik-Tok of Oz, The Scarecrow of Oz, and *Rinkitink in Oz,* the eighth, ninth, and tenth Oz books respectively, all contain quests that Baum uses to string his plots together. In these three books, however, the plots basically consist of the "exciting adventures, unexpected difficulties [...], and marvelous escapes" that Baum in "Modern Fairy Tales" says children want (140). In works like *The Wonderful Wizard of Oz, The Marvelous Land of Oz,* and *Ozma of Oz* character, plot, and setting exist for one another and interact with one another. These three books are full of "exciting adventures, unexpected difficulties [...], and marvelous escapes," but most of them contribute to the organic structure of the plots. In *Tik-Tok of Oz, The Scarecrow of Oz,* and *Rinkitink in Oz* character, setting, and even plot often seem to exist merely for the sake of producing those "exiting adventures, unexpected difficulties," and "marvelous escapes."

Toward the end of Baum's eighth Oz book, *Tik-Tok of Oz,* Tik-Tok says to Ozma that Betsy Bobbin "is al-most as nice as Dor-o-thy her-self" (240). These are high words of praise from the mechanical man whom Dorothy liberates from the room in which the King of Ev locked him (*Ozma* 41–45). With these words Baum makes explicit what is implicit throughout *Tik-Tok of Oz*: the reader should compare Betsy to Dorothy. They are "almost of one size" (250), and they come from neighboring states in the United States, Dorothy from Kansas and Betsy from Oklahoma. Both are also nice, resourceful little girls. Yet the differences between Dorothy as she appears in *The Wonderful Wizard of Oz* and *Ozma of Oz*, the first and third Oz books, and Betsy are tremendous, just as the differences between the two earlier books and the later book are tremendous. In the first two books in which she appears, Dorothy is a genuine hero: in *The Wonderful Wizard of Oz* she frees the Munchkins, Winkies, and inhabitants of the Emerald City from tyrannical or at least inept rule; and in *Ozma of Oz* she takes the magic belt from Roquat, thus enabling Ozma and her party to escape from the underground kingdom. Actually, Betsy more closely resembles the Dorothy of the later Oz books who tends not to be heroic or decisive at all but just a little girl who participates in adventures others lead, just as the episodic plot of *Tik-Tok of Oz* tends to be in many ways typical of the plots of Baum's later Oz books even though it contains material from earlier books.

Although many critics examine *The Wonderful Wizard of Oz*, hardly any even mention *Tik-Tok of Oz*. Those who do usually say negative things. For example, Gary D. Schmidt calls the book a "less than riveting addition to the Oz series," prefacing his remarks by saying, "I shall try to be gentle here" (463). Frank Joslyn Baum and Russell P. MacFall call it, "a veritable slumgullion of Ozzy tidbits" (197). Similarly, Raylyn Moore writes that it "is little more than a reworking of the tailings of Baum's earlier and more successful 'strikes'" (169). One critic who does not treat the work negatively is Celia Catlett Anderson, who looks at the humor in it, especially humor growing out of Tik-Tok's "literal mindedness" (237). Anderson points out that on the frontispiece Tik-Tok "looks decidedly Quixotic [...]" (237). Certainly his attempt to serve as the only private in Ann Soforth's army is Quixotic. Ann Soforth is the Queen of Oogaboo, "the smallest and the poorest" kingdom "in all the Land of Oz" (1). She decides to conquer the world. At Ann's command, Tik-Tok tries to conquer the Nome King, who is now named Ruggedo since he forgets his original name, Roquat, after drinking from the Forbidden Fountain, the water of which makes him forget everything. Tik-Tok fails miserably because Kaliko, the king's high chamberlain, "stole softly behind the copper man and kicked his knee-joints so that they suddenly bent forward and tumbled Tik-Tok to the floor, his gun falling from his grasp" (160), producing an ignominious end to a gallant attempt. At least, Anderson's comments on the whole tend to be neutral.

In surface matters, parts of the plot of *Tik-Tok of Oz* resemble parts of *Ozma of Oz*. Betsy and Dorothy get to Oz in similar ways. In *Ozma of Oz* during a storm at sea Dorothy is blown overboard from a ship going to Australia. She drifts ashore with Billina the Hen in the Kingdom of Ev, and after going to the realm of the Nome King, she eventually gets to Oz. Betsy is the sole human survivor of a ship that a storm at sea destroys. As she watches, the ship explodes. The only other survivor is Hank the Mule. Betsy and Hank also have several adventures before they get to Oz, including going to the realm of the Nome King. Yet in *The Wonderful Wizard of Oz* and in *Ozma of Oz* Dorothy is a decidedly heroic, quick-thinking, decisively acting protagonist. In addition, Dorothy's adventures in these two books help her grow significantly. In the first she learns how to do housework, including washing, cleaning floors, and sewing, all of which will enable her to help Aunt Em when she gets back to Kansas. More importantly, she learns about her own capabilities, including the ability to love selflessly. In the second book she helps save Ev and Oz from chaos as she learns to look beneath appearance to reality.

For all of her niceness, Betsy is certainly not heroic. If she is on a quest, it is a strange one, for it has no apparent goal. She does not seek home; after Polychrome returns to her home on the rainbow, Betsy says, "Once, [...] I, too, had a home. Now, I've only–only — dear old Hank" (233). Although she is definitely not a picaro, her initial intention seems to be to wander wherever her adventures take her until Dorothy, Ozma, and the Wizard intervene and enable her to go to Oz (240–43). In *Tik-Tok of Oz* Betsy becomes one of several characters who compose a protagonal party, none of whom are particularly heroic. The only ones who approach heroism are Tik-Tok and Files. When Tik-Tok tries to obey Queen Ann Soforth's command to conquer Ruggedo, he could become a hero, but Kaliko easily prevents the conquest and makes Tik-Tok look foolish in the process (155–56); thus, he is more of a clown than a hero. Files is one of Ann's subjects, the only one who hopes to help her conquer the world. However, he resigns his "position as the Army of Oogaboo" when Queen Ann orders him, he feels, "to bind harmless girls" (71). His resignation is a simple act that separates him from the generals in the army who are too cowardly to do anything on their own, except run from danger. Thus, any heroism he may display comes from a kind of renunciation of his role in Ann's army.

Ann Soforth is on a definite quest, one she gladly relinquishes before the book's end: she declares, "I am going to conquer the world" (6). She and her army of one private and many officers illustrate Baum's fairly typical anti-militarism and provide additional comic relief for the book. The Shaggy Man is on a successful quest for his brother, whom he discovers the Nome King holds captive.[1] But none of these quests have much significance beyond the desires of the questers themselves. Like Betsy, Polychrome just joins the protagonal party to have something to do until she can rejoin her father and sisters on the rainbow. Incidentally, although Baum has Shaggy and Polychrome share extensive adventures in *The Road to Oz*, the two do not know each other when they meet in *Tik-Tok of Oz*.

Tik-Tok of Oz has a basically episodic plot. The protagonal party itself consists of separate groups of questers who join together for convenience. Several of the episodes are connected only by storyline, including the Great Jinjin's sending Quox the Dragon to conquer the Nome King because Ruggedo uses the Hollow Tube in his attempt to get rid of the protagonal party (124–25). After Ann and her army enter the Nome King's underground realm and crawl through the secret tunnel to get to the Metal Forest, they see "more plunder than they had ever dreamed of; yet they were prisoners in this huge dome and could not escape with the riches heaped about them." Baum comments, "Perhaps a more unhappy and homesick lot of 'conquerors' never existed than this band from Oogaboo" (206). When they reunite with the rest of the protagonal party, Ann decides that she has had enough of conquering the world: "If I could find my way back to Oogaboo," she says, "I'd take my army home at once, for I'm sick and tired of these dreadful hardships." When Betsy asks her about conquering the world, Ann replies, "I've changed my mind about that [...]. The world is too big for one person to conquer and I was happier with my own people in Oogaboo" (235). Otherwise, the members of the protagonal party remain basically unchanged throughout their adventures. Even Ann changes only at the end when she is exhausted, tattered, and dirty as a result of crawling through the tunnel (206). Whereas Dorothy is basically dynamic in *The Wonderful Wizard of Oz*, Betsy, like Dorothy in the later Oz books, is basically static.

In *The Wonderful Wizard of Oz* Dorothy is intent upon returning to Kansas. In fact, the whole book involves Dorothy's quest for home. Moreover, her references to Kansas repeatedly remind the reader of her quest. Also, wherever she goes in Oz, she carries her Kansas virtues of practicality and cleanliness with her. Obvious examples involve her putting on, before she begins her trip to the Emerald City, her gingham dress with white and blue checks that "happened to be clean" and her putting on the silver shoes of the wicked Witch of the East because her own shoes are "old and worn." The witch's shoes fit her perfectly, and she is sure "They would be just the thing to take a long walk in, for they could not wear out" (20–21). Moreover, when she leaves her house, "She closed the door, locked it, and put the key carefully in the pocket of her dress" (21). Betsy, on the other hand, seems uninterested in returning to Oklahoma. Possibly Baum considered Kansas worth returning to but Oklahoma not worth returning to.

Baum shows his lack of concern for what he is doing in *Tik-Tok of Oz* when he has Shaggy, who in earlier Oz books is from our world and has been to Kansas, introduce Betsy to Tik-Tok, saying, "The small girl here is Betsy Bobbin, from some unknown earthly paradise called Oklahoma, and with her is Mr. Hank, a mule with a long tail and short temper" (67). Even the flippant tone of the passage does not help explain how Shaggy could think of Oklahoma as an "unknown" place, much less an "earthly paradise." At any rate, toward the end of the book Baum has Betsy indicate that she has nothing to return to in Oklahoma. She possibly loses her whole family on the ship that explodes, but if she does, she shows no sorrow at that time (27–29). At any rate, before Ozma decides to allow her to go to Oz, Betsy thinks that her future will consist of wandering the world with Hank, the Shaggy Man, and his brother, hunting for adventures.

In *The Wonderful Wizard of Oz*, storyline, character development, and setting all work together. In *Tik-Tok of Oz* Baum depends essentially on storyline and setting. The characters go from one adventure to the next, and the setting is at times decidedly bizarre and gimmicky. Storyline and setting do not interact the way they do in the first Oz book. Moreover, in *Tik-Tok of Oz* the personalities of most of the characters remain static, except possibly Ann, who does decide not to continue trying to conquer the world, and Files and Ozga the Rose Queen, who enjoy each other's company and seem to find each other attractive. However, even though Moore calls *Tik-Tok of Oz*, the only "'adult'

Oz book" by Baum (131), Baum seems unwilling to go so far as to have Ozga and Files grow into any kind of love that may seem to involve sex or sexuality. At the book's end Ozma sends them both to Oogaboo because, she says, "They have become such good friends that I am sure it would make them unhappy to separate them" (237). The operant word here is *friends.* No mention is made of their being in love. Ruggedo also finds Polychrome attractive, asking her to remain underground and be his daughter or wife or aunt or grandmother (171). By including "daughter," "aunt," and "grandmother" in his list, here too Baum seems to be trying to avoid references to any kind of sexual activity at the same time that he makes the passage humorous.

A good example of the kind of gimmickry associated with setting occurs as Betsy, Ozga, Shaggy, Tik-Tok, Ann, and her army approach the underground kingdom. First, they unknowingly enter the Rubber Country where they find themselves bouncing unexpectedly off rocks they are using as stepping-stones to cross a stream. After Tik-Tok and two of Ann's officers have mishaps, Polychrome and Betsy bounce successfully across the stream. However, when Hank lands in the water, Betsy goes after him and emerges completely dry. Polychrome remarks, "It's dry water." Betsy then suggests that the others can wade across and remain dry. They all do (85–88). The idea of having rubber rocks and dry water is clever, but it leads nowhere. The travelers never return to this part of the country, nor do they seem to learn anything of value from their adventures in it.

At one point, Ruggedo makes the travelers fall through a Hollow Tube that goes through the earth to the kingdom ruled over by Tititi-Hoochoo, the powerful Jinjin. The Jinjin told Ruggedo never to use the Tube. The penalty for those who go through the Tube is to "be tortured for nine days and ten nights and then thrown back into the tube" (111). But the Jinjin recognizes that Betsy and her friends are not responsible for their trip, so he punishes the responsible person — Ruggedo — instead. He sends the dragon Quox along with the travelers back through the Tube, making their journey much easier for them by having them sit on seats on Quox's back and having them illuminated by an electric light on Quox's tail. Eventually, after Ann and her army fail to conquer Ruggedo as part of Ann's plan to conquer the world, Quox takes away Ruggedo's ability to perform magic and banishes him from the underground realm (180–86).

Tik-Tok of Oz is full of interesting characters, especially Ruggedo,

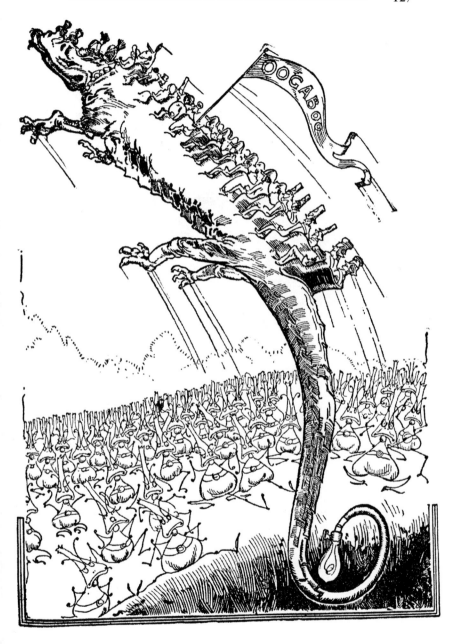

Quox in midair. *Tik-Tok of Oz* (illus. John R. Neill; Chicago: Reilly & Lee, 1914), p. 163.

who is "proud of his hatred and abhorred love of any sort," so he avoids looking at the Love Magnet Shaggy carries (164). Still, he admits to Polychrome, "I hate everybody — but you," and tries to get her "to live always in this beautiful cavern [...]" (170). Sometimes he does act like a spoiled child and a bully. For example, when the Long-Eared Hearer tells Ruggedo that Queen Ann and her army intend to conquer the Nome King, in a fit of anger he bellows with rage, dances "up and down, rolling his eyes, clicking his teeth together and swinging his arms furiously," and then seizes the Hearer's ears and pulls and twists "them cruelly" (92). But he is often magnificent in his wickedness, especially when he changes Ozga into "a fiddle" and tries unsuccessfully to change Files into "a fiddle bow" (179).[2] Even though Ruggedo is at times a comic figure, he seems anything but harmless in this book.

Thus, *Tik-Tok of Oz* is full of interesting adventures with some interesting characters. In his essay entitled "Modern Fairy Tales," Baum writes that what children "want is action — 'something doing every minute' — exciting adventures, unexpected difficulties to be overcome, and marvelous escapes" (140). In several of his earlier Oz books he gives all of these things and much more — unified stories that involve significant growth on the part of their central characters and that lead to definite climaxes. Yet in *Tik-Tok of Oz* Baum tends to concentrate wholly on the "exciting adventures, unexpected difficulties [...], and marvelous escapes."

The Scarecrow of Oz and *Rinkitink in Oz* also involve quests. However, on the whole, they consist of little more than the series of adventures that Baum in "Modern Fairy Tales" says that children want. *The Scarecrow of Oz*, with its underground adventures, is wonderfully scary. In a small boat Trot and Cap'n Bill get sucked into a whirlpool. They end up in an underground cavern where at first they think that they face starvation. At one end of the cavern is a "dark hole" that Trot urges Cap'n Bill to let them enter. However, the captain replies, "Some things are more hard to face than starvation [...]" (16). Eventually, they do enter the hole, which is a tunnel leading to a cliff and then another tunnel (32–33). While in the second tunnel Cap'n Bill says, "There's somethin' queer about this 'ere tunnel, I'm certain [...]. Here's three candles gone a'ready, an' only three more left us; yet the tunnel's the same as it was when we started. An' how long it's goin' to keep up, no one knows" (34). Consequently, the travelers decide to journey ahead in darkness, with the Ork — a bird with a propeller tail who also gets caught in a whirlpool and pulled into the cavern — in front, since if the Ork comes across another precipice, he will not be hurt by the fall. The idea of traveling underground in the dark with no idea what, if anything, lies ahead or at the end of the tunnel is terrifying.[3] When the travelers finally do get above ground, they find themselves stranded on a small island. Still, Trot says that "it's better than those terr'ble underground tunnels and caverns," to which Cap'n Bill replies, "You are right, little one [...]. Anything above ground is better than the best that lies under ground" (44).

A little man named Pessim lives on the island. He was stranded there because nobody liked him and he liked nobody. Cap'n Bill tells Pessim that the Ork can fly, but the captain and Trot are stuck on the island. When Pessim says to Trot and Cap'n Bill, "You can go back into the hole you came from," Baum writes, "Cap'n Bill shook his head; Trot shuddered at the thought; the Ork laughed aloud" (60), indicating the horror the two people — and possibly the Ork — feel about going back underground.

Once Trot and Cap'n Bill reach Oz, their adventures in Jinxland, a country on Oz's edge but separated from the rest of Oz by rugged mountains, are also scary, especially the transformation of Cap'n Bill into a grasshopper that, like the captain, has a wooden leg and what Baum calls a meat leg, and the freezing of the heart of Princess Gloria, both of which are caused by an "old and ugly" witch named Blinkie (135). When the witch freezes Gloria's heart, Trot and Pon, the gardener's boy who loves Gloria, watch:

> Trot saw the body of the Princess become transparent, so that her beating heart showed plainly. But now the heart turned from a vivid red to gray, and then to white. A layer of frost formed about it and tiny icicles clung to its surface. Then slowly the body of the girl became visible again and the heart was hidden from view. (166)

Like the episode involving Mr. Yoop in *The Patchwork Girl of Oz*, the episodes involving Cap'n Bill's transformation mix horror and comedy. When the Ork finds out that the captain is a grasshopper, the bird asks, "How do you like it?" The captain replies, "Why, it worries me a good deal [...]. I'm always afraid o' bein' stepped on, and I don't like the flavor of grass an' can't seem to get used to it. It's my nature to eat grass, you know, but I begin to suspect it's an acquired taste." The Ork then asks, "Can you give molasses?" to which the captain replies, "I guess I'm not that kind of grasshopper [...]. But I can't say what I might

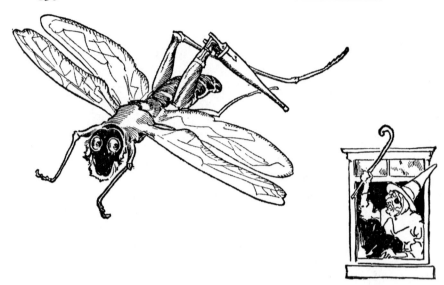

Cap'n Bill as grasshopper in *The Scarecrow of Oz* (illus. John R. Neill; Chicago: Rand McNally, 1915), p. 182.

do if I was squeezed — which I hope I won't be" (197). As so often occurs in Baum's writing, for some readers the humor makes the horror all the greater.

But Trot and Cap'n Bill, along with Button-Bright, whom they find in Mo as they travel toward Oz, apparently gain no self-knowledge during their adventures. Again, like Betsy, they are certainly not rogues but travel where fortune takes them, even though they do hope to get to Oz sometime.[4] Incidentally, it is ironic that Jinxland is a part of Oz, but getting there brings no happiness, at least at first, to the travelers.

The Scarecrow, however, goes on a quest with a definite goal: Glinda sends him to Jinxland "to protect Trot and Button-Bright and Cap'n Bill" and to end the rule of King Krewl, who, Glinda says, "has no right to" be king (153–54). Since Jinxland is part of Oz, Glinda here indicates that Oz is not a eutopia and that all the people are not content. To fulfill the quest, the Scarecrow must change the government of Jinxland, removing King Krewl from his throne that he holds unrightfully and putting Gloria on her rightful throne. At no time does Glinda question whether she has the right to impose a particular ruler on Jinxland, nor does Baum consider such a question. Since Glinda's actions lead to what she (and Baum) consider better rule for Jinxland, from Baum's point of view she has every right to impose a new ruler. The Scarecrow does give the people a chance to choose their own ruler. But before he does so, the people of the country assemble, and "the Scarecrow declared that the only one in all Jinxland who had the right to sit upon the throne was Princess Gloria, the daughter of King Kynd" (222). Still, the people want the Scarecrow to rule them, an honor he refuses. Then, although some of the residents want Pon to rule, the majority pick Gloria to be their ruler.

At this point in the story Baum comes as close as he ever does to introducing possibilities of sexual activity into an Oz book. After the people name Gloria their queen, she takes Pon's hand and raises "him to the seat beside her." She then says to her subjects, "You shall have both a King and a Queen to care for you and to protect you, [...] for Pon was a King's son before he became a gardener's boy, and because I love him he is to be my Royal Consort" (223). Baum's child readers may not know that Pon's being a royal consort would make him Gloria's husband, but the term *royal consort* does mean that and thus has sexual implications. At any rate, from the vantage point of the twenty-first century Glinda's imposing a new ruler on Jinxland appears imperialistic, even though that ruler is undoubtedly better than the ruler who gets deposed. As Gloria declares, she intends to "care for" and "protect" her subjects instead of exploiting them as King Krewl does. At least the people of Jinxland get some say in who shall rule them.

Although the Scarecrow ultimately succeeds in his quest, he almost gets burnt at the stake, an episode that may be an ironic reference to the idea of burning witches at the stake: the Scarecrow comes to Jinxland in part to free it from a terrible ruler who depends in part on witchcraft for his power. One of the Scarecrow's tasks is to take away all of Blinkie's magical powers. At any rate, at the last minute a group of Orks rescue the Scarecrow (206–07), so he does not share the fate of so many people who in the real world have been labeled witches. The book, then, has exactly the kinds of narrow escapes Baum says children love, but it has no overall pattern.

Rinkitink in Oz is similar. It began as a non-Oz book onto which Baum tacked Oz material.[5] King Rinkitink happens by chance to be on the island of Pingaree, ruled by King Kitticut and Queen Garee, when warriors from Regos and Coregos capture the island and lead off its inhabitants into slavery. Rinkitink and Inga, prince of Pingaree, along with Rinkitink's talking goat, Bilbil, manage to remain free. Inga uses magic pearls to release the inhabitants of Pingaree and other slaves the people of Regos and Coregos hold, but King Gos of Regos takes Inga's parents to the land of the Nome King to be held as captives there. In this book Kaliko is Nome King since Ruggedo gets dethroned near the end of *Tik-Tok of Oz*. Inga follows King Gos to the land of the Nomes, where, with the help of Dorothy and the Wizard of Oz, he eventually frees his parents. Throughout the book the fat Rinkitink rides Bilbil. Near the book's end the Wizard recognizes that the goat is the enchanted prince of Boboland. With difficulty, Glinda undoes the enchantment, first turning the goat into a lamb, then into an ostrich so that it has "two legs and feet instead of four." Then she fails to transform the ostrich into Prince Bobo, so she turns it into "a tottenhot — which is a lower form of a man" (261–62). Tottenhots play a role in *The Patchwork Girl of Oz*. As John R. Neill's illustration for the transformation episode in *Rinkitink in Oz* implies, Baum's (and Neill's) racism is at work here, just as it is in *The Patchwork Girl*: Neill's Tottenhot looks not like a Khoikhoin but like a stereotypical caricature of an African native wearing some kind of fur and carrying a club. Baum's statement, moreover, that the Tottenhot is "a lower form of a man" follows turn-of-the-twentieth-century racist ideas that blacks are racially inferior to other human beings.

Then, Glinda turns the Tottenhot into a Mifket — one of Baum's imaginary creatures that Neill illustrates as being round and pudgy with an angry face and pointed head. In *John Dough and The Cherub* (1906), a work that pre-dates *Rinkitink* by eight years, Baum describes Mifkets as follows:

> Their heads had the appearance of coconuts, and were covered with coarse hair clipped close, and turning upward until it ended in a sharp peak at the very top. Their faces were like putty, with small, beady eyes that glittered brightly, flat noses, and wide, grinning mouths. The Mifkets' bodies were shaped like pears, and their legs were short and their arms long. For clothing they wore gay leaves of the for est [sic] plants, twisted and woven together in quite a clever way; and taken all together, they were as unlike any creatures that inhabit our part of the world as can well be imagined [82].

According to Baum in *Rinkitink in Oz*, a Mifket "was a great step in advance" of a Tottenhot (262), but apparently still a lower form of humanity, thus increasing for Baum and his readers the supposed gap between Africans and African-Americans on the one hand and white

From goat to prince, as shown in *Rinkitink in Oz*. (illus. John R. Neill; Chicago: Reilly & Lee, 1916), pp. 294–95.

people on the other hand. Then, Baum writes, "finally, Glinda transformed the mifket into a handsome young man, tall and shapely [...]" (262). Here too Baum's decided preference for good-looking people over ugly people appears. However, Baum's racism in this book seems entirely gratuitous as does his having Bilbil the Goat be an enchanted prince: Bilbil's being an enchanted prince seems to have no real connection to the rest of the plot; nothing in it demands that the goat be an enchanted person.

By the time the book is over, the Oz people return to Oz, and Inga and Rinkitink return to Pingaree. But Rinkitink's subjects find where he is and force him to return to his own land so that he can rule them.

Even as brief a plot summary as given here indicates that the book is fairly haphazard. The only times Inga is in danger are when the warriors come to his island because he then does not hold the magic pearls, when he temporarily loses his pearls on Regos and Coregos, and when in the Nome Kingdom he lets Rinkitink have the pink pearl that protects its bearer from all danger. Otherwise, the pearls make him so powerful and impregnable and give him such good advice that he seems in no danger at all. The underground episodes are slightly scary, especially when Inga has to travel alone through the Nomes' caverns without the aid of his pink pearl, but even then, his tremendous strength from the blue pearl and the advice of the white pearl protect him in such a way that the reader is sure of the outcome of his adventures before they begin. The underground episodes, thus, do not attain the kind of claustrophobic grandeur that underground scenes in *Dorothy and the Wizard in Oz*, *Ozma of Oz*, or even *The Scarecrow of Oz* attain.

Nonetheless, the book has some interesting touches. After the people of Pingaree have been taken into captivity, for example, the narrator describes the island as follows:

> The sun shone upon the beautiful green isle as brilliantly as if no ruthless invader had passed and laid it in ruins. The birds still chirped among the trees and the butterflies darted from flower to flower as happily as when the land was filled with a prosperous and contented people [38].

More important than the recognition of the former contentment of the residents of Pingaree is the indifference of nature to what has happened. In this passage Baum writes like a late-nineteenth- or early-twentieth-century Realist — possibly even a Naturalist, showing a complete divorce between humankind and the environment in which humankind finds itself. The landscape here is, in effect, opposite that in Kansas in the first Oz book, except for a very important similarity: in both cases the landscape seems utterly indifferent to the people who do or do not inhabit it.

Rinkitink in Oz also contains explicit moralizing and social criticism, things that tend to weaken the book. In *Rinkitink in Oz* Kaliko gives a speech about strong kings having to trample weak ones under their feet, making him seem like a stereotypical capitalist. In addition, when Inga puts to route the savage warriors under the command of King Gos, Baum writes, "Like all bullies and marauders, Gos was a coward at heart, and now a panic seized him and he turned and fled before the calm advance of Prince Inga of Pingaree" (101). After King Gos flees Inga, Queen Cor tells King Gos, "only soldiers and bullies are cowards" (130), claiming that she can handle Inga, and at first she does. But ironically, she too ends up fleeing Inga in fear. *Rinkitink in Oz* also contains some explicit social criticism when Baum comments on the bravery of Zella and her family: "poor people are often obliged to take chances that rich ones are spared" (142). In fact, Baum's sympathy in the Oz books seems pretty consistently associated with the poor, as his treatment of Dorothy, Em, and Henry's life in Kansas shows.

In *Rinkitink in Oz* Inga promises Zella that he will make her family "rich and prosperous." Nikobob, a poor charcoal burner, is Zella's father. He pleads with Inga to forget his promise, explaining, "I have been safe from molestation for many years, because I was poor and possessed nothing that anyone else could envy. But if you make me rich and prosperous I shall at once become the prey of thieves and marauders and probably will lose my life in the attempt to protect my fortune." About Nikobob's words Rinkitink says, "Perhaps [...] the charcoal-burner has more wisdom concealed in that hard head of his than we gave him credit for" (191). Nikobob further explains:

> What you call my wisdom [...] is merely common sense. I have noticed that some men become rich, and are scorned by some and robbed by others. Other men become famous, and are mocked at and derided by their fellows. But the poor and humble man who lives unnoticed and unknown escapes all these troubles and is the only one who can appreciate the joy of living.

Hearing these words, Bilbil the goat wishes he had a hand so he could shake Nikobob's hand and adds, "But the poor man must not have a cruel master, or he is undone" (191–92). So even being poor and unnoticed does not necessarily ensure that one "can appreciate the joy of living." Instead, in Baum's Oz books, the fairly consistent key to being able to lead such a life is living in a well regulated state governed by benevolent rulers. Nikobob ends up going to Pingaree, where he will have such rulers and thus not have to worry about having anything stolen from him.

Baum even becomes preachy in the book when he writes about Inga's thinking how to escape from a predicament in the Nome Kingdom. Baum writes, "This is the way to get ideas: never to let adverse circumstances discourage you, but to believe there is a way out of every difficulty, which may be found by earnest thought" (231). Moralizing of this sort actually disrupts the flow of Baum's narrative. At his best, as in *The Marvelous Land of Oz* when Ozma speaks of "the riches of content," the morals grow out of the material Baum presents. In *Rinkitink in Oz*, however, he does not even give the morals a chance to grow out of his story. He hurls them at the reader, creating repeated blemishes in his book.

The moralizing and social criticism in *Rinkitink in Oz* do not raise the book above the level of mediocrity. Actually, they help anchor it at that level. Repeatedly, they disrupt the flow of the otherwise exciting narrative. Baum could write an interesting, lively book when he followed his formula of "exciting adventures," "unexpected difficulties," and "marvelous escapes." When he transcended the formula, he could and did write some great books. In *Rinkitink in Oz* he barely lives up to the formula. He has the adventures, difficulties, and escapes, but at times he slows them down with his repeated moralizing, producing one of his weakest Oz books.

True to Baum's formula the characters in *Tik-Tok of Oz, The Scarecrow of Oz,* and *Rinkitink in Oz* do not grow, and the adventures within each book have no logical connection to each other except that they involve events in sequence. The settings, moreover, seem merely to be interesting places through which the characters must travel. In these three books Baum strings together episodes, depending on them and their settings and characters to be interesting enough to carry his readers to the end of each book. David L. Greene points out that, when first published, *Tik-Tok of Oz* sold nicely, but soon sales fell, so much so that Baum ultimately "termed the 1914 sales 'disastrous.' [...]" The lower sales, Baum's publisher speculated, may have resulted from the "War and business depression," and Greene implies that the low sales of *Tik-Tok* accompanied low sales of all the Oz books until 1918 or 1919 (17). Nonetheless, the episodes in the book seem interesting enough to generate sales, for the book still is available in several editions, including inexpensive paperbacks, indicating that it, like *The Scarecrow of Oz* and even *Rinkitink in Oz,* still has a reading audience long after it was published. However, Betsy and Trot are not Dorothy, and *Tik-Tok of Oz, The Scarecrow of Oz,* and *Rinkitink in Oz* are not masterpieces of the sort that *The Wonderful Wizard of Oz* is, nor do they have the kind of coherence that many of the other Oz books have. In them Baum really is guilty of what so many critics say he is guilty of in all of his Oz books: weak plotting.

10

The Lost Princess of Oz
RESCUING PERSEPHONE

In very general terms *The Lost Princess of Oz* follows the story of the Greek goddess, Persephone or Kore. Ugu the Shoemaker's stealing of Ozma is the equivalent of Hades' ravishment of Persephone.[1] Hades takes the goddess to his underground kingdom; Ugu buries Ozma in a peach pit in his orchard, and at one point, Ozma even enters a hole in the ground when Button Bright, who carries the peach pit in his pocket, falls into one (224). Persephone's mother, Demeter, seeks Persephone; all the major Oz characters seek Ozma. By means of a divine compromise Persephone is allowed to return to the Earth's surface part of each year; her rising coincides with the coming of spring and the return of order to the Earth after the chaos of winter. In Baum's book the Wizard releases Ozma from her burial place in the peach pit, and harmony and order return to the Land of Oz. These resemblances between the myth and Baum's book, however, are very general, and the differences are great: no mother longs for and seeks Ozma, although Glinda is anxious that Ozma return. No one destroys crops because of lamenting Ozma's loss. No divine marriage occurs. Frankly, the Greek myth plays a minimal role at best in *The Lost Princess of Oz*. The myth plays a far more important role in Baum's last Oz book, *Glinda of Oz*.

In a letter of 17 January 1916 to Frank K. Reilly of Reilly & Britton, the firm that was his publisher at that time, Baum wrote that the manuscript that would become his eleventh Oz book, *The Lost Princess of Oz*, "was exactly in line with the style of the first four Oz books" (qtd. by David Greene 19). Rogers agrees with Baum: *The Lost Princess of Oz*, she says, is written "in the style of his early Oz books," and she calls it "one of his best." It is, she claims, "well-plotted" and "full of fine inventions" (215).

Three of Baum's first four Oz books — *The Wonderful Wizard of Oz, Ozma of Oz*, and *Dorothy and the Wizard in Oz* — involve quests that begin in the so-called real world, go to Oz, and then return to the real world. Unlike these three books, however, but like Baum's second and sixth Oz books, *The Marvelous Land of Oz* and *The Patchwork Girl of Oz*, the quest in *The Lost Princess of Oz* begins and ends in Oz. Like *The Marvelous Land of Oz, The Lost Princess of Oz* involves a search for a transformed Ozma, the rightful ruler of the Land of Oz. Like *The Wonderful Wizard of Oz, The Marvelous Land of Oz*, and *Ozma of Oz, The Lost Princess of Oz* treats political issues, especially the need for political stability and the ways in which magic can preserve and threaten that stability. Yet unlike any of the first four Oz books, but like *The Emerald City of Oz, The Lost Princess of Oz* has a double plot. One involves the search for the missing Ozma and the missing magical apparatus of the Wizard and Glinda. The other involves the search for the missing dishpan of Cayke the Cookie Cook of Yip. These two separate quests at first seem unrelated but eventually merge.

Dorothy's quest in *The Wonderful Wizard of Oz* is largely structured on the traditional hero quest, on what Joseph Campbell calls the monomyth. Although on the surface the quests in *The Lost Princess of Oz* seem similar to Dorothy's in the first Oz book, the later book does not really involve any hero quests. It is more of a detective story — a search for a thief — combined with a suspenseful travelogue through interesting, unknown parts of the Land of Oz. The parts traversed seem to have no organic relationship to one another. Like the landscape in *Tik-Tok of Oz*, parts of the landscape of *The Lost Princess of Oz* seem to exist merely for the sake of being interesting, unusual places the ones in search of Ozma travel through. Places of this sort are the Merry-Go-Round Mountains, the turning lands around Thi, and the thistle field outside the city of Thi that supplies food for the inhabitants of the city, the Thists. Even the strange shape of the inhabitants of Thi along with their insides being gold-lined seem mere gimmickry on Baum's part, an attempt to entertain the children reading the book rather than a necessary part of the book. Weakest of all seems to be the fact of Toto's losing his growl, something apparently added to the story simply for the sake of pathos and humor. Still, *The Lost Princess of Oz* reveals some interesting things about the role of magic in the politics of Baum's Oz.

The more important quest in terms of its value for the entire Land of Oz is the one for Ozma, the magic picture, the great book of records, and the magical apparatus and elixirs of both Glinda and the Wizard. The less important one involves the search for Cayke's missing dishpan. However, both quests actually have the same goal. All of these things disappear in the course of one night. All of these disappearances are united, and both quests are thus united, since they involve searches for the same thief.

Early in the book the people of the Emerald City discover that someone has taken all the magical apparatus and elixirs belonging to the Wizard and Glinda as well as taken Ozma herself. The thefts have disastrous potential: they threaten to place a tyrant as ruler over the Land of Oz or to destroy political stability in Oz altogether and plunge the land back into the kind of anarchy that characterizes Oz before Ozma assumes the throne at the end of the second Oz book, *The Marvelous Land of Oz*. Before that time the Land of Oz is ruled by two wicked witches, whom Dorothy destroys; a humbug Wizard, who leaves in a balloon; and two good witches, the relatively weak good Witch of the North and Glinda, the powerful good Witch of the South. Dorothy's destruction of the wicked witches and unmasking of the humbug Wizard leads to the Scarecrow's rule over the Emerald City, the Tin Man's rule over the Country of the Winkies, and the Cowardly Lion's reign as King of the Beasts. The Scarecrow's rule, however, receives its legitimacy from the Wizard, who, because he has no real magic and, at least in *The Marvelous Land of Oz*, no legitimate claim to the throne of the Emerald City, is in Oz not an adequate source of political power. Accordingly, General Jinjur and her all-female army quickly overthrow the Scarecrow's rule. Jinjur, a bad ruler, spends her time as queen eating candies and neglecting her country. Then, Glinda reestablishes harmony and order by putting Ozma in her rightful place as ruler of the Emerald City. As a result of her recognition of the potential harm magic can do and of the good it can do in the right hands, in later Oz books Ozma decrees that only Glinda, the Wizard, and Ozma herself are permitted to practice magic.

In *The Lost Princess of Oz* the stealing of the magical apparatus and of Ozma herself clearly indicates that someone is violating Ozma's decree. As it turns out, the thief is ultimately interested in gaining political power: "He wanted to be powerful and great and he hoped to make himself master of all the Land of Oz, that he might compel everyone in that fairy country to obey him" (212). Note the word *compel* here: Ugu intends to rule Oz not through love but through force. He hopes to put into action the totalitarian potentiality that things like Ozma's magic picture and Glinda's great book of records involve.

Several parties leave the Emerald City to search for Ozma in different parts of the country. Dorothy puts together the party that searches in Winkie Country, where Ugu the Shoemaker, who has committed the thefts, lives. Dorothy's party includes Dorothy herself, Trot, Betsy Bobbin, Button-Bright, Scraps the Patchwork Girl, the Cowardly Lion, Hank the Mule, the Sawhorse, the Woozie, and Toto. The Wizard also goes with the party, he says to Dorothy, "to protect you from harm and to give you my advice. All my wizardry, alas, is stolen, so I am now really no more a wizard than any of you; but I will try to protect you from any enemies you may meet" (54–55). He feels that "[...] a wizard without tools is as helpless as a carpenter without a hammer or saw" (248), yet he still retains his knowledge of magic, which enables him to solve some problems along the way.

After crossing the Rolling Plains and the Merry-Go-Round Mountains and visiting the cities of Thi and Herku, the members of Dorothy's party meet Cayke, the Frogman, the Lavender Bear, and the Little Pink Bear, who search for Cayke's dishpan. Joining forces, they enter Ugu's wicker castle and eventually defeat him.

In spite of all the adventures the searchers have, only two characters in the book seem dynamic: the Frogman and the villain, Ugu the Shoemaker. And both change largely as a result of forces external to themselves. The Frogman begins the quest as a pompous showoff. His large size and his pretense at great wisdom make the residents of Yip regard him with awe. In other words, the Frogman's appearance fools them. Being able to see through appearances to reality is a central idea in *The Lost Princess of Oz*, just as it is in so many of the Oz books. The party searching for Ozma are fooled by what seems to be a wall surrounding the city of Thi (102) and by the thinness of the inhabitants of Herku. Moreover, after both search parties join together, they are fooled by illusions Ugu creates around his wicker castle, especially an all-girl army with spears that proves to be an illusion (234–35).[2] But as the Czarover of Herku tells them, "you must never trust appearances, which have a way of fooling one" (143). At any rate, the Yips come to the Frogman to settle their disputes, and he is in effect their ruler.

Tiring of the adulation of the Yips, the Frogman decides to accompany Cayke in her search for her dishpan by going with her into the world below Yip so that others can recognize how magnificent he is. When he reaches the lowlands, he soon discovers that people there are less easily fooled: no one will admire him as the Yips do. When Cayke announces to Wiljon the Winkie that the Frogman is "the wisest creature in all the world," Wiljon replies sarcastically, "Does the Scarecrow admit that this over-grown frog is the wisest creature in the world?" Cayke and the Frogman admit they have never heard of the Scarecrow, but the Frogman says that his brains "grew in my head," so they "must be better than any wizard brains"; and he brags, "I am so wise that sometimes my wisdom makes my head ache. I know so much that often I have to forget part of it, since no one creature, however great, is able to contain so much knowledge." Wiljon replies, "It must be dreadful to be stuffed full of wisdom. [...] It is my good fortune to know very little." Wiljon's indifference disappoints the Frogman, but he hopes that "others in this unknown land might prove more respectful" (41–44). Before the Frogman has a chance to find out whether his hopes will be fulfilled, however, he bathes in the Truth Pond, the water of which makes one always tell the truth. Consequently, he admits to Cayke that he is not at all wise (155–58). However, his new-found honesty is not the result of growth on his part but of his drinking from the Truth Pond. Before the book is over, however, he shows in additional ways that he learns true humility and even selflessness.

Incidentally, Cayke is very upset when she discovers that the Frogman is not as wise as he earlier claims. Hearing his confession "shattered one of her most pleasing illusions," and she tells the Frogman that he was "foolish" to bathe in the pond. Like the Scarecrow, Tin Man, and Lion in *The Wonderful Wizard of Oz*, she cherishes her illusions and does not like having them dispelled. In that first Oz book the Wizard says to himself, "How can I help being a humbug [...] when all these people make me do things that everybody knows can't be done?" (169). That the Frogman's supposed wisdom is one of Cayke's "most pleasing illusions" indicates that she, like the people of the Emerald City, prefers being fooled.

Ugu the Shoemaker steals all the missing things. A magician himself, he recognizes that magic is the main basis of political power in Oz. By stealing the magic of the three people who by Ozma's law monopolize magic, Ugu hopes to make his power irresistible. Using his magical powers, he says, "[...] I mean to be the Ruler of Oz myself [...]" (243). But he knows that Ozma, the legitimate ruler of Oz, has outlawed the practice of magic by all except Glinda, the Wizard, and Ozma herself. So he fears that if any of them finds that he is practicing magic, they will all work together to stop him. For that reason, he steals Cayke's dishpan that has powers that enable one to move quickly from one place to another by riding in it, and he uses it to steal the rest of the magical apparatus and Ozma, who surprises Ugu as he steals the magic picture (216) and whom he imprisons in the pit of a peach in a tree in a giant orchard near his wicker castle.

When the questers enter the castle, the Shoemaker easily captures them. Then, Dorothy uses the magic belt, one magical thing Ugu conveniently does not steal, to free the questers and to turn the Shoemaker into a dove, but the Shoemaker uses his magic to become a "Dove of War." The giant dove tries to attack Dorothy, who cannot be hurt because of the magic belt. Having had a dose of zosozo, a potion that makes him very strong (244), the Frogman, not knowing that Dorothy is protected, attacks the dove, knocking it out of the air. But the dove "got free and began to bite and claw the Frogman, beating him down with its great wings whenever he attempted to rise." Then, Dorothy "feared for her champion and by again using the transformation power of the Magic Belt she made the dove grow small, until it was no larger than a canary bird" (257). Ugu flies away, but by then the Frogman has demonstrated his courage. He really is Dorothy's "champion" in his selfless attempt to protect the little girl. Earlier, he is a pompous, selfish frog, wanting "his fame" to "spread throughout the land of Oz": "He wanted others to see his gorgeous clothes and listen to his solemn sayings [...]." And he commanded three Yips to slide down the mountainside at the top of which Yip is located ahead of him to break a path among the brambles and cactus plants so that "he would not tear his splendid clothes" (32–33). In Ugu's palace he risks his own safety (and clothing!) for Dorothy.

Before the questers enter the castle, Button-Bright gets lost, gets hungry, and picks and eats the peach containing Ozma. He saves the pit since it is solid gold and he wants to show it to the girls who are

Ugu stealing Ozma in *The Lost Princess of Oz* (illus. John R. Neill; Chicago: Reilly & Lee, 1917), p. 217.

also searching for Ozma. The Little Pink Bear, who can answer any question as long as it does not deal with the future, repeatedly tells the questers where the princess is, but they misunderstand his answers, so all except the Lavender Bear think the Little Pink Bear is mistaken. When the questers finally examine the things in Button-Bright's pocket after the Pink Bear says that is where Ozma is, they find the peach pit, the Wizard cuts it in half, and out pops Ozma (265).

Then, "The Frogman took off his tall hat and bowed low before the beautiful girl [...]" (265–66). His bow expresses the willingness of this former pompous ruler of Yip to subjugate himself to Ozma's rule. Simultaneously, the truthful Frogman's bow symbolizes the willingness of almost all the inhabitants of the Land of Oz to subjugate themselves to Ozma's benevolent rule, for they know that her needs and desires coincide with their needs and desires, resulting in true political stability and harmony. Under her rule most of them are contented. Early in the book one of the Yips says, "Contentment with one's lot is true wisdom" (31), a kind of wisdom, incidentally, that the Frogman lacks early in the book. Later, the Wizard says, "those who are contented have nothing to regret and nothing more to wish for" (117), words that echo Ozma's about "the riches of content" at the end of *The Marvelous Land of Oz*. Even the Cowardly Lion recognizes the virtue of contentment, explaining to the other animals searching for Ozma, "To be individual, my friends, to be different from others, is the only way to become distinguished from the common herd. Let us be glad, therefore, that we differ from one another in form and in disposition" (124). Had the Lion stopped here, he would look like a snob because of his use of the term, *common herd*. However, he adds, "Variety is the spice of life and we are various enough to enjoy one another's society, so let us be content" (125). In contrast, Ugu intends to use his magical powers to force his rule on the residents of Oz. Thus, he would become a tyrant unconcerned with the contentment of his subjects.

Like the Frogman, Ugu learns humility. As a small dove he uses the dishpan to get to Quadling Country, where the Tin Woodman and the Scarecrow still search for Ozma, since they do not know that she has been found. They find the dishpan and take it to the Emerald City where Ozma herself returns it to Cayke, indicating that Ozma's law monopolizing magic does not apply absolutely. Still, like Cayke, who seems to know only that the dishpan contains a kind of magic that enables her to bake good cookies (44), Ozma may not know the kinds of magical power the dishpan possesses.

When the Scarecrow and Tin Man find the dishpan, they discuss what good a dishpan made of gold and studded with diamonds is, and they decide that it is of no real value, since it is "unnatural" (277), not for a moment recognizing how unnatural they both are and how extremely valuable the dishpan is. It appears to be of little actual value since jewels and gold are common in the Land of Oz and since jewels and gold in no way contribute to the purpose the dishpan seems designed to serve. But its magic makes it of great value, especially to Cayke, who without it cannot bake excellent cookies. It also, of course, is potentially very harmful to political stability in Oz, as Ugu recognizes and displays.

After finding the dishpan, the Scarecrow says, "If I could not be a Scarecrow — or a Tin Woodman — my next choice would be to live as a bird does." Ugu listens carefully to the Scarecrow's words (276). Later, Ugu flies to Dorothy and asks for forgiveness. He says, "many days of quiet thought have shown me that only those things one acquires honestly are able to render one content," and he begs Dorothy to allow him to remain a dove:

> As Ugu the Shoemaker I was skinny and old and unlovely; as a dove I am quite pretty to look at. As a man I was ambitious and cruel, while as a dove I can be content with my lot and happy in my simple life. I have learned to love the free and independent life of a bird and I'd rather not change back [279].[3]

Dorothy grants his request (279–80). Here too *content* is a key word. Fairly consistently in Baum's Oz books the greatest good for an individual is to be content. Once Ugu becomes content, he no longer desires political power and consequently no longer poses a threat to stability in Oz. But the fact remains that he and the Frogman initially are discontent. Moreover, the ferryman whom Cayke and the Frogman meet remains discontent because he cannot understand the words of animals and they cannot understand his words. As long as discontent exists in Oz, there is room for revolt and other threats to political stability.

The Lost Princess of Oz also contains one of Baum's feminist statements. When the all-girl army apparently marches out of and surrounds Ugu's castle, the Patchwork Girl says, "They're only girls!" to which the now-truthful Frogman responds, "Girls are the fiercest soldiers of all [...]. They are more brave than men and they have better nerves. That is probably why the magician uses them for soldiers and has sent them to oppose us." Baum then adds, "No one argued with this statement [...]" (235–36). Still, in the context of Baum's Oz books, where Baum on the whole seems to prefer pacifism to militarism, these words may not involve praise for women.

Baum's assertion that *The Lost Princess of Oz* is "exactly in line with the style of the first four Oz books" seems, then, only partially true, unless he uses "style" mainly to refer to the way he puts sentences together. In *The Lost Princess of Oz*, although the characters have many exciting adventures and achieve a happy ending, most of the plot episodes are loosely connected at best. The Frogman and Ugu, however, change significantly. Both become wiser, humbler creatures. The Frogman learns to be less concerned about fooling people and about appearance, and Ugu learns to be content living the life of a bird.

Nevertheless, *The Lost Princess of Oz* clearly illustrates the potential for incredible political and personal damage that magic has in the Land of Oz. The book thus shows the need for Ozma's decree monopolizing at least most forms of magic in the hands of the Wizard, Glinda, and Ozma herself. In Ugu's hands magic spells potential disaster for the Land of Oz. In the right hands it brings stability, peace, happiness, prosperity, and, above all, contentment.

Like so many of Baum's late Oz books, *The Lost Princess of Oz* follows Baum's formula involving "exciting adventures, unexpected difficulties [...] and marvelous escapes" ("Modern Fairy Tales" 140). However, it is roughly unified by the idea of the quests for the dishpan and Ozma and by the latter quest's following in very general ways the pattern of the Greek myth of Persephone, a pattern Baum also follows, but more closely, in his last book, *Glinda of Oz*.

11

The Tin Woodman of Oz
BAUM'S *ODYSSEY*

In several ways, *The Tin Woodman of Oz* parodies aspects of the more traditional quest in which a hero returns home. As Northrop Frye writes,

> The hero of a quest first of all goes "away": that is, there must be some direction for his movement. Home, as [T. S.] Eliot says, is where one starts from. If the quest is successful, he normally returns home, like a baseball player, the great model for this returning journey being of course the *Odyssey* [213].

Whether Baum had Homer's *Odyssey* in mind when he wrote his third from last Oz book is unknown, nor is there any hard evidence that Baum read *The Odyssey*; but given the educational system of his day and his extensive knowledge of myth, it would be extremely surprising if he had not. Moreover, Baum's novel can be profitably read in the context of *The Odyssey*.

Named Nick Chopper in *The Tin Woodman of Oz*, as he is beginning in *The Marvelous Land of Oz*, the Tin Man, like Odysseus, seeks his home: he is returning to the Munchkin land from which he came. Also like Odysseus, the Tin Man feels that his beloved — or at least his former beloved — awaits him at the end of his journey. However, the Tin Man does not seek Nimmie Amee because he loves her; he claims that the Wizard gave him "a Kind Heart instead of a Loving Heart" (18). These words echo *The Wonderful Wizard of Oz*. Before Dorothy and her companions travel to the land of the wicked Witch of the West, the Wizard tells the Tin Man that if he helps Dorothy kill the wicked witch, he will give the Tin Man "the biggest and kindest and most loving heart in all the Land of Oz" (115), a promise he cannot keep. When he gives the Tin Man a heart, it is "made entirely of silk and stuffed with sawdust" (168). Thus, it is hardly a loving or kind heart. Nonetheless, the Tin Man asks the Wizard, "is it a kind heart?" The Wizard replies, "Oh, very!" (168). In *The Tin Woodman of Oz*, when Woot the Wanderer tells the Tin Man, "it was unkind of you to desert" Nimmie Amee, the Scarecrow comments, "This boy is right," so the Tin Man decides to go in quest of her because "if I can make her happy, it is proper that I should do so, and in this way reward her for her faithfulness" (19), words full of the kind of dramatic irony that permeates this book. It is interesting to note that in *The Wonderful Wizard of Oz* the Tin Man declares that if he gets a heart, he will "go back to the Munchkin maiden and marry her" (48), a declaration that he apparently forgets until Woot reminds him of his obligation.

David L. Greene calls *The Tin Woodman of Oz,* "the most flawed of Baum's later Oz books. Much of it," he writes, "is spent in an episodic tour of Oz, without any real connection with the quest and without any particularly interesting episodes or characters" (51). Yet the book does not seem nearly as flawed as Greene indicates. Katharine M. Rogers correctly writes that the Tin Man is involved in an "absurd," "passionless pseudo-romance" (225). Shortly before they actually confront Nimmie Amee, Woot suggests that they go back. The Tin Man replies, "No, [...] I have decided that it's my duty to make Nimmie Amee happy, in case she wishes to marry me" (238). The Tin Man earlier meets the Tin Soldier, named Captain Fyter, who also is engaged to Nimmie Amee and also does not marry her because he rusts. About marrying her, the Tin Soldier says that he too feels it is his duty to make her happy and adds, "A good soldier never shirks from doing his duty" (238). As it turns out, however, Nimmie Amee wishes to marry neither of them.

Like that of Odysseus, the Tin Man's return is delayed, but unlike Odysseus, who never forgets Penelope, the Tin Man forgets Nimmie Amee until Woot reminds him of her; thus, he causes most of the delay himself. Although Woot instigates the Tin Man's search for Nimmie Amee, the boy wonders about the Tin Man's motives: he says to the Scarecrow, "It's too bad he hasn't a Loving Heart," and adds, "This Tin

Man is going to marry a nice girl through kindness, and not because he loves her, and somehow that doesn't seem quite right" (24). Yet the Tin Man thinks all along that he is doing some kind of favor for Nimmie Amee, and the Scarecrow apparently agrees, for he answers Woot, "Even so, I am not sure it isn't best for the girl [...], for a loving husband is not always kind, while a kind husband is sure to make any girl content" (24). Thus, both the Scarecrow and Tin Man appear chauvinistic as well as tremendously naïve. The Scarecrow's use of one of Baum's key words here, *content*, emphasizes his naiveté. Significantly, both the Scarecrow and Tin Man appear more than a little foolish throughout the quest. Baum thus parodies their chauvinism and naiveté.

Also, once the Tin Man decides to find Nimmie Amee, his vanity makes him refuse to travel through the Emerald City: he wants as few witnesses to his meeting with Nimmie Amee as possible, when, he says, "[...] I confess to Nimmie Amee that I have come to marry her because it is my duty to do so [...]" (25), a confession that he seems to feel is bound to make her happy. His attempt to keep his friends there from knowing that he is seeking Nimmie Amee causes him to be delayed repeatedly as he seeks the woman he intends to make his wife. Ironically, his friends in the Emerald City know from the start that he is on a journey, but they don't know what he seeks.[1] If they did not know about the journey, Ozma would not be able to rescue the travelers from the transformations Mrs. Yoop causes (135–37).

At the end of Odysseus's journey waits the faithful Penelope; at the end of the Tin Man's journey is the faithless Nimmie Amee. After Odysseus reveals himself, overcomes all of Penelope's suitors, and proves his identity by answering Penelope's question about the marriage bed, she greets her husband's return with great love, indicating her faithfulness. The Tin Man overcomes no suitors; instead, he unites with one — the Tin Soldier — and is vanquished by another. Nimmie Amee greets the return of her former fiancé with no love at all. In fact, when he arrives, she asks, "But who can *you* be?" (240). She then says to him, "Even sweethearts are forgotten after a time [...]" (241). Unlike the faithful Penelope, Nimmie Amee has taken a husband; she explains to the Tin Man and Tin Soldier, "All I knew is that neither of you came to marry me, as you had promised to do. But men are not scarce in the Land of Oz" (243). Thus, in terms of general outline, *The Tin Woodman of Oz* does resemble the traditional quest and Homer's *Odyssey* in particular. Both are tales of return, tales of homecomings. Yet there are obviously some important differences.

Even some of the individual episodes are similar to those in *The Odyssey*, especially those involving Mrs. Yoop, who is a giant and the wife of Mr. Yoop, the giant whom Dorothy, Ojo, Toto, the Patchwork Girl, and the Scarecrow encounter in *The Patchwork Girl of Oz*. Odysseus encounters several giants on his journey: the human-eating Laestragonians and Cyclopes. Unlike her husband, however, and the giants Ulysses encounters, Mrs. Yoop shows no desire to devour human beings. She is, though, a kind of Circe, but unlike Circe, Mrs. Yoop does not try to attract people to her home. When some arrive, she transforms them, not into swine but into whatever form she chooses. Odysseus avoids being transformed by Circe, but he allows Athena to transform him so that he looks like an old man, a disguise that can help him overcome the suitors and test Penelope's faithfulness. Against the Tin Man's will, Mrs. Yoop transforms him into a tin owl. Baum may be playing a subtle joke in this transformation and making a subtle allusion again to Greek mythology (perhaps to *The Odyssey* itself), since the owl is associated with Athena, goddess of wisdom, and Athena repeatedly helps Odysseus. In Baum's book, however, the Tin Man seems anything but wise. The joke, however, works even without the allusion, since in the twenty-first century, folklore still associates owls with wisdom, as does Baum himself in *The Patchwork Girl of Oz* where he has the Wise Donkey say about the Foolish Owl, "Owls are supposed to be so very wise, generally, that a foolish one is unusual [...]" (84). Mrs. Yoop also resembles Calypso, who tries to get Odysseus to remain on his island through eternity: Mrs. Yoop wants the Tin Man, Woot the Wanderer, the Scarecrow, and Polychrome to remain with her always.

Like the Mr. Yoop episode in *The Patchwork Girl of Oz*, the adventures with Mrs. Yoop are especially interesting because of the way they combine comedy and horror. Rogers recognizes the horror in the episode — she calls it "really frightening" (226), but it is also funny. The humor centers around the Tin Man's and especially the Scarecrow's dismay at the forms into which Mrs. Yoop changes them. As soon as Mrs. Yoop transforms the Tin Man, the Scarecrow says, "Madam, [...] I consider this action very impolite. It may even be rude, considering we are your guests" (72). Mrs. Yoop then transforms the Scarecrow into a straw-stuffed bear. Before he is transformed, the Scarecrow is

Right to left: Mrs. Yoop, the Scarecrow, the Tin Man, and Woot. From *The Tin Woodman of Oz* (illus. John R. Neill; Chicago: Reilly & Lee, 1918), pp. 76–77.

extremely clumsy: Baum writes that he "was awkward in his movements and decidedly wobbly on his feet" (22). In addition, scarecrows are hardly dignified. Yet after his transformation he growls, "[...] I don't like walking on four legs; it's undignified" (75). In this episode he thus repeatedly looks like a pompous fool.

One of the most horrifying yet funny parts of the book involves what may be a parody of the part of the hero quest that involves an expansion of consciousness on the part of the hero: the Tin Woodman's conversation with his own meat head. He finds the head in a cupboard in the shop of Ku-Klip the Tinsmith, the man who replaced Nick Chopper's and Captain Fyter's meat bodies with tin. The head does not recognize the Tin Woodman, is not glad to see him, and resents being disturbed. Were it not for the humor, this section of the book would be pure nightmare. Even the title of the chapter in which the conversation occurs — "The Tin Woodman Talks to Himself" — adds humor to the episode. When he first discovers that he is talking with his own head, the Tin Man asks, "If you are Nick Chopper's Head, then you are *Me*—or I'm *You*—or—or What relation *are* we, anyhow?" (185), a question no one can answer. Immediately after the conversation, he says, "Yes; I'm rather surprised at my head, myself [...]. I thought I had a more pleasant disposition when I was made of meat" (188).

Odysseus successfully completes his quest, even discovering that a part of his true identity is inextricably connected with his home — Ithaca, a thing he shows when, realizing he is in Ithaca, he "rejoiced at finding himself again in his own land, and kissed the bounteous soil" (Homer 207). He prefers to be mortal and return to Ithaca rather than to be immortal and remain with the nymph Calypso. He admits to Calypso that she is more beautiful than Penelope, but adds, "Nevertheless, I want to get home, and can think of nothing else" (Homer 77). William G. Thalmann comments that "this hero of the very broadest possible experience wants only home and family" (11), something Odysseus' statement to Calypso certainly shows. The Tin Man, on the other hand, does not value his original home: although at one point in his journey he says, "I was born in this grand forest," and he laments his years rusting in the woods, when the travelers approach his actual "old home," he says, "my little cabin stands not a great way off, but there is no occasion for us to visit it," and travels on in his search for Nimmie Amee (163–65). His old home, thus, has no appeal for the Tin Man, who, unlike Odysseus, fails to recognize any real ties to the past.

Actually, the general outline of the plot of *The Tin Woodman of Oz* resembles that of many tales involving quests full of trials undertaken for the sake of a beloved, ranging from *The Odyssey* to the part of the German tale "Rapunzel," in which the blinded prince wanders through the woods until he stumbles on Rapunzel and her twin children. Similar also is the Scandinavian tale, "East o' the Sun and West o' the Moon," in which the farmer's daughter endures hardships to find her prince who is being held in a castle located east of the sun and west of the moon. The fairy tales, however, are not tales of return like *The Odyssey* and *The Tin Woodman of Oz* are.

In terms of motivation for the quest — duty rather than love — *The Tin Woodman of Oz* is closer to Vergil's *Aeneid* than it is to Homer's tale. Aeneas finds his true love, Dido, in Carthage in North Africa, but he must go to Italy where he must marry Lavinia, for that is his fate, even though leaving Carthage results in Dido's suicide and his own loss of a chance for real happiness. He must accept his fate and, like a good ancestor of the Romans, do his duty. For Aeneas, duty is more important than love, and fulfilling his destiny is more important than fulfilling his own desires. As Harry Slochower writes, "Aeneas' heroism lies in his obedience to the demands of his Roman authority. He is brave, fearless, persistent, but always within the framework of his public duty" (340). Similarly, in searching for Nimmie Amee, the Tin Man chooses to do what he considers his duty rather than what he thinks will make him happy. When his quest fails, he is glad to be relieved "of any further anxiety concerning" Nimmie Amee (246). For her part, Nimmie Amee, anything but a true Penelope or Dido, is "glad to be rid of" the Tin Man and her other unwanted visitors (248). The Tin Man has no concern for his original home or for family, and Nimmie Amee is quite content with the family she has.

Part of the Tin Man's quest involves becoming small and traveling through a rabbit's tunnel to get to Nimmie Amee's house. The underground journey will lead to the Tin Man's discovery of what the future holds for him. Here too the Tin Man is more like Aeneas than Odysseus. Odysseus travels across an ocean to a Hades apparently located aboveground in order to hear a prophecy of what the future holds for him; Aeneas travels underground to Hades to hear his father prophesy his future. Granted, some of these resemblances may seem far-fetched, but when added together, they clearly place *The Tin Woodman of Oz* in the context of epic tradition, and when the book is placed in that tradition, it is easy to see Baum's humor at work.

The Tin Woodman of Oz is, in fact, a kind of mock-heroic novel. In it, like the true epic hero, the Tin Woodman has many opportunities to learn about himself, his capabilities, and his place in the world. However, unlike the true hero, he takes no advantage of those opportunities. Like Odysseus, the Tin Man at times seeks adventure for its own sake. For example, he and his companions go to Loonville, even though a sign tells them not to do so (32). But that episode teaches him neither to avoid possible problems nor to enjoy them when they occur. Later, even though Nimmie Amee has erected a wall of solid air to keep people out, he and his companions enter her house; and although his meeting with her relieves him of what he thinks of as his responsibility to Nimmie Aimee, the Tin Man certainly does not enjoy the encounter (233–46). He gains none of the self-knowledge a true hero should gain. Nor does he bring back any boon from his quest. For him, as the book's ending suggests, the entire trip is just an adventure that he and the Scarecrow can discuss (254–55). Frye claims, "The genuine quest-cycle is of the type in which the conclusion is the starting point renewed and transformed" and adds that "[...] Virgil's *Aeneid* is a quest of this type" in which "Aeneas moves from old to new Troy, setting up a new cycle of history with the same race of people" (214) However, the Tin Woodman is neither an Odysseus nor an Aeneas. From the start his quest is completely sterile, even though he ostensibly seeks a wife. His quest renews nothing, including himself. He is a kind of antihero who, instead of performing heroic deeds, performs deeds that make him look foolish. Victor Brombert points out that "The antiheroic mode [...] involves the negative presence of the subverted or absent model" (1–2). By reading Baum's novel in the context of Homer's and Vergil's epics, one can see just how much Baum subverts the idea of the truly heroic quest and just how foolish the Tin Man is.

In the last analysis, the Tin Woodman is very different from Odysseus, who is, as Paolo Vivante says, "so convincing as a real character" (103). At one point, the Scarecrow says of the Tin Man, "You are too hard and stiff" (163), and the Scarecrow is correct in more than just a physical sense. In *The Tin Woodman of Oz* the Tin Man has none of the humanity of Odysseus, whose "great theme" is, Vivante says, "grief" (106). The Tin Man feels no grief about his lost home or about his lost love. He just feels, he claims, a sense of duty, but even that sense slumbers until Woot wakes it.

The Tin Woodman of Oz, then, is basically a comic novel, a mock heroic tale in which the Tin Woodman's apparently pointless wanderings, when placed in the context of true epics, produce humorous contrast.

The Emerald City of Oz and *The Tin Woodman of Oz* give Baum's most explicit descriptions of what Katharine M. Rogers calls his "ideal society" (168).[2] Suzanne Rahn, following the lead of several earlier critics, uses passages from these two books to place Baum in the tradition of Edward Bellamy (*Wizard of Oz* 34–35). However, it seems doubtful that Baum really intended to describe in either of these books some kind of eutopian or ideal society, especially in connection with the later book, since it is so comical. Perhaps this book is both a mock epic and a mock eutopian novel.[3] At any rate, in *The Tin Woodman of Oz* Baum contradicts some of the eutopian ideas he states. He creates in this book a new myth about the origins of Oz as a fairyland, calling Ozma not the daughter of Pastoria, former ruler of the Emerald City, as she is in *The Marvelous Land of Oz*, or the daughter of a man named Oz, as she says she is in *Dorothy and The Wizard in Oz*. Rather, here she is a member of the fairy band of Queen Lurline, whom Lurline left behind to rule Oz (132). In *The Tin Woodman of Oz* Baum also introduces the idea that no one ever dies in Oz and another idea: no one ever ages (132–33). And Baum asserts, "the Oz people were as happy and contented as can be" (133).

Yet the story itself contradicts this final idea, unless one understands "as can be" simply to mean "as they are." Tommy Kwikstep hardly seems "happy and contented" with his numerous legs, although he is happy when Polychrome reduces him to just two legs (116–19); Mrs. Yoop also does not seem "happy and contented," especially when she becomes a green monkey (156–57). Even the Tin Woodman and the Scarecrow seem more bored than happy and contented, except when they are on their journey. Baum does admit, "Perhaps all parts of Oz might not be called truly delightful, but it was surely delightful in the neighborhood of the Emerald City, where Ozma reigned" (133). Yet Mrs. Yoop's valley does not seem all that far from the Emerald City itself. It takes the Tin Woodman and his friends two days to get there from the Tin Woodman's castle. Since their journey involves detouring around the Emerald City, the valley cannot be that far from the city. In *The Tin Woodman of Oz*, then, just as Baum subverts the idea that the Tin Man is a hero on a magnificent quest, so he subverts the idea that Oz is a kind of eutopia. It contains discontented and bored inhabitants. It even has inhabitants, like Mrs. Yoop, who are genuinely evil.

12

The Magic of Oz
MAGIC AND POLITICS IN OZ

Baum's penultimate Oz book, *The Magic of Oz*, experiments with three plots, each involving a quest. The first treats the attempt of Ruggedo, the ex-Nome King, and Kiki Aru, a Hyup who lives on Mount Munch in Munchkin Country, to conquer the Land of Oz and enslave its people. Ruggedo wants to take over Oz for revenge; Kiki wants to do so for adventure and wickedness. As readers would guess after reading *The Emerald City of Oz*, each of the would-be conquerors intends to betray his co-conspirator. Kiki can work transformations using a magic word. The heartless Kiki at one time intends to "transform the old Nome into a marble statue and keep him in that form forever" (30), an idea that places him on a level with Mombi in *The Marvelous Land of Oz*, who wanted to transform Tip into a statue. At another point, Kiki intends to transform Ruggedo "into a tree, for he lies and I cannot trust him" (76). And the apparently even more heartless Ruggedo hopes to steal the magic word from Kiki and then transform Kiki into "a bundle of faggots and burn him up and so be rid of him" (31), thus destroying Kiki completely. The narrator comments: "This is always the way with wicked people. They cannot be trusted even by one another" (31). Thus, Baum again injects morality and unpleasantness into his tale in spite of his assertion in the Introduction to *The Wonderful Wizard of Oz* that since "Modern education includes morality," "the modern child seeks only entertainment in its wonder-tales and gladly dispenses with all disagreeable incidents" (vii). Again, Baum does not follow what he claims are his own critical principles.

The second plot involves Cap'n Bill and Trot's quest for the Magic Flower as a birthday present for Ozma. The third involves the Wizard and Dorothy's journey to the Forest of Gugu to get some monkeys which the Wizard will make small, teach tricks, and put into a birthday cake for Ozma. The three plots come together in the Forest of Gugu when the Wizard foils the plot of Ruggedo and Kiki Aru, and the Glass Cat tells the Wizard that Cap'n Bill and Trot have taken root on the Magic Isle where the Magic Flower is. While trapped on the island, Trot and the captain are growing smaller. Both are in danger of disappearing completely; as Trot says to the Wizard, "If you can't save us soon, there'll be nothing left of us" (183), words that may echo Alice's words in *Alice's Adventures in Wonderland* when she wonders whether her shrinking might not end with her "going out altogether, like a candle" (12). Thus, horror is present in both Alice's world and that of Trot.

Just as the two plots in *The Emerald City of Oz* are ironically related to each other, so in *The Magic of Oz* the plot involving the Nome King and Kiki is ironically related to the other two plots. Were the king and Kiki to be successful, Ozma would have no birthday party, thus in a way making the search for presents for her a waste of time. At any rate, the attempt to conquer Oz presents what at least seems to be real danger to the inhabitants of Oz, and the searches for birthday presents cause genuine anxiety and real danger to the ones on the two searches.

In *The Magic of Oz* the three plots dovetail nicely. In the Forest of Gugu, Kiki uses the magic word to transform the Wizard into a fox, Dorothy into a lamb, the Cowardly Lion into a Munchkin boy, and the Hungry Tiger into a rabbit. Kiki, who earlier changes himself and Ruggedo into eagles and Li-Mon-Egs (part lion, part monkey, and part eagle), changes Ruggedo into a goose. When Kiki changes some monkeys into giant soldiers to use as an army to conquer Oz, the Wizard foils their plot by overhearing the magic word and using it on Kiki and Ruggedo. Two of the three quests are successful — the two that involve getting gifts for Ozma, of course, and near the story's end occurs a grand celebration of Ozma's birthday. Again, however, the quests involve no inner exploration or growth on the part of the questers. In fact, by the end of the book, Kiki and Ruggedo drink some of the water of the

Trot and Cap'n Bill growing roots in *The Magic of Oz* (illus. John R. Neill; Chicago: Reilly & Lee, 1919), p. 115.

Fountain of Oblivion and forget their pasts entirely. About Kiki, Ozma says, "He seems a nice boy, now that all the wickedness has gone from him [...]. So we will keep him here with us and teach him our ways — to be true and considerate of others" (230–31). About the Nome King she says, "we must find a place for him in the Land of Oz, and keep him here. For here he can learn no evil and will always be as innocent of guile as our own people" (234). However, at the beginning of the book, Kiki, who is one of Ozma's "people," is hardly "innocent of guile." Nonetheless, the happy ending apparently rewards Kiki and Ruggedo for their evil deeds with eternal life in or near the Emerald City.

Central to the uses of magic in *The Magic of Oz* and L. Frank Baum's other Oz books is his concern for political unity, stability, and virtue. In Baum's books numerous people try to destabilize Oz, some of whom, like Ann Soforth, Ugu the Shoemaker, and Kiki Aru, are originally from Oz.

Born in 1856, Baum lived through the Civil War, an event that impressed upon the nation the need for political unity and stability.

He also lived through the Grant administration and the Gilded Age, the corruption of which impressed the nation with the need for political and corporate virtue. In 1890, in Baum's editorials for the *Aberdeen Saturday Pioneer*, he repeatedly shows his desire to purge corruption from local politics.[1] Neil Earle shows that Baum was part of what Earle calls "The era of missionaries and muckrakers that we associate with the Progressive period in American history [...]" (47). It is not surprising, then, that Baum has as one of his central concerns the need to purge corruption from politics and achieve and maintain political stability and unity in the Land of Oz; and magic is central to that concern.

Most discussions of magic in Baum's Oz books deal with his using magic and technology to produce what Hugh Pendexter, III, calls "technological magic" ("Magic in Post-Thompson Oz" 2). In Baum's Oz the relationship between magic and technology is so close that in *The Lost Princess of Oz* the Wizard says, "[...] a wizard without tools is as helpless as a carpenter without a hammer or saw." This reliance on technology leads critics to agree with Baum himself that in his Oz books he created modern, American fairy tales. Perhaps, however, it is even more important that in Baum's Oz books, magic almost always occurs in overlapping psychological, philosophical, and especially political contexts.

Henry M. Littlefield theorizes that events close in time to the composition of the first Oz book — *The Wonderful Wizard of Oz* — affected Baum's attitudes about politics; Littlefield mentions a "frightful depression" beginning in 1893 and the Spanish American War of 1898 (40). Fred Erisman argues that by the time Baum started writing the Oz books, he felt "an insoluble conflict between a [basically rural] value system no longer applicable (but held too firmly to be given up) and the recognition that new ways are needed" ("L. Frank Baum and the Progressive Dilemma" 622). Following these same lines, Jack Zipes theorizes that Baum created Oz to show "disenchantment with America, if not with the course of western civilization" (121). And Michael O. Riley writes about Baum's concern about "directions America was taking — directions that decreased the wonder, beauty, and quality of life in the country" (194) However, Littlefield's, Erisman's, Zipes', and Riley's theories rest on very slender biographical evidence.

According to Russell P. MacFall and Frank Joslyn Baum, the creator of Oz had little concern with real-world politics or social criticism. In fact, MacFall and F. J. Baum assert that even though Baum "had felt the bitter breath of failure and hard times in the Dakota territory" and "had suffered [...] long, lean years in Chicago," "he did not turn to resentful social criticism" (124).

Zipes sees Baum as having grown so disenchanted with America, especially America's economic system, that at the end of the sixth Oz book, *The Emerald City of Oz*, he had Glinda use magic to make Oz invisible (130). Erisman views this sixth Oz book as "Baum's surrender to the demands of reality, and the beginning of his escape to Oz" ("L. Frank Baum and the Progressive Dilemma" 622). Riley writes that Baum shut off Oz from the world to "keep his imaginary world free" of "the unbridled growth" he saw in American cities (165). Most people who examine Baum's life, however, follow MacFall and F. J. Baum's lead, explaining that Baum made Oz invisible because he had grown "tired of Oz" and wanted to spend his time working on non-Oz books, a theory for which ample biographical evidence exists.[2] Readers may never know whether Baum's creation of Oz had primarily political, psychological, literary, monetary, or other motives. Readers also may never know exactly why he tried to end the Oz books after the sixth in the series by cutting Oz off from the rest of the world. Nonetheless, readers do know that in his Oz books he repeatedly shows concern for political stability and virtuous leaders, and this concern very well may have grown out of his reaction to political events in the America of his day.

Sarah Gilead finds in fantasy a link between "modern culture" and "the lost wholeness and stability of an imagined (and largely imaginary) past" (288). Baum may not have found "wholeness and stability" in any kind of past, and he may not have found them in his own time, but he made them central concepts in his Oz books. And in Oz magic is central to his idea of how political stability and unity are achieved and maintained as well as threatened, a set of facts that in itself indicates that he might have felt that political stability and wholeness were unattainable in the United States of his day.

In *The Wonderful Wizard of Oz*, when Dorothy arrives in Oz from Kansas, she finds a fragmented land that even includes several small totalitarian countries. Of the places she travels, only the Quadling Country, ruled by Glinda, has a strong ruler who is concerned about her people.[3] Dorothy herself kills the wicked Witches of the East and West, thus ending tyrannical rule in their kingdoms and introducing possibilities of benevolent reigns. Dorothy is also instrumental in ridding the Emerald City of the fraudulent Wizard, whose reign, though less fanatically tyrannical than those of the witches, seems primarily designed to ensure his own comfort and safety. By the time Dorothy comes to the Emerald City in *The Wonderful Wizard of Oz*, he hides in his throne room. A man with whom Dorothy stays before she enters the Emerald City tells her, "[...] I have never been permitted to see the Great Oz, nor do I know of any living person who has seen him" (52). Not even the soldier who guards the Palace has seen the Wizard (103). After Dorothy discovers that the Wizard is a fraud, he tells Dorothy that he is "tired of being such a humbug. If I should go out of this Palace my people would soon discover I am not a Wizard, and then they would be vexed with me for having deceived them" (173), words that indicate his fear of his own subjects. When he first meets Dorothy, he also seems afraid that, if he leaves the Palace, the wicked Witch of the West may find that he is a humbug and attack the Emerald City. Why else would he send a child, a Tin Man, a Scarecrow, and a Cowardly Lion to kill the witch? Still, the Wizard shows some concern for his people and for political stability and smooth succession, when, just before he leaves in his balloon, he tells the people of the Emerald City, "While I am gone the Scarecrow will rule over you. I command you to obey him as you would me" (175).

At the end of the first Oz book the Tin Man and Scarecrow replace the wicked Witch of the West and the Wizard as rulers, and the Cowardly Lion rules in the forest as King of the Beasts, introducing possibilities of benevolent rule to places hitherto governed by rulers either completely unconcerned with the well-being of their subjects or unable to keep the peace except, in the case of the Wizard, through humbuggery. Glinda, who has true magical powers at her command, shows her lack of corruption and her commitment to good rule when she uses the three wishes she gets when Dorothy gives her the golden cap not for selfish purposes but to have the winged monkeys carry the Scarecrow, the Tin Man, and the Lion to their kingdoms (214–15). Thus, Dorothy leaves behind her a Land of Oz much better governed than when she first arrives, but it still has a number of small kingdoms, some of which have relatively powerless rulers. In *The Marvelous Land of Oz*, the second of Baum's Oz books, General Jinjur's successful rebellion illustrates the need for a ruler with greater power than the Scarecrow, working with a mandate from a humbug Wizard and even with the blessing of Glinda, can supply. And in Oz magic helps provide the basis of that power.

Baum's most interesting philosophical statement about magic occurs in *The Marvelous Land of Oz*, when the Scarecrow says, "All magic is unnatural, and for that reason is to be feared and avoided" (156). At first glance, this statement seems unequivocal but, when placed in context, becomes complex. The speaker of the words about magic's being "unnatural" is, after all, the Scarecrow, whose very life is "unnatural." Clearly, magic is involved in his being alive. The irony (and humor) of the Scarecrow's saying that that which is "unnatural" is to be "feared and avoided" is obvious to a careful reader, since the lovable Scarecrow is certainly not to be feared and avoided, except by one wishing to harm others.[4]

In Baum's later conception of the Land of Oz, magic is central to Ozma's rule. In *The Tin Woodman of Oz*, for example, he writes of Oz's having been "much like other lands" until the ruler of a band of fairies — Queen Lurline — "enchanted the country and so made it a Fairyland." Lurline left one of her fairies — Ozma — to rule over the land (132).

The kind of magic that is most prevalent in Baum's Oz books and is most often associated with evil or selfish characters is transformation. When Glinda discovers that Ozma, rightful ruler of the Emerald City, has been transformed into Tip, Tip says that he is willing to try being Ozma for a while but only if Glinda will change him back into Tip if he does not like being a girl. Glinda responds, "I never deal in transformations, for they are not honest, and no respectable Sorceress likes to make things appear to be what they are not. Only unscrupulous Witches use the art [...]" (259–60). Glinda's words indicate that transformations, even those done for good purposes, are evil. Her words about making "things appear to be what they are not" indicate that even transformations involving only illusion, such as the ones the Wizard practices in *The Wonderful Wizard of Oz* when he appears as "an enormous Head," "a most lovely Lady," "a most terrible Beast," and "a Ball of Fire" (106–115), are also to be avoided by honest creatures. Glinda does not object to undoing transformations, as she shows when Mombi the Witch changes Jellia Jamb so that she appears to be Mombi. Spotting the change, Glinda "quickly transformed the girl into her proper shape" (240). Still, on the whole, Baum sticks to his condemnation of transformations, but there are some exceptions. As the Wizard says in *Glinda of Oz*, the last Oz book Baum wrote, "It is wicked to transform any living creatures without their consent [...]" (227), but sometimes creatures give their consent, as Ugu does after Dorothy transforms him into a dove, and some other transformations seem justified, as does that of Mrs. Yoop into a green monkey since that is the form into which she transformed Woot. In Baum's last Oz book, *Glinda of Oz*, even Glinda works transformations of a sort.

Although Mombi is a witch and voluntarily uses her magic to support General Jinjur's irresponsible rule, she ironically performs the work of magic that serves the highest good in *The Marvelous Land of Oz*. She, not Glinda, undoes her own transformation, changing Tip back into Ozma, rightful ruler of the Emerald City, thus introducing the possibility of permanently ending the fragmentation that characterizes Oz up to this time. Mombi, however, reverses the transformation only under threat of death from Glinda (254).

At the end of *The Marvelous Land of Oz* Ozma is called Queen of the Emerald City. Her subjects stand in "awe" of "her magical powers," saying, "The Wonderful Wizard was never so wonderful as Queen Ozma, [...] for he claimed to do many things he could not do; whereas our new Queen does many things no one would ever expect her to accomplish" (270–72). Yet having Ozma rule only the Emerald City does not seem sufficient. Baum seems to desire the greater stability in Oz that comes with lack of fragmentation, for in the third book in the series, *Ozma of Oz*, Ozma declares, "I am ruler of the Land of Oz" (96), a position she retains through the rest of Baum's Oz books. The political fragmentation of *The Wonderful Wizard of Oz*, then, gives way to the unity and stability of a land under the benevolent rule of Ozma.[5] It is interesting to note that Timothy E. Cook, focusing on five of Baum's books (but only three of the five are Oz books: *The Wonderful Wizard of Oz*, *The Marvelous Land of Oz*, and *Ozma of Oz*), says that for Baum, "Authority figures are seen as distinctly fallible," more valuable "as vaguely likable individuals than as competent, omnipotent protectors." Actually, authority in politics may threaten "the ordinary, extraordinary individual [that Cook says inhabits Oz] by having the capabilities of violating the norms of equality and individualism" (332–33). Still, Ozma and Glinda, although certainly not omnipotent, repeatedly prove themselves not only extremely powerful but also competent and dedicated to preserving equality and individualism. In fact, they almost always appear to cherish both.[6]

In Baum's Oz books that follow *The Marvelous Land of Oz*, preserving unity and stability becomes of paramount importance. The foiling of explicit attempts of would-be tyrants to overthrow Ozma's rule is central to *The Emerald City of Oz, Tik-Tok of Oz, The Lost Princess of Oz*, and *The Magic of Oz*. In addition, *Ozma of Oz* involves the possibility of Ozma's being unable to rule if she remains a piece of bric-a-brac in the Nome King's palace. Even *The Scarecrow of Oz* and *Rinkitink in Oz* treat the dual ideas of political stability and rightful rule, although neither involves a threat against Ozma; and *The Patchwork Girl of Oz* treats the necessity for rule by law complemented by mercy and benevolence. In *Glinda of Oz*, moreover, Ozma works to extend her peaceful rule to the Skeezers and Flatheads, inhabitants of Oz ruled by feuding, corrupt tyrants. Thus, of Baum's fourteen Oz books, eleven deal directly with problems involving politics and benevolent rule.

In *Ozma of Oz* Roquat the Nome King uses his magic belt to transform members of the Royal Family of Ev and members of Ozma's court, including Ozma herself, into pieces of bric-a-brac to decorate his private chambers. Clearly what he does is wrong: his motives are entirely selfish as he shows by his unwillingness to change the people and creatures he transforms back into their original forms without some sort of dangerous, unfair test being involved. To escape the Nome King, Dorothy ultimately uses the magic belt to change some of Roquat's warriors into eggs, which roll around the cavern and cause the rest of the Nome army to flee in panic (211–12).

Here, Dorothy works a transformation that strikes horror in the remaining Nomes, for they fear eggs above all else. The morality of Dorothy's transforming the Nomes is questionable. Still, Baum seems to have felt that it is all right, since it saves Ozma and her party and the Royal Family of Ev, consequently restoring the rightful ruler to the throne of Ev and allowing Ozma to return to her rightful place as ruler of Oz. Thus, Dorothy restores order to what in Ev was a kingdom ruled by Langwidere, an incompetent, unconcerned ruler, and Dorothy preserves order in Oz; Dorothy's act serves the common good, so her working transformations is, Baum indicates, more selfless than selfish. In spite of what Glinda says about transformations in *The Marvelous Land of Oz*, Pendexter is undoubtedly correct in insisting that "[...] Baum normally saw magic as neither intrinsically good nor bad" ("Magic of Baum" 2). Riley calls the fairy magic that Ozma performs "inherently good," but he writes, for other magic-workers in Oz, their magic, "like science," is "neither good nor bad," depending instead on the morality of the one who uses the magic (224). Still, Baum sometimes shows that he knows that good people can accomplish bad things for good reasons, and bad people sometimes do good things for bad reasons. The transformation of Coo-ee-oh, discussed later in this chapter, is a case in point. In *Glinda of Oz* Glinda says to the Wizard that "[...] Ozma's magic is fairy magic, while you are a Wizard and I am a Sorceress. In this way the three of us have a great variety of magic to work with [...]" (216–17), but neither Glinda nor Baum clearly differentiates between these three kinds of magic, except for indicating that Glinda's and the Wizard's depends mostly on magical apparatus while Ozma's depends mostly on a wand or scepter.

Actually, the key to differentiating between good and bad magic in the Land of Oz seems to have nothing to do with the way the magic is produced. Bad magic helps only its performer and hurts others; it tends to destabilize the community. Good magic serves the community at large. Bad magic threatens the "wholeness and stability" that Gilead says characterize fantasy. Repeatedly, Baum indicates that "wholeness and stability" are extremely difficult to establish and maintain in Oz, especially because of the wicked witches and sorcerers who desire power for themselves. Only after Dorothy visits Oz and frees the land of two wicked witches and a humbug wizard can the land begin to move in the direction of the "wholeness and stability" of which Gilead speaks. And even after the end of the second Oz book, characters repeatedly threaten the unity and stability that Ozma and Glinda establish. Fairly consistently in Baum's Oz books bad magic destabilizes both the individual and society. Good magic restores stability and wholeness.

In *The Patchwork Girl of Oz* the Shaggy Man sings a song, the second stanza of which is:

> Our Ruler's a bewitching girl whom fairies love to please;
> She's always kept her magic sceptre to enforce decrees
> To make her people happy, for her heart is kind and true
> And to aid the needy and distressed is what she longs to do [134].

As Allen Eyles notes, in Oz under Ozma's rule, "official authority is used only for the benefit of all" (53). There is one obvious exception to Eyles' statement: when Ozma sentences Eureka the cat to death for a crime she does not commit. Nonetheless, the Shaggy Man enters Oz in the fifth Oz book, and Eureka's trial is in the fourth, so he may not be aware of Eureka's trial, or the inconsistent Baum may have forgotten it or ignored it. At any rate, the Shaggy Man's words show that he feels that Ozma's magic is the foundation of benevolent authority.

Recognizing the great potential for destabilization and fragmentation that magic has as well as its ability to preserve unity and order, Ozma forbids anyone in the Land of Oz from working magic except the Wizard, Glinda, and Ozma herself.[7] In *The Patchwork Girl of Oz* Ozma explains the prohibition and monopolizing of the practice of magic when discussing the specific law against picking a six-leafed clover. According to Ozma, "no law is ever made without some purpose, and that purpose is usually to protect all the people and guard their welfare." Then, she explains:

> Years ago there were many Witches and Magicians in the Land of Oz, and one of the things they often used in making their magic charms and transformations was a six-leaved clover. These Witches and Magicians caused so much trouble among my people, often using their powers for evil rather than good, that I decided to forbid anyone to practice magic or sorcery except Glinda the Good and her assistant, the Wizard of Oz, both of whom I can trust to use their arts only to benefit my people and to make them happier. Since I issued that Law the Land of Oz has been far more peaceful and quiet [...] [229].

When she says that she trusts Glinda and the Wizard "to use their arts only to benefit my people and to make them happier," Ozma indicates that she herself wants the ruler's wishes to coincide with the wishes of the ruled. She also shows her concern with political stability and unity when she says that Oz is "far more peaceful and quiet" now than it was before the law was issued, presumably referring to the pre-Dorothy days and the time of General Jinjur's revolt, when fragmentation resulted largely from the powers of various witches. Ozma's use of "peaceful" implies that she is aware that, before the outlawing of magic, Oz was at times disturbed by the selfish misuse of magic (or in the case of the Wizard, humbuggery), which led to things like the Wizard's attempt to invade the realm of the wicked Witch of the West and Mombi's attempts to support Jinjur's rule of the Emerald City. Ozma, then, monopolizes magic in large part to prevent the refragmentation of Oz and any harm to her subjects that might result.

Glinda, the Wizard, and Ozma herself do not perform magic for selfish purposes. In *The Tin Woodman of Oz* Baum writes that Ozma "knew a lot of magic, but she only used it to benefit her subjects" (134). In *The Scarecrow of Oz* Baum writes that Glinda, "has wonderful magical powers and uses them only to benefit the subjects of Ozma's kingdom" (148). Even the Wizard, who earlier pretends humbuggery is magic and uses it to make people fear and obey him, can in later Oz books be trusted to use magic for the common good: Baum writes in *The Magic of Oz* that the Wizard uses magic "to perform such wizardry as Ozma commanded him to do for the welfare of her subjects."[8] In addition, in *The Emerald City of Oz* the Wizard says that he is learning magic from Glinda (151) and that "Glinda the Good's magic, that I am trying to practice, can never hurt anyone" (246), a statement perhaps contradicted in *The Lost Princess of Oz* when Ugu the Shoemaker steals Glinda's magical apparatus and elixirs and seems intent on using them for evil purposes. Although readers cannot be sure that he actually is able to use them for evil purposes, readers do know that Ugu also steals from Ozma the magic picture (12), and he does use that to spy on the Wizard and his party as they try to rescue Ozma (201). However, being consistent throughout the Oz books seems to have interested Baum little.

Even the prohibition against the practice of magic is enforced inconsistently: it does not seem to apply to all forms of magic or to all magicians. In *The Lost Princess of Oz*, for example, a book in which the prohibition is explicitly stated, Ozma makes no attempt to deprive Cayke the Cookie Cook of her magic dishpan that enables her to bake excellent cookies; to deprive the Little Pink Bear of the magic that enables him to tell people anything they wish to know, except the future; to deprive the Lavender Bear of the magic that the fairies dropped into his stuffing that allows him to create true images of things; or to stop Dorothy from wearing and using the magic belt. In fact, Ozma herself returns the dishpan to Cayke (278). Although Baum is often inconsistent, here, except in the case of the magic belt and perhaps Cayke's dishpan, he seems to be distinguishing between powerful forms of magic that can do great harm and relatively weak but useful forms that in the hands of their practitioners do no harm.

When Ugu the Shoemaker uses magic to kidnap Ozma and imprison her in a golden peach pit, he deprives the realm of its rightful ruler. Ultimately, "he hoped to make himself master of all the Land of Oz" (212). When Dorothy, using the magic belt, changes Ugu into a dove that Ugu makes large and then Dorothy transforms him into a small dove so that he cannot hurt the Frogman, who is trying to protect Dorothy (255–57), she works magic that eventually leads to the freeing of Ozma and the reestablishment of stability. Again, unlike Ugu's transformation of Ozma, Dorothy's transformation of Ugu serves a good purpose, so good that Ugu himself eventually sees the justice in it and desires to remain a dove (279).

Another case that shows the inadequacy of the Scarecrow's declaration that all magic is "to be feared and avoided" occurs in *Glinda of Oz*. Queen Coo-ee-oh uses magic to rule wickedly and tyrannically over the Skeezers. Because she has been the Su-dic's enemy for a long time, having transformed his wife into a golden pig, the Su-dic of the Flatheads transforms Coo-ee-oh into "a beautiful White Swan" covered with diamonds (112). As a swan Coo-ee-oh is unable to use her magic, but the change delights her, for she no longer has any worries, and she feels that "swans are lovelier than girls, especially when they're sprinkled with diamonds" (118–19). Her people too are ultimately much better off with her as a swan. Thus, even though she is transformed for selfish, wicked purposes, her transformation ultimately serves the common good, and she remains a swan.

In *Glinda of Oz*, incidentally, Glinda herself works transformations of a sort: Baum writes that "the great Sorceress transformed, in a way, every Flathead on the mountain" by making their heads rounded and putting their brains inside their heads rather than in cans where they hitherto carry them (253). Now that they are transformed so that they resemble everyone else and so that their brains are distributed evenly and they cannot steal them from one another, the Flatheads no longer desire to conquer their enemies or each other. Thus, Glinda's transformations serve the common good and contribute to peace and stability, again indicating that for Baum magic is to be judged on the basis of what it accomplishes.

One of the most extensive treatments of magic in Baum's Oz books occurs in *The Magic of Oz*, where again the main form magic takes involves transformations. Kiki Aru learns about a magic word that when pronounced properly "can transform anyone into beast, bird or fish, or anything else, and back again" without the use of "tools or powders or herbs [...]" (3–4). Kiki and the Nome King plan to use Kiki's powers to conquer Oz; at Ruggedo's urging, Kiki, like Circe in *The Odyssey*, intends to transform all the people of Oz into beasts and enslave them (28–29). Overhearing Kiki use the magic word, the Wizard uses it to transform Kiki into a hickory nut, Ruggedo into a walnut, and himself back into his own form (139–40).

The transformations that the Wizard performs obviously contribute to the common good and help preserve order, peace, and stability. Baum further illustrates the good of the Wizard's transformations when the Wizard turns Kiki and Ruggedo back into their natural forms but makes them very thirsty so that they immediately drink the water of the Fountain of Oblivion. Then, Kiki forgets his magic word, and Kiki and Ruggedo forget their evil purposes. Again, the Wizard's transformations and then his undoing them both serve the common good by ending an incipient political insurrection.

From these relatively few episodes, it is clear that what makes magic good or bad in Baum's Oz is the purposes it serves. In recognizing the way magic can tempt even good people to do evil things, Ozma rightfully limits its official practice to the Wizard, Glinda, and Ozma.

Although the Scarecrow says, "All magic is unnatural, and for that reason is to be feared and avoided," his very life contradicts his words. In Oz some kinds of magic seem natural, a part of the landscape itself, for Oz is a place in which tin men live and love; creatures stuffed with straw, cotton, or hair walk, talk, and think; and machines have lives of their own. Magic seems to lie in the very soil.[9] As Baum writes in his first Oz book, the flying monkeys belong to Oz "alone, and cannot leave it" (180); put the china dolls in Kansas, and they "can only stand straight and look pretty" (196).[10] In *The Patchwork Girl of Oz* the Shaggy Man is right when he says to the Patchwork Girl, "In America a girl stuffed with cotton wouldn't be alive." Then he ironically adds, "nor would anyone think of making a girl out of a patchwork quilt" (177), anyone, that is, except L. Frank Baum. Take away the magic, convert the Scarecrow into a mere bundle of straw stuffed into clothes and propped on a pole, and Oz loses its charm and its ability to fascinate generations of readers.

Yet in Baum's Oz books magic can destroy peace and order and can fragment society. Remembering the days when "Witches and Magicians caused so much trouble," Ozma wisely concentrates magic in the hands of three virtuous people who use it to serve the common good and preserve a benevolent order. Thus, Baum has Ozma try to ensure that under her rule the Land of Oz is not plagued by the kinds of disunity and corruption that characterized large chunks of American history during Baum's lifetime. In Oz under Ozma, the will of the ruler and that of the ruled almost always coincide, resulting in political equilibrium; and at least in one of Baum's conceptions of Oz, in which there is no death (*Tin Woodman* 132), Ozma's rule should, at least in theory, last eternally, but as *The Magic of Oz* indicates, there is always the possibility of revolution or outside conquest.

Whether Baum wrote the Oz books, as Zipes theorizes, in reaction to what he considered the horrors of the American system or, as Baum indicates, to please children or even to amuse people, including himself, and to make money, or for some other reason or reasons remains unclear. Nonetheless, these children's books treat important aspects of politics. They can easily be seen as embodying Baum's reaction to the corruption, instability, and lack of unity that characterized America during large portions of his life. And since the solutions to the problems of government in Oz involve magic, it is easy to theorize that Baum felt that in the real world of his day, many political problems were insoluble.

13

Glinda of Oz
BAUM'S TALE OF DEMETER
AND PERSEPHONE

Glinda of Oz is L. Frank Baum's fourteenth and last Oz book. He revised it during the last year of his life, working from fall 1918 until the time of his death on 6 May 1919 (Carpenter and Shirley 121; Rogers 234–38). It was published posthumously in 1920. It is, as David L. Greene and Dick Martin write, a "somber" tale. It is also, they say, "the most tightly plotted of all of Baum's books" (56). Although it is unclear how one measures which of Baum's books is "the most tightly plotted," *Glinda of Oz* indeed has a tightly knit plot quite different from the episodic plots that characterize most of Baum's late Oz books.

According to Michael O. Riley, *Glinda of Oz* is "the best" of the four Oz books Baum wrote at the end of his career; it has "no unnecessary incidents" to slow down the story (221). However, early in the book are episodes involving giant spiders and mist fairies that seem tangentially related at best to the rest of the book: they simply involve obstacles unrelated except by space that Ozma and Dorothy overcome to reach their goal. Moreover, many of the escapades of the group that accompany Glinda to rescue Ozma and Dorothy also seem merely tacked onto the story for amusement, especially the episode involving Button Bright's getting lost; so the book is probably not as tightly plotted as it could be.[1]

Nonetheless, *Glinda of Oz* has a fairly tight structure based in part on the myth of Demeter and Persephone. In the best known version of the myth, Hades seizes Persephone and takes her to his realm in the underworld. Demeter wanders the earth hunting for her daughter. Since Demeter is the goddess of agriculture, fertility, and marriage, the people go hungry during her wanderings. Finally, after discovering where her daughter is, Demeter gets Zeus to agree to have Persephone return to the surface to be with her mother, but it is discovered that the daughter has eaten some seeds from a pomegranate that grows in Hades' garden, as a result of which she must stay underground. Zeus enforces a divine compromise: during three months of the year — winter — Persephone will remain underground. During the other nine months — spring, summer, and fall — she will rise to the surface and remain there with her mother until she returns underground in the late fall. That way, Demeter can be with her daughter; people can plant, raise, and harvest their crops; and Hades can have his wife. Persephone thus becomes a vegetation deity.

In *Glinda of Oz*, Glinda functions somewhat like Demeter, and Ozma functions somewhat like Persephone. Both Glinda and Ozma are immortal, and both have powers that go beyond those of other inhabitants even of a fairyland like Oz. Ozma has fairy powers, which are, she says, greater than those of "any other inhabitant of Oz," but she is, she says, "not as powerful as Glinda the Sorceress, who has studied many arts of magic that I know nothing of" (41). Glinda is, in effect, the power behind the throne, and in *Glinda of Oz* both Glinda and Ozma use their powers, they feel, "to make" the inhabitants of the Land of Oz "more happy and contented — although they were already the happiest and most contented folk in all the world" (3). Thus, Ozma and Glinda really do have a kind of status that resembles that of Greek goddesses. Incidentally, this passage, like so many passages in Baum's Oz books, emphasizes the importance of contentment and indicates the concern Glinda and Ozma have for the contentment of Ozma's subjects. It is interesting that Baum made Glinda and Ozma much more concerned about the welfare and contentment of the residents of Oz than the Greek gods are about mortals.

Why during his last years, on a sickbed, Baum regained some of his old power to produce tightly constructed plots is a matter of speculation. It seems that at least with *Glinda of Oz* he regained it in part because the book's central issues are some of what seem to be his most important concerns, ones he treats repeatedly in his children's books: the absurdity of war and the need for just, stable, and benevolent government. These two concerns are related, for war certainly tends to destabilize government and interfere with justice. Baum's dealing with these two serious concerns can also help explain why the book is so somber.

David L. Greene and Dick Martin also point out that the villains in *Glinda of Oz* "are proud, cruel and vindictive, without any of the comic touches that make us laugh at the Nome King" (56). The villains thus resemble those of *Dorothy and the Wizard in Oz*. Their desire to make war on one another involves the potential destruction of both of their people, and the Su-dic or Supreme Dictator of the Flatheads nearly does destroy the Skeezers when he turns their Queen Coo-ee-oh into a swan, since as a swan she forgets the magic that would enable her to raise her city from its submerged position.[2] Only through the help of Glinda (and Dorothy) is Ozma able to raise the city and thus save the Skeezers.

Greene and Martin also claim that the magic in this last Oz book "is more mechanistic than" in any of Baum's other Oz books: "the most important magic is no longer a simple device, but a complex machine," and they consider the machine "more important than the person who makes it function" (56). Although their use of the term "mechanistic" probably is imprecise, their main point is essentially correct: the magic devices in *Glinda of Oz* that Coo-ee-oh uses indicate, as Greene and Martin write, that even in the Land of Oz, "technology, like war, can be destructive" (56); and in *Glinda of Oz* technology and war are combined. One can even see echoes of World War I in the technology, especially in Coo-ee-oh's submarines.

Glinda of Oz begins like so many of Baum's late books. People discover a problem, set out to solve it, and at first have a series of unconnected adventures in the course of solving it. In this case, the problem involves a coming war between the Skeezers and Flatheads. Ozma says, "[...] I cannot allow any wars or troubles in the Land I rule, if I can possibly help it" (6). Although the countries of the Skeezers and Flatheads are in Oz and therefore part of Ozma's kingdom, they do not acknowledge her rule; in fact, almost all of their inhabitants are unaware of her existence. Instead, the Flatheads are ruled by a wicked Su-dic or supreme dictator; and Coo-ee-oh, a Krumbic witch (whatever that may be), rules over the Skeezers. Like the Su-dic, Coo-ee-oh

Ozma and the Su-Dic in *Glinda of Oz* (illus. John R. Neill; Chicago: Reilly & Lee, 1920), p. 81.

too is a dictator who uses her magic to enforce total obedience (90–91). Both the Su-dic and Coo-ee-oh practice magic, a practice that Ozma outlaws for all except the Wizard, Glinda, and Ozma herself (8). More importantly, the Su-dic and Coo-ee-oh use their magic solely for their own purposes with no regard for their subjects' happiness and contentment.

Ozma and Dorothy go on a quest to establish Ozma's rule over the Skeezers and Flatheads and thus bring peace and contentment to them. They travel to the mountain of the Flatheads, where the Su-dic proves uncooperative. He is determined to conquer Queen Coo-ee-oh and the Skeezers because Coo-ee-oh changed his wife into a golden pig when his wife tried to poison the water of the Skeezers' lake (61). Ozma later discovers that the wife tried to poison the lake in an attempt to kill three fishes. Coo-ee-oh transformed the three Adepts of Magic, who used to rule the Flatheads before the Su-dic took over, into fishes. Coo-ee-oh is determined to protect the fishes, since when they were transformed, they told Coo-ee-oh that if anything happened to them, she would "become shrivelled [sic] and helpless" (95).

When the Su-dic tries to take Dorothy and Ozma prisoners, they escape (66) and go to the lake of the Skeezers, hoping to find Coo-ee-oh more cooperative than the Su-dic, but they are disappointed. Coo-ee-oh makes Ozma and Dorothy her prisoners and declares that she now rules the entire Land of Oz since she rules Ozma (86). She then uses magic to cause the city on the Magic Isle to sink beneath the surface of the lake where a glass dome protects it (103). The next day, she faces the Su-dic in battle, and he wins, transforming her into a white swan, but he fails to poison the lake's water and thus kill the three fishes (111–12). The rest of the book involves ultimately successful attempts by Ozma and then Glinda to raise the sunken city and bring peace and Ozma's rule to the lands of the Skeezers and Flatheads.

Central to *Glinda of Oz* is Ozma's attempt to extend her benevolent, peaceful reign. Without the help of Glinda, Ozma would not succeed. She and Dorothy would have to spend eternity under the glass dome under the water. And without the unintentional help of the Su-dic, who transforms Coo-ee-oh into a swan, Ozma might indeed remain Coo-ee-oh's prisoner, thus destabilizing the entire Land of Oz.

In Baum's Oz books Glinda seems closely related to an archetypal figure, the Good Mother aspect of the Great Mother. As Raylyn Moore recognizes, Glinda is "the supportive mother-figure [...] of the Oz cycle" (127). In *The Magic of Oz* Glinda assumes the role of Ozma's mother as she leads Ozma to the table where her birthday presents are (223). In *Glinda of Oz* Glinda displays some of her motherly attributes explicitly in the scolding she gives Button Bright after he gets lost and is found (160), but more important is her implicit role as figurative mother to all of the characters in the Land of Oz, especially Ozma. In terms of overall form *Glinda of Oz* seems a kind of replay of the myth of Demeter and Kore, who, later, when she returns from the land of the dead, is called Persephone. This is one of the myths Erich Neumann treats in his seminal work on the Great Mother (305–11).[3] Just as Demeter rescues her daughter from the underworld where she has been taken and imprisoned by Hades (an episode often referred to as the "rape" of Kore), so Glinda rescues Ozma from underwater where Coo-ee-oh imprisons her. And just as the return of Persephone to the surface of the earth reestablishes order by allowing spring to occur and crops to grow, so Ozma's release from the lake of the Skeezers enables peace and harmony to reign in the Land of Oz. Repeatedly, Neumann refers to the "unity of mother and daughter, Demeter and Kore" (307), and

Ozma and Glinda function as a team, with Glinda using her magic to serve Ozma, which in turn means serving Ozma's subjects, and with Ozma seeking out and following Glinda's advice.

According to Neumann, "The one essential motif" in the Demeter-Kore myth and indeed "in all matriarchal mysteries" is "the 'finding again' of Kore by Demeter, the reunion of mother and daughter." "Psychologically," Neumann explains, "this 'finding again' signifies the annulment of the male rape and incursion, the restoration after marriage of the matriarchal unity of mother and daughter" (308). The *Glinda of Oz* version of this "finding again" occurs after Coo-ee-oh, a female, seizes Ozma and takes her not underground but underwater. Then, Glinda goes on a quest to find and rescue Ozma, and, of course, Dorothy, who is underwater with her. When Glinda enters the submerged city and raises it above the water, allowing her figurative daughter to return to her life on the surface of the world, the mythic cycle is complete. In the best-known Greek version of the myth, Persephone must spend one season of the year, winter, in the underworld as a result of eating seeds of a pomegranate that grew in Hades' garden. Neumann says that "The redness of the pomegranate symbolizes the woman's womb, the abundance of seeds its fertility" (308) and that in effect "the daughter becomes identical with the mother; she becomes a mother and is so transformed into Demeter" (309). In *The Emerald City of Oz* Baum writes of Ozma, "The people were her children [...]" (22). Hearn, moreover, writes that under Ozma's rule, Oz becomes "The Land of Love," and Ozma becomes "like an all-embracing mother" (xcvi). However, since in Baum's later conception of the Land of Oz, people live forever and never age, with the infant remaining always an infant and the old remaining elderly, there is no need for sexual reproduction (and, incidentally, no need for Baum to treat any aspect of sexual attraction). So the idea of Ozma's being pregnant in any literal sense is unthinkable. Since her being a mother is purely metaphorical, Baum omits the sexual reproduction part of the myth from his book. When rescued from the submerged Great Dome, she is free to remain outside the city of the Skeezers yet chooses to extend her reign into it, in a sense remaining present there through her representative, Lady Aurex (250).

Thus, in Baum's version of the Demeter-Kore myth, Ozma does not take Glinda's place as the mother and certainly does not become a literal mother. Instead, she always remains a young child, a Kore (kore means maiden)[4] both in appearance and many of her activities.

In the course of their adventures in Baum's last Oz book, Dorothy, Ozma, and Glinda apparently do not grow in any significant way. That is one of the problems with Baum's later Oz books. Once the residents of Oz become immortal and once physical growth becomes arrested, what happens to emotional growth? It too seems arrested, except perhaps in the cases of the Frogman and Ugu the Shoemaker. The best one can do is accept the boredom and sameness, the way that Reera the Red seems to do,[5] or seize on any adventure, as Dorothy does, in a land that the narrator says "is usually peaceful and uneventful" (4). At the end of the tale, the reader and the Oz residents may have a better appreciation of Glinda's magical powers, and Ozma's peaceful, benevolent rule is extended to the lands of the Skeezers and Flatheads. But these things involve no internal growth for the main characters.

That her magic and Ozma's magic should ultimately be victorious over the magic of the tyrants, Coo-ee-oh and the Su-dic, should be no surprise. In Baum's Oz, as the flying monkeys in the first Oz book point out, "the Power of Good [...] is greater than the Power of Evil" (*Wizard* 128), and Glinda and Ozma, who are good, ultimately use their powers for selfless purposes. The Su-dic and Coo-ee-oh, both of whom are evil, use their powers for selfish purposes. That the tale should also be, as Greene and Martin say, "somber," is no surprise since it treats what Baum considered important topics and since Baum places those topics as well as the larger clash between good and evil into a specific yet universal context that itself is somber in spite of its happy ending — that of the Demeter-Persephone story. Just as in the Greek myth the return of Persephone reestablishes order in the world of humankind, so the return of Ozma reestablishes order in Oz, a land that Baum repeatedly shows needs its rightful ruler. Ozma is, she says, happy that she "went to see" the Skeezers and Flatheads, for, she says, "I not only prevented any further warfare between them, but they have been freed from the rule of the Su-dic and Coo-ee-oh and are now happy and loyal subjects of the Land of Oz" (255), and the book ends as she adds, "Which proves that it is always wise to do one's duty, however unpleasant that duty may seem to be" (255). Thus, her quest is successful in that she extends her peaceful rule and simultaneously brings happiness and contentment to more of her subjects. Incidentally, Baum here too does not hesitate to teach explicitly the very morality that he says, in the Introduction to *The Wonderful Wizard of Oz*, should be dispensed with in modern "wonder-tales," yet here, unlike similar statements do in *Rinkitink in Oz*, the moral statement grows directly out of the tale.

Whether Baum had the Demeter-Persephone story consciously in mind when he wrote this book may be doubted, but in the last analysis, it does not matter. By having Ozma and Dorothy escape from the living death involved in being trapped underwater, Baum's story follows the archetypal pattern of birth, life, death, and rebirth, the very pattern that anthropologists say lies at the heart of the Demeter-Persephone tale. Baum's book, then, is a story of the cycle of human life. Baum manages to adapt this story to his fairyland in which people neither die nor age and accordingly reproduction becomes unnecessary. He works into his tale two successful quests — that of Ozma to end the enmity between the Skeezers and Flatheads and the bad rule from which both groups suffer and that of Glinda to rescue Ozma. In so doing, Baum produces a tale of great power.

14

Boundaries
Oz as Sacred Space

According to Raylyn Moore, Oz's being surrounded by deserts "suggests the undiscovered paradise which *might have been* an oasis at the core of the Great American Desert itself, if such a desert had existed on the scale imagined by map-makers and early explorers" (96). According to Michael O. Riley, before the publication in 1914 of *Tik-Tok of Oz*, "the most general impression of the location of Oz had been that it is in our world, hidden away and difficult to get to, but a magical, marvelous, undiscovered part of America" (187). Since Dorothy first arrives in Oz by means of a tornado, such ideas seem plausible for the first Oz book. She arrives in Oz the second time, however, as the result of a storm at sea when she is on the way to Australia, making it difficult to conceive of Oz as part of America. Instead, Baum's Oz apparently exists in a kind of space very different from that in which people really live and very different from that of America in Baum's day, a space in which magic works.

Moore recognizes that Oz also resembles "mythical islands for which explorers searched" (98), an idea that hints that Oz is to be thought of as being outside the physical world as people know it, a "mythical" rather than a real place. It is interesting that F. J. Baum (L. Frank Baum's son) and Russell P. MacFall write, "In looking for prototypes of *The Wonderful Wizard of Oz*, one finds little except two

179

long-forgotten tales by a Boston poet and painter, Christopher C. [sic] Cranch" (126–27), referring to *The Last of the Huggermuggers: A Giant Story* (1856) and *Kobboltozo: A Sequel to The Last of the Huggermuggers* (1857) by Christopher Pearse Cranch, a minor Transcendentalist poet and friend of Ralph Waldo Emerson. In both of these books Cranch has his protagonist, Jacky Cable, go to an island where the Huggermuggers, a race of giants, live. In the earlier of the books Jacky tries, unsuccessfully, to bring the last living Huggermugger back to civilization. Cranch's books obviously derive from Jonathan Swift's *Gulliver's Travels* and Daniel Defoe's *Robinson Crusoe,* but if Moore is right about Oz's resembling "mythical islands," then Baum's work probably descends in part at least from Cranch, Swift, and Defoe, thus having American as well as European antecedents. At any rate, on Baum's "island" — surrounded not by water but by desert — magic works. As Trot says in *The Magic of Oz*, in Oz "magic is so common" (145).

Most discussions of magic in Baum's books deal quite rightly with his mixing magic and technology to produce "technological magic" that sometimes involves complicated machines that work by magic, such as those that raise and lower the Magic Isle in *Glinda of Oz* (Pendexter, "Magic in Post-Thompson Oz" 2).[1] According to Katharine M. Rogers in her excellent biography of Baum, his fascination with modern technology was reinforced by his visits to The World's Columbian Exposition of 1893 in Chicago, where Baum became interested especially in the possibilities of electrical power, leading him to write *The Master Key: An Electric Fairy Tale* (43–44). Rogers calls the work "science fiction" (97), as does Martin Gardner in his introduction to Baum's *Queen Zixi of Ix* (xi). But it seems closer to science fantasy, with its Demon of Electricity, a figure that violates the laws of the world as Baum understood and people now understand them.

Rogers' and Gardner's labeling *The Master Key* science fiction rather than fantasy is an indication of a kind of blurring of boundaries that many critics feel Baum engages in. As Hugh Pendexter, III, writes, "much of Baum's magic reflects the technological advances that were going on in his time" ("Magic of Baum" 8). S. J. Sackett writes, "one might well scoff that the Utopia of Oz was made possible by the existence of magic and [...] human nature is too corrupt for so perfect a fairyland" (212). But, Sackett says, people have a tremendous amount of "magic" available to them in the form of electricity and atomic power, and Sackett insists that Baum felt that human nature is changeable (212).

Rogers claims that Oz is "a slightly heightened version" of some of the pleasant "rural parts" of America, like the ones where Baum grew up (77), and insists that Baum forces readers to inquire about the difference "between what is 'objectively' true and what is believed to be true" at the same time that "he blurs" distinctions between his "magical worlds," which become "real in our imaginations, and the everyday world." However, even she notices that Baum in the first Oz book uses Kansas "to contrast with Oz" (73). Actually, it seems that one cannot have it both ways: either Oz is distinctly different from "the everyday world," or it isn't.

Baum recognizes irreconcilable differences between the so-called real world as it is embodied in his books and Oz. In the first Oz book the Flying Monkey King acknowledges that the monkeys cannot fly Dorothy to Kansas because they "belong to this country alone [...]." In addition, the Monkey King says, "There has never been a Winged Monkey in Kansas yet, and I suppose there never will be, for they don't belong there" (180). The princess of the china dolls knows that in Kansas she "can only stand straight and look pretty" (196); in *Ozma of Oz* Glinda explains that the magic belt cannot work outside of a fairyland (243). In *The Patchwork Girl of Oz* Dr. Pipt declares that he will perform "one of the greatest feats of magic possible to man, even in this marvelous Land of Oz. In no other country could it be done at all" (37). Thus, in spite of what Sackett and Rogers write, Baum seems to have had in mind some kind of clear "distinction" between his "magical worlds [...] and the everyday world," at least as Baum embodies those worlds in some of his works. In fact, the real world in Baum's works tends to be decidedly grim. His Kansas is a place of unremitting poverty, a place where Uncle Henry cannot succeed even though he "worked in the fields as hard as he could," as Baum writes in *The Emerald City of Oz* (13). The same book is also set at a time "when," Baum writes, "fairies are supposed no longer to exist" (14). Thus, unlike Oz, Baum's version of Kansas is decidedly prosaic.

Oz is a *utopia*, or no place, but it is not a *eutopia*, or good place. It is too full of dangers and discontent; otherwise, Oz books would probably be extremely boring. And Oz is not even Baum's idea of a eutopia, or good place, although in many ways it might be better than America of his day as he conceived of it. The basic difference between the world readers perceive and the world in the Land of Oz is, of course, that in Oz real magic works, so the real world cannot reproduce what happens there; it is the stuff of fantasy. With the science and technology available in Baum's day and even in our own, there is no way to replace all the parts of a human being with tin, and there is no way to make a man of straw come to life. Nor can people enable animals to think rationally, act on those rational thoughts, and communicate those thoughts in English to humankind. So Oz is indeed what J. R. R. Tolkien calls a "Secondary World," one quite distinct from what Tolkien calls the "Primary World" in which real people live (36). Actually, since Baum's conception of Oz changes from book to book, it might be more accurate to call Oz a series of Secondary Worlds, distinct from the Primary World. And there appears to be no possible blurring of boundaries between Oz and what Rogers calls "the everyday world." Although Oz can be reached from the real world as it exists within the Oz books, it cannot be reached from the real world in which real people live. Thus, it serves as sacred space within the Oz books but as unattainable space within the real world.

Baum's mixture of science and fantasy in his fantasy worlds continues from *The Master Key* to his last Oz book, including a continuing fascination with electricity (as manifested repeatedly, for example, in *Tik-Tok of Oz*). His last Oz book, *Glinda of Oz* (published posthumously in 1920), is especially interesting in connection with the elaborately conceived machines powered by magic. But the critics who explore his mixing of magic and technology ignore that this particular mixture simultaneously allows the blurring of boundaries between the real world and Oz in very interesting ways *and* provides quite distinct boundaries between the world as people conceive of it and Oz. Actually, a blurring of some boundaries pretty consistently occurs in Baum's Oz books, while one boundary at least seems to remain quite distinct.

To cross the boundary from the real world as it is embodied in Baum's books to Oz takes incredible force: one needs ferocious natural forces like a tornado, as in the first Oz book, *The Wonderful Wizard of Oz*; terrible storms at sea, as in the third book, *Ozma of Oz,* and the eighth one, *Tik-Tok of Oz*; a whirlpool, as in the ninth book, *The Scarecrow of Oz*; or magic itself, as in the fifth book, *The Road to Oz,* and the sixth book, *The Emerald City of Oz*. In the fourth Oz book, *Dorothy and the Wizard in Oz*, an earthquake enables Dorothy and the Wizard separately to reach a fantasy land, and magic enables them eventually to get to Oz. Yet once they are in Baum's fairyland, people find themselves in a radically different kind of space from that in which people at least think they find themselves in the so-called real world.

Though magic works in the first Oz book, the Land of Oz itself is not a pleasant place. It has several kingdoms with good rulers, two large kingdoms that wicked witches rule, and one that a humbug Wizard rules. The Emerald City at the center of Oz appears to be an *axis mundi* or world axis. According to Mircea Eliade, an *axis mundi* is a holy place at the world's center, "where heaven and earth meet" (*Cosmos and History* 12). Eliade further defines sacred space as a place where "an opening has been made, either upward (the divine world) or downward (the underworld, the world of the dead)." It is, Eliade writes, "sometimes expressed through the image of a universal pillar, *axis mundi*," something simultaneously connecting and supporting "heaven and earth and whose base is fixed in the world below (the infernal regions)," and adds, "Such a cosmic pillar can be only at the very center of the universe, for the whole of the habitable world revolves around it" (*Sacred and Profane* 36–37). Joseph Campbell uses the terms *world axis* and *world navel* interchangeably; for him, the navel is "the point of entry" at "the center of the symbolic circle of the universe" at which "Grace, food substance, energy [...] pour into the living world [...]." A world navel constitutes "the immovable Spot [...] around which the world may be said to revolve" (*Hero* 40–41). The true shaman or priest can establish any area as sacred space, as an *axis mundi*. In existing as sacred space, then, Oz is not heaven. It is a connecting point between the earthly and the divine. Baum makes the Emerald City the center of Oz, and makes the Royal Palace the center of the center. In *The Magic of Oz* he explicitly writes, "In the center of the Emerald City of Oz, the capital city of Ozma's dominions, is a vast and beautiful garden, surrounded by a wall inlaid with shining emeralds, and in the center of this garden stands Ozma's Royal Palace, the most splendid building ever constructed" (36). In the first Oz book, however, the Emerald City is ruled by a humbug Wizard, who is a kind of false god or priest or shaman with no real power. Also, humbug lies at the heart of the city's beauty: the green glasses everyone in the city must wear make it appear more magnificent than it really is. Thus, in *The Wonderful Wizard of Oz* the city is a parody of a world axis in which no real interpenetration of earthly and divine can occur. Significantly, in this first book Dorothy cannot return to Kansas from the Emerald City; she must travel south to the land ruled by Glinda, a good witch powerful enough to create a true world navel, and from there Dorothy can return home.

Only at the end of *The Marvelous Land of Oz* does the Emerald City start to become a true world navel when Ozma takes her place as rightful ruler of the Emerald City and uses her real magical ability to rule it. A true priest or shaman, Ozma is able to establish Oz as a place in which the earthly and divine interpenetrate. By the beginning of *Ozma of Oz*, Baum's conception of Ozma has changed: she now rules the entire land of Oz (96), and the Emerald City itself becomes a kind of center not only for Oz but also for the rest of the world. As Moore astutely comments, "In Oz the Emerald City is the axis and Ozma its personification" (125). From the Emerald City Dorothy goes to Australia in *Ozma of Oz,* and in *Dorothy and the Wizard in Oz* the power found in the Emerald City enables her to go to Oz and return to Kansas.

It is impossible to judge how strong Baum's commitment to Theosophy was. His mother-in-law, Matilda Joslyn Gage, an early suffragette and associate of Elizabeth Cady Stanton and Susan B. Anthony, was a devoted Theosophist. Baum seems to have both admired and loved his mother-in-law. Baum and his wife Maud joined the Ramayana Theosophical Society in Chicago in 1892. Yet Baum's membership in the society may have simply reflected what Rogers calls his "disregard for conventional religion" (66) rather than a strong commitment to Theosophy itself. Michael Patrick Hearn also notes about Baum's commitment to the tenets of Theosophy, "Whether he actually believed all of this is debatable" (xciii). His adherence to any religion seems to have been minimal. Still, Rogers claims that Theosophy influenced Baum's creation of his fantasy worlds by affirming "a reality beyond the everyday visible world" and by providing Baum with a "vision of a cosmos in which physical and spiritual reality were part of one great whole, filled with beings seen and unseen and governed by the same laws" (51). Baum, however, could have gotten these same ideas from many branches of traditional Christianity, including Methodism, in which his mother strongly believed and in which she raised her children, and Episcopalianism, to which Baum and Maud belonged during their years in Aberdeen, South Dakota.[2] As Eliade points out, "Every temple or palace—and by extension, every sacred city or royal residence—is a Sacred Mountain, thus becoming a Center" or *axis mundi* (*Cosmos and History* 12). Thus, most religions can and do establish such centers. At any rate, from any of the religions to which he belonged, Baum could have gotten ideas about constituting part of the world as a world navel or axis, although he may have been unfamiliar with these terms.

In Baum's later conception of the Land of Oz magic is central to Ozma's rule, and the magic centers around the Emerald City. Ozma has what Baum calls "fairy magic" (*Glinda* 216–17), for which she needs no magical instruments of the sort Glinda and the Wizard, at least in later Oz books, need. The Wizard also lives in the Emerald City. Glinda still lives in her own castle outside of the city, but she always uses her magic to serve Ozma.

In the fourth book, *Dorothy and the Wizard in Oz*, Baum has Ozma give voice to a myth of an Oz "united under one Ruler" whose "name was always 'Oz,'" which means in our language 'Great and Good'; or, if the Ruler happened to be a woman her name was always 'Ozma.'" But Mombi "stole" Ozma's grandfather and kept him prisoner. Four wicked witches then ruled Oz until good witches came to power in the North and South. When Ozma was born, Mombi transformed her into a boy. However, Ozma escaped and became, she says, "the Ruler of my people" (167–68). In the sixth Oz book, *The Emerald City of Oz*, Ozma tells of a wicked king of Oz who "made himself and all his people very miserable and unhappy." As a result, Glinda put the Forbidden Fountain with the Water of Oblivion in it on the palace grounds in the Emerald City, "and the King drank of its water and forgot all his wickedness." But since the people remembered how wicked the king was, they still feared him, so he made them drink of the water of the fountain. "After that they all grew wise together, and their wisdom was good, so that peace and happiness reigned in the land" (273–74). Whether this myth about the fountain is a part of the one involving all the male rulers being named Oz and female rulers named Ozma is impossible to say. Since it involves someone Ozma calls a "King" rather than just ruler or prince (the equivalent of what she calls herself, a princess), it may be part of a separate myth of Oz's past.

In the twelfth Oz book, *The Tin Woodman of Oz*, Baum creates yet another myth about Oz's having been "much like other lands" until the ruler of a band of fairies — Queen Lurline — "enchanted the country and so made it a Fairyland." Lurline left one of her fairies — Ozma — to rule over the land (132). In this myth the fairy Lurline changed Oz in such a way that people there live forever, never getting older than they were when Lurline and her fairy band first passed over Oz (132).

These later conceptions of Oz differ radically from Baum's first conception, in which creatures — such as wicked witches and Kalidahs — die, and people age, and in which Pastoria, Ozma's father, rules the Emerald City before the Wizard arrives (*Land* 228). For example, in *The Marvelous Land of Oz* Baum writes of Tip's growth (2) and of providing for Mombi's old age (261), and in *The Emerald City of Oz* he writes of Omby Amby's boyhood (93). In *The Patchwork Girl of Oz* Dr. Pipt assures the Glass Cat that Ojo, a Munchkin boy, "will grow big and become as tall as Unc Nunkie," Ojo's uncle (33).

By the twelfth book, nonetheless, the whole Land of Oz constitutes divine space in which mortals from the United States who are lucky enough to get there achieve a kind of immortality. No one knows whether they, unlike the native inhabitants of the land, may still die, although in the natural — which is to say the unnatural — course of events they will live for a long, long time. In *The Magic of Oz* the narrator says that "it is doubtful whether those who come to Oz from the outside world [...] will live forever or cannot be injured. Even Ozma is not sure about this, and so the guests of Ozma from other lands are always carefully protected from any danger, so as to be on the safe side" (62).[3]

In *The Emerald City of Oz,* Oz becomes constituted as a completely separate space, wholly cut off from the mundane world in which real people live. Because of the invention of and expanding use of airships and because of an invasion from the lands surrounding Oz, Glinda makes it "impossible for anyone [living outside Oz] to ever communicate with us [that is, the beings in Oz] in any way, after this. Then, we may live peacefully and contentedly" by making Oz "invisible to all eyes but our own." She performs a feat of magic that enables the inhabitants of Oz to "separate ourselves forever from all the rest of the world" (295). Baum conceived of this as being his last Oz book. In fact, Dorothy writes a note on a feather from a stork's wing announcing, "*You will never hear anything more about Oz, because we are now cut off forever from all the rest of the world. But Toto and I will always love you and all the other children who love us*" (298).

Why Baum erected this supposedly impenetrable barrier between Oz and the everyday world remains a source of debate. In one of the first works to take Baum seriously as a "subversive" writer and thus one worthy of close attention, Jack Zipes argues that at the beginning of *The Emerald City of Oz* Baum "developed" and announced "principles for his utopia [...]" (128) in one of the most-cited passages in discussions of Oz as a eutopia.[4] That Baum did not stick to these principles apparently does not bother Zipes, who writes of "Baum's socialist utopia," claiming, "he grasped that technology in the hands of capitalist entrepreneurs would mean the doom of utopian developments like Oz," and adding that making Oz invisible was Baum's way of indicating that any chance of achieving an American "utopia" "had been canceled and forfeited." According to Zipes, for Baum "the real American world of finance" destroyed the American dream that Baum tried to embody in Oz (130). Zipes probably exaggerates here. Baum's making Oz invisible and unreachable may merely have been part of his attempt to stop writing Oz books and spend his time working on other things.

When he started writing Oz books, Baum himself was a failed "capitalist entrepreneur," and he continued investing time and energy in entrepreneurial activities, such as his various attempts to make stage shows and films connected with his Oz works, most of which failed. Even in Baum's Oz books there are people resembling Zipes' "capitalist entrepreneurs," most notably Ugu the Shoemaker, who, in *The Lost Princess of Oz*, tries to use magical machinery and objects, most of which he steals, to overthrow the legitimate ruler of Oz and put himself in her place. The Nome King also is a kind of entrepreneur who in Baum's books twice (in *The Emerald City of Oz* and *The Magic of Oz*) tries to take over the Land of Oz but does not succeed. As long as Glinda and her assistant, the Wizard, have "the knowledge of magic" (*Lost Princess* 17), they will find a way to preserve Ozma's rule even if others steal their tools or develop magic of their own. In addition, Ozma is very concerned about keeping magic out of the wrong hands, so much so that she decrees a monopoly on the practice of it, allowing only the Wizard, Glinda, and Ozma herself to use magic in any form.[5]

Still, at the end of *The Emerald City of Oz* it seems as though Oz stories will end. The boundary between Oz and the rest of the world, not just the real world as it is embodied in Baum's books but also the rest of his magical kingdoms, is sealed, with no more possibility of people or ideas or tales crossing the boundary. The real world embodied in the books is deprived of its navel, and no interpenetration of the divine and the earthly can occur. Yet after *The Emerald City of Oz* Baum wrote eight more Oz books, and in some of them, such as *Tik-*

"Farewell." From *The Emerald City of Oz* (illus. John R. Neill; Chicago: Reilly & Lee, 1910), frontispiece.

Tok of Oz and *The Scarecrow of Oz,* people from the United States enter Oz. Obviously, Baum decided not to maintain the rigid boundary that separated Oz from the America found in his works. And technology supplies one of the ways that he penetrates that boundary.

In the Prologue to the seventh Oz book, *The Patchwork Girl of Oz,* Baum summarizes the material from the sixth book about Oz being "rendered invisible to all who lived outside its boundaries." He then explains that at the suggestion of one of the children who clamored for more Oz books, he decided to have Dorothy communicate with the outside world "by wireless telegraph." Baum says that he himself learned to use wireless telegraphy and started sending messages to Dorothy, which Glinda found out about in her "big book in which is recorded every event that takes place anywhere in the world, just at the moment it happens." The Shaggy Man, "who knew how to telegraph a wireless reply," then reestablished contact between Oz and the rest of the world (ix-x). So the Oz books can continue, and within the worlds they create, Baum can remain what he calls the Royal Historian of Oz.

The mixture of technology and magic in terms of literary history establishes a kind of difference or boundary between Oz and previous fairylands, in part helping make the first Oz book what Baum calls "a modernized fairy tale" (*Wizard* ix) and making all the Oz books into American fairy tales different from European and other tales in part because of their great dependence on technology, a dependence thought more immediately typical of American life than of life elsewhere. Even here, however, the boundary is blurred, since the Oz books draw on many of the elements of European fantasy and fairy tale, including talking animals, wicked and good witches, and a repeated structural use of variations on the hero quest.[6] In his book from 1901, *American Fairy Tales,* Baum blurs the boundaries also. Martin Gardner begins his introduction to the Dover edition with the following assertion: "The title of this book is somewhat of a misnomer. Not all its stories occur in America, and not all are about fairies" (v). That the stories are not all "about fairies" should be no surprise since so many of the tales classified as *fairy tales* have no creatures called fairies in them. "Little Red Riding-Hood," "Hansel and Gretel," and "Jack and the Beanstalk" are some very well known examples. The main point here is that Baum obviously felt that to write fairy tales, he had to draw on European tradition, something he also did when writing the Oz books.

At one point in the Oz books, magic itself shuts off the bound-

ary between Oz and the rest of the world, including, of course, the
United States, with a supposedly impenetrable barrier. But the powerful forces of technology later enable that barrier to be penetrated, and
in other Oz books forces of nature continue to penetrate that boundary.

After Dorothy's initial journey in *The Wonderful Wizard of Oz* and
after Ozma attains her throne in *The Marvelous Land of Oz*, Oz becomes
and remains sacred space, and Ozma establishes the Emerald City as
a world axis or navel to which creatures from the United States as it is
embodied in the Oz books must journey to get permission to remain
in Oz and thus become immortal or at least almost immortal. However, as books like *The Road to Oz* and *The Scarecrow of Oz* indicate,
people can enter Oz from places other than the Emerald City itself, so
the whole of Oz remains a kind of sacred space. Oz itself, then, has a
kind of divinity associated with it, and the Emerald City, with Ozma
ruling from there, becomes the usual locus at which the worldly and
divine interpenetrate. But, alas, even though Baum portrays himself as
an historian rather than creator of fantasy, both Oz and the Emerald
City remain unattainable for real people.

Within the Oz books Baum usually makes the boundary between
the real world and Oz permeable, but the two worlds are markedly
different: Oz contains boundless possibilities; the real world as it
appears in Baum's Oz books contains few possibilities but much
unremitting and unrewarding hard labor. Moreover, the boundary
between Oz and the world people really inhabit is not permeable. It
cannot be both ways: either Oz is distinctly different from the real
world, or it is not. Baum's Oz is part of a series of works of fantasy,
and, as David Russell writes, "In the broadest sense, *fantasy* is any story
of the impossible" (194). Deborah O'Keefe also calls fantasy "a type of
fiction containing something impossible, contrary to the laws of nature
as we know them" (22). Technology is not magic. People may talk of
the magic of Hollywood, the magic of television, and the magic of
computers, but they know that these things involve no real magic. So
people know that it is impossible, at least in their waking lives, to reach
Oz or an Oz-like land, a place dependent on real magic for its existence. Perhaps that fact explains in part why the makers of the 1939
MGM movie made Dorothy's journey a dream. In waking life people
seem forever shut off from the sacred space that Baum's Oz constitutes.

15

Baum's Oz
(Dys)(Eu)(U)Topia?

In 1929 Edward Wagenknecht published a booklet, *Utopia Americana,* that is usually considered the first recognition by a serious literary scholar of the value of L. Frank Baum's Oz books. It treats the books as creating an essentially American utopia. Since Wagenknecht's booklet appeared, critics have repeatedly called Oz a *utopia*, meaning good place (*eutopia*) as well as no place (*utopia*), but have rarely examined the implications of this label.

This chapter attempts to deconstruct the notion that Baum's Oz is a *eutopia* or "good place," although it is indeed a *utopia* or "no place." It comes closer to being a totalitarian state ruled by a marriage of technology and magic than it does to being a eutopia. Ozma's magic picture and Glinda's great book of records give Princess Ozma of Oz the ability to spy on every action of her subjects. With her monopoly on magic, she is able to exert total control. Actually, Oz is not a totalitarian state. It is a fairyland in books for children. Although these books often do express philosophical and political ideas, they do not put forth a consistent political philosophy.

In a highly provocative and insightful essay entitled "Utopian Tension in L. Frank Baum's 'Oz,'" Andrew Karp sees within the Oz books an attempt to create a "framework for social harmony"; Baum tries "to eliminate prejudice" and replace it "with cooperation and respect not just between" people but also between people "and the world around them," including "animals, vegetables, minerals, and machines [...]" (119). However, only when those vegetables, minerals, machines, and animals become, for all practical purposes, human do the people of Oz show any real respect for them. Oz residents eat vegetables and go fishing.[1] And in several Oz books Billina eats bugs.[2] The Cowardly Lion, moreover, apparently eats animals that he kills. In *The Lost Princess of Oz*, for example, Baum writes that "the Lion had stolen away and found a breakfast to his liking; he never told what it was, but Dorothy hoped the little rabbits and the field mice had kept out of his way" (137). Oz residents also do not hesitate to use minerals for decorative purposes, putting shoes of gold on the Sawhorse and using emeralds extensively to adorn the Emerald City. As for eliminating prejudice, Baum's Oz does emphasize toleration, except for those groups against which Baum himself, apparently, is prejudiced.

Karp points out that many "scholars dismiss Baum's utopian society as a fairy tale paradise rife with inconsistencies and superficialities" and consequently neglect Baum's "central political and philosophical concerns," especially "the conflict between the individual and the community" as well as the difficulty of creating "a unified and harmonious society out of a rag-tag of wildly diverse individuals" (103). Incidentally, several scholars have, indeed, explored what they feel are Baum's "central political and philosophical concerns" in his Oz books, including Jack Zipes and Michael O. Riley, who tend to see the works consistently rejecting the American system of government, especially aspects of it involving support of capitalism. Others, such as William Leach and Stuart Culver, see Baum's Oz books as supporting the capitalist system and teaching children to be good consumers in that system. Once again readers are faced with the fact that the books tend to be inconsistent or at least so ambiguous that scholars can find polar-opposite meanings in them.

Karp says that Baum apparently personally supported the ideals of the United States, so Karp wonders why Baum made "his utopian world [...] a socialist monarchy" (111). Karp answers his own question by noting the centrality of royalty to "fairy tale tradition," and Karp adds that by giving Oz "a Queen," Baum furthers "his attempt to create a series of uniquely American fairy tales" (111).[3] Given Baum's extensive knowledge of fairy tales and his repeated assertions that Oz is a fairyland, Karp's idea here seems correct.

Karp still feels, however, that for Baum, a land that has "a strong, benevolent monarch" controlling the land and functioning "as a loving mother" to her subjects is "more harmonious than" one "potentially ravaged by competitive democracy or uncontrollable passions and instinctual urges" (111). Karp certainly slants his argument here, although he may be right. But being "more harmonious" than Karp seems to feel the America of Baum's day was does not necessarily make Oz a eutopia.

For Karp, individualism is preeminent in the Land of Oz, but the land's society can "function" only when its inhabitants "squelch their pride and arrogance" so that they can work together for the country's welfare rather than act in their own self-interest (118). That Oz does not always "function," however, indicates that it is not a eutopia. In fact, Karp's vision of Oz involves what seems to be a basic contradiction. How can individualism be preeminent if cooperative action is always a necessity?

Even if all Oz people always work together, there still might be problems. In his essay on "Marxism and Utopia" Pavel Kovaly indicates that when cooperation is stressed over individual rights, totalitarianism may result; Kovaly writes that for George Lukács, "authentic freedom can be reached only through discipline and the unconditional absorption of the total personality in the practice of the movement" (91). Is such "authentic freedom" worth attaining? Kovaly indicates that it is not; for him, given Lukács' ideas,

> A utopian promise justifies not only external forces of oppression in social and political practice, but requires individual inner submission and subjection as well. Both from outside and in his inner life, a concrete living being has been reduced to an object. The great, magnificent utopian vision has turned man into a mere cog in the wheels of political apparatuses. Man has become negligible [92].

Kovaly believes that just this kind of thing happened in the Soviet Union, producing a totalitarian state.

Oz under Ozma has a real danger of also becoming a totalitarian state: as freedom of choice disappears, eutopia becomes dystopia. And in Baum's Oz freedom of choice is in danger of disappearing — or in some of the Oz books perhaps has disappeared. In *The Patchwork Girl of Oz*, for example, the Shaggy Man tells the Patchwork Girl, "In this country [...] people live wherever our Ruler tells them to" (181). If what the Shaggy Man says is true, then individual choice vanishes unless

Ozma chooses to respect it. Moreover, in the same book the Wizard tells the Patchwork Girl, "You're a stranger here, Miss Patches, and so you don't know that nothing can be hidden from our powerful Ruler's magic picture — nor from the watchful eyes of the humble Wizard of Oz" (225–28). Later in *The Patchwork Girl of Oz* Ozma herself says, "Nothing that happens in the Land of Oz escapes the notice of our wise Sorceress, Glinda the Good" (338). In such a society one can still exercise one's individual will, but only if one is willing to bear consequences for doing so if that individual will conflicts with the will of the rulers. Moreover, the idea of being constantly watched bothers some people tremendously.

Obviously, not until after Dorothy has her first series of adventures in Oz does it approach being any sort of Eden. Pre-Dorothy Oz is closer to dystopia than eutopia. Decidedly unfit rulers, including two wicked witches and one humbug Wizard, control the lives of most of the inhabitants. When Dorothy leaves Oz for the first time, the selfish rule of the two wicked witches and of the Wizard is over. At the end of the first Oz book, *The Wonderful Wizard of Oz*, Glinda is ready to send the Scarecrow to the Emerald City to rule, the Tin Woodman to the land of the Winkies to rule, and the Lion to the forest to become King of the Beasts (213–15). So Oz would seem to be on its way to being well governed.

Riley places the conversion of Oz into a utopia or no place in *Tik-Tok of Oz*: in that book, he writes, "[...] Oz has been removed from our world and now exists apart from it" (187). In fact, Riley explains Betsy's being able to get there after a shipwreck by writing, "the argument leans toward the idea of heaven." [4] He adds that only with difficulty can one "disregard" what he calls "the religious overtones" of this Oz book, even though, Riley claims, Baum himself may not have been aware of those overtones. Still, Riley admits that he cannot "prove" his idea that Baum at any time considered "Oz as a vision of heaven" (150). Although Oz becomes a kind of sacred space, it does not become heaven, at least as people in America usually conceive of heaven. In fact, in *The Magic of Oz* Baum explicitly introduces the idea that "Ozma is not sure" that people from our world who enter Oz "will live forever or cannot be injured" (62). Accordingly, though Baum is often inconsistent, in this one Oz book, written after *Tik-Tok of Oz*, if Oz is heaven, it is indeed an unusual kind of heaven.

That what some people consider Baum's eutopia in later Oz books should be made from the same stuff as his dystopia initially found in *The Wonderful Wizard of Oz* should not be surprising. In his study of *The Dystopian Impulse in Modern Literature* M. Keith Booker notes that dystopian and eutopian thought work "with rather than against" each other and that "it may be that dystopian warnings of impending nightmares are ultimately necessary to preserve any possible dream of a better future" (177). As Joseph H. Wellbank writes, "if the demands of justice are ignored, the 'good place' (EUTOPIA) portrayed in constructive utopia can turn into the 'no place' (UTOPIA) of a satire, or worse, it can degenerate into the 'bad place' (DYSTOPIA) of the anti-utopia or dystopia" (31).

What passes for justice in Oz is sometimes problematical. In *Dorothy and the Wizard in Oz*, for example, Dorothy's kitten, Eureka, when accused of eating a piglet, is considered guilty from the start and actually found guilty since, the jury says, "Kittens have no consciences, so they eat whatever pleases them" (213–14). Ozma is "about to order Eureka's head chopped off" when the Tin Man tries to save her by lying (214). Even when it turns out that the piglet is still alive, Eureka is "in disgrace" and "forbidden to wander around the palace" (218). Similarly, in *The Patchwork Girl of Oz*, when Ojo, the book's protagonist, gets arrested for picking "a six-leaved clover" (178), his being found guilty seems a foregone conclusion. Although the Soldier with the Green Whiskers does say, "Anyone accused of a crime is given a fair trial by our ruler and has every chance to prove his innocence" (186), no such thing happens to Eureka. Also, Shaggy assumes Ojo is guilty (191), and Tollydiggle, the jailer, says to Ojo, "When you are tried and found guilty" (198), not "*If* you are found guilty."

In *The Wonderful Wizard of Oz* Baum uses the word "gray" to characterize Kansas. The land is gray, the house Dorothy lives in is gray, and Uncle Henry, the rightful inhabitant of the land, is gray. The landscape, moreover, is exceptionally dry and lacking in fertility. The sun beats relentlessly on the land, turning the grass "the same gray color to be seen elsewhere" (2). On the contrary, the Oz Dorothy enters is, except for the Land of the Winkies, full of flowers, grass, and trees along with abundant brooks and rivers (10). The land of the Winkies is treeless, and the sun beats on it unmercifully (120), perhaps an indication that the rule of the wicked Witch of the West has sapped it of its fertility. It seems that Baum indicates that misrule can change Oz into something that resembles Kansas. Still, the Land of the Munchkins, over whom the wicked Witch of the East rules until Dorothy's house drops on her, is characterized by great fertility.[5] Everywhere Dorothy goes in Oz (except in the land of the wicked Witch of the West), she finds an abundance of food and water. When she initially arrives, the landscape of Oz in which she first finds herself is in many ways similar to the "fresh, green breast of the new world" that F. Scott Fitzgerald in *The Great Gatsby* (1925) says greeted the Dutch sailors' eyes when they first approached Long Island (227). The good Witch of the North even says that "the Land of Oz has never been civilized" (*Wizard* 14). Dorothy may be seen as one who brings the beginnings of civilization to the wilderness of Oz, but civilization may not be such a wonderful benefit.

The Oz that Dorothy first enters has only one city, the Emerald City. In the second Oz book, *The Marvelous Land of Oz*, Baum mentions "the City of the Winkies" (111), but it appears to be no more than a village and is not mentioned elsewhere in Baum's Oz books. Other cities in Oz, such as Thi and Herku in *The Lost Princess of Oz*, seem relatively small and isolated. So Baum's Oz is basically a rural, agrarian country of the sort Thomas Jefferson in his *Notes on the State of Virginia* (1784) hopes the United States will remain.[6] In fact, in the Oz books, especially the first in the series, Baum displays a pro-rural, anti-urban bias. In the Emerald City the humbug Wizard can only fool people into thinking that he gives them what they already have. The city's grandeur is based on illusion: the green glasses make it look more magnificent than it really is. Thus, the city itself, built under the Wizard's direction, is a reflection of his humbuggery. And thus in the city Dorothy's wish to return to Kansas cannot be granted.

For Baum in 1900, unlike for the makers of the 1939 movie based on his book, no eutopia or good place is to be found in a city. In later Oz books, after Ozma inhabits the capital, wishes are granted there, and it becomes the place from which the whole of Oz is ruled. But at the time of the setting of the sixth Oz book, *The Emerald City of Oz*, the Emerald City itself has, Baum says, 57,318 inhabitants (21). In contrast, by 1900 New York City had 3,347,202 inhabitants, and Chicago had 1,698,575. In the United States 38 cities had populations over 100,000, and 64 had populations over 59,000 (*U. S. Census Bureau*). By the standards of 1910, then, when *The Emerald City of Oz* was first published, American readers would hardly consider Baum's Emerald City a great metropolis. By giving it a definite population, Baum makes it more real for his readers. He also, more importantly, depicts it as a large town or small city rather than a huge city, so it can serve appropriately as the capital of a basically rural land like Oz and can become a place where wishes can rightfully be granted after Ozma becomes its ruler.

According to Eric Rabkin, "Each reader moved by utopian literature is responding intellectually to a vision of the future, but emotionally to a felt memory of his past" (1). Baum's Oz plays on both of these aspects of utopia (and eutopia), for in it, the imagined past and future of America come together to form what many people see as an agrarian paradise. Rogers, for example, calls Oz "an American version of the pastoral ideal [...]" (245). Rabkin adds, "Often the utopian world is a pastoral one by virtue of the exclusion of technology [...]" (3). Granted, Oz is largely pastoral, but Baum does not exclude technology, and the technology is intimately connected with magic.

Rabkin theorizes that what he calls the "garden of our past" in pastoral utopias "serves as an appealing fictional indulgence of a normal nostalgia for the pre-sexual time when we were protected and provided for, when the demands of our selves were less troubling and when we more willingly followed the patterns set down for us" (3). And he adds, "writers revert again and again to the old place, the lost Garden, Eden, our atavistic hope and home." However, he warns, "there is trouble in paradise, and that trouble is sex" (4). Baum seems to have recognized this problem. Except possibly for the relationship between Files and the Rose Queen in *Tik-Tok of Oz*, that between the Nome King and Polychrome in *Tik-Tok of Oz*, and that between Gloria and Pon in *The Scarecrow of Oz*, hints of explicit sexual attraction and activity do not enter Baum's fairyland. In fact, in later Oz books he gets around the problem of sex by making up a myth in *The Tin Woodman of Oz* in which long ago the fairy Lurline changed Oz so that people there live forever and people never get any older than they were when Lurline and her fairy band first passed over Oz (132). In this conception of Oz, infants in their cribs remain infants forever, a prospect that may be the best form of birth control ever devised. How many people would choose to change diapers through eternity? Also, it seems, adolescents would remain adolescents forever, preventing Oz from ever being a eutopia for their unfortunate parents. At any rate, the separation of Oz from the rest of the world that occurs at the end of *The Emerald City of Oz* may really be designed to exclude sexual activities since it precludes

Glinda, Ozma, and Dorothy. *Glinda of Oz* (illus. John R. Neill; Chicago: Reilly & Lee, 1920), p. 155.

Dorothy's reaching an age of sexual maturity. Certainly, the work of the fairy Lurline to keep people from aging in Oz is at least in part designed to have that effect, for with immortality the need to propagate the species disappears. It seems significant that the tale of Lurline appears in *The Tin Woodman of Oz*, a book about what would have been a loveless marriage between a tin man and a flesh woman.

By seemingly ending the ravages of time in Oz, Baum seems to put it outside of history. Yet things happen in Oz after it gets separated from the rest of the world, and people from the United States still enter it; there is even a Royal Historian of Oz, as Baum calls himself in later Oz books.[7] But he is not in Oz. As Zeese Papanikolas points out, "Utopia hates history [...]. Utopia is all stillness, order, balance; the last place, the place where time stops" (95). In Oz, however, time continues to pass, and all certainly is not "stillness, order, balance," as the adventures in the later Oz books show. People from our world who manage to get to Oz may age and die. Still, most characters in the late Oz books as Baum seems to have conceived of them do not suffer any of the ravages of time, except perhaps boredom. They do not age, and they do not die, although the possibility remains that the people from our world will one day die; and even in the conception of Oz voiced in *The Tin Woodman of Oz* the Oz people may "be totally destroyed" (133).

In discussing what he considers to be "American" aspects of Baum's utopia, Wagenknecht points to the "use of machinery in the Oz books," a use which he calls "typically American. In general, magic may be said to inhere not in persons but in things. Whoever has the magical instrument can perform magic deeds" (*Utopia Americana* 27). Yet when he calls the Land of Oz an American utopia, Wagenknecht writes, he does "not mean that the Oz books are full of social criticism [...]. Yet the utopia element in them is strong, and if the children do not forget it all by the time they grow up, perhaps it is not too fantastic to imagine that it may do some good" (*Utopia Americana* 30).

Wagenknecht focuses his reading of Oz as eutopia on the description of the magical land that appears in the beginning of *The Emerald City of Oz*. Here, Baum writes, "every inhabitant of that favored country was happy and prosperous." The people do not get sick or die. Also, there are no poor people in Oz, "because there was no such thing as money, and all property of every sort belonged to the Ruler [...]. Each person was given freely by his neighbors whatever he required for his use [...]." Some of the people raise crops; others manufacture things. "Each man and woman, no matter what he or she produced for the good of the community, was supplied by the neighbors with food and clothing and a house and furniture and ornaments and games." If shortages ever occur, "more was taken from the great storehouses of the Ruler, which were afterward filled up again" (22–23).

All Oz residents, Baum writes, "worked half the time and played half the time, and the people enjoyed the work as much as they did the play, because it is good to be occupied and to have something to do." So each "was proud to do all he could for his friends and neighbors, and was glad when they would accept the things he produced" (23). About life in Oz Baum comments, "I do not suppose such an arrangement would be practical with us, but Dorothy assures me that it works finely with the Oz people" (23). Baum obviously writes tongue-in-cheek in the first clause of this last sentence. Still, there is a possibility that he may not think the system really is all that good.

About the inhabitants of Oz he writes, "There were all sorts of queer characters among them, but not a single one who was evil, or who possessed a selfish or violent nature. They were peaceful, kind-hearted, loving and merry, and every inhabitant adored the beautiful girl who ruled them, and delighted to obey her every command" (*Emerald City* 24). Fortunately, Baum was not too concerned about being consistent from book to book or within books. Otherwise, only external threats should be of interest to the readers of the Oz books, and all external threats would be eliminated at the end of the sixth Oz book. Yet in later Oz books one of Baum's central concerns involves internal threats to Ozma's rule: residents of Oz, like Ugu the Shoemaker in *The Lost Princess of Oz*, Queen Ann Soforth in *Tik-Tok of Oz*, Kiki Aru in *The Magic of Oz*, and Queen Coo-ee-oh and the Su-dic in *Glinda of Oz*, are discontented enough to disobey or try to overthrow Ozma. In addition, these characters indicate that discontent really does exist in Oz itself as Baum conceived of it. Minor characters are also unhappy: in *The Lost Princess of Oz* Baum entitles one of his chapters "The Unhappy Ferryman." It treats a man who has lost the ability to understand the words of animals because he once cut off a fox's tail and made an omelet from some bird's eggs. The Tin Woodman punished him by making him unable to communicate "with beasts, birds, or fishes." He cannot, he says, "understand them when they speak to me, although I know that other people can do so, nor can the creatures understand a word I say to them. Every time I meet one of them I am reminded of my former cruelty, and it makes me very unhappy" (167–68). Blinkie the Witch and King Krewl, who initially rules over Jinxland (a part of Oz), in *The Scarecrow of Oz* are also not content or nice. And Pon and Gloria through most of the parts of *The Scarecrow of Oz* in which they are present are miserable. Moreover, in *Glinda of Oz* some of Glinda's maids of honor look "enviously" at Ozma and Dorothy as they approach Glinda's castle (2), so even there discontent exists.

Sackett declares that Baum's Oz books "represent an ideal country," but Baum never shows how "to bring the ideal conditions to actual existence or even whether it would be desirable to do so" (207). Since political power in Oz is based on magic, it would seem that Baum feels that conditions in Oz cannot possibly be brought into "actual existence";

he writes in *The Emerald City of Oz* that he does not think such "an arrangement would be practical with us." Still, utopian or no-place thinking as well as eutopian or good-place thinking is usually not meant as a blueprint for the real world. Instead, as Peyton E. Richter points out, it usually helps people "envisage an ideal social order by means of which to evaluate and to reform both states of affairs and affairs of state" (3). Thus, again, it resembles dystopian thinking.

In Sackett's view of Oz, individuals and individual communities have a great deal of freedom, except that individual communities are not allowed to fight each other and unauthorized people cannot practice magic (209). Even this assertion, however, is questionable since in *The Lost Princess of Oz* giants are slaves of the Herkus because the Herkus are so strong. If the Herkus were not so strong, the giants, the Czarover of Herku says, "would soon become our masters." The Czarover even throws one of the giants out of a window for disobeying him (145). Incidentally, Baum never even hints that any attempts will be made to end the Herkus' enslavement of the giants.

Oz has no crime, Sackett argues, because it has "no money and therefore no temptation to rob anyone" (211). This statement, however, seems wishful thinking on Sackett's part, since various characters in various books, including *The Patchwork Girl of Oz*, *The Scarecrow of Oz*, *The Lost Princess of Oz*, *The Magic of Oz*, and *Glinda of Oz*, commit crimes. According to Sackett, "The only way to acquire goods and services [...] is to be so lovable that other people want to give them to you. A person can steal goods, but there is no need to, since one can get whatever one wants from others" (211). Still, robberies do occur: in *The Lost Princess of Oz*, Ugu the Shoemaker steals Ozma herself.

Sackett claims that "utopias" usually "imply a wish to implement them in the real world," an idea that a theoretician like Richter contradicts. Still, Sackett adds that Baum may never have seriously considered that the real world could become more like Oz "except perhaps in small details [...]," and he adds that "one might well scoff that the Utopia of Oz was made possible by the existence of magic and that human nature is too corrupt for so perfect a fairyland" (212). Sackett says, however, that America has a tremendous amount of "magic" in the form of electricity and atomic power, and Sackett insists that Baum believed that human nature could change (212). So perhaps for Sackett, if not for Baum, America should and can become more like Oz.

Zipes also believes that Oz is a eutopia. He calls it "a fairy-tale utopia" and says that in his Oz books Baum uses "strong socialist and matriarchal notions to express his disenchantment with America [...]" (121). Zipes, like Wagenknecht, focuses much attention on *The Emerald City of Oz*, at the beginning of which, Zipes says, Baum "developed precise principles for his utopia [...]" (128), and Zipes then refers to some of the material from Baum's book quoted earlier in this chapter. Zipes calls "Baum's socialist utopia" "strange" because though a princess governs it, it lacks a "hierarchy or ruling class" (129). Yet there really does seem to be a hierarchy, with Ozma and Glinda and their trusted friends at the top, with almost everyone else beneath them, and with inhabitants like the giants enslaved by the Herkus at the bottom. Zipes calls Ozma "a symbol of matriarchy" who regulates magic and bans "black magic" to guarantee "the development of socialist humanism in Oz" (129), and he asserts that Baum "grasped" the idea "that technology in the hands of capitalist entrepreneurs would mean the doom of utopian developments like Oz." Zipes adds that making Oz invisible was Baum's way of indicating that chances of realizing "utopia in America had been canceled and forfeited" (130), thus arguing the exact opposite of what Sackett argues.

When he started writing Oz books, Baum himself was a failed "capitalist entrepreneur." And in Baum's Oz books there are people resembling Zipes' "capitalist entrepreneurs," most notably the Nome King, who wants to possess all the jewels and precious metals in the world, and Ugu the Shoemaker, who in *The Lost Princess of Oz* tries to use magical machinery and objects, most of which he steals, to overthrow the legitimate ruler of Oz and put himself in her place.

Papanikolas calls Oz "the Kansas of our hearts, [...] that home we are always searching for, that green, good place" (107). If one is concerned only about landscape, Papanikolas' words may be true. But Baum's Oz does not seem to be "that home we are always searching for." Nor can it accurately be labeled "Utopia Americana," as Wagenknecht does. As the critics who claim Oz is a eutopia point out, Princess Ozma rules Oz by monopolizing magic. She has her magic picture, and Glinda has her great book of records. Thus, Ozma can spy on her subjects at any time and control those subjects, if need be; and in book after book she uses that ability. As Allen Eyles notes, "Oz has an absolute ruler [...]" (53). Thus, Ozma has tremendous power, and the inhabitants of the Land of Oz have an absolute lack of privacy.

Perhaps such benevolent despotism and such intrusions on privacy represent Baum's ideal and that of many of his readers. And perhaps a classed society that involves slaves such as the giants may also represent an ideal to some people. Still, changing diapers through eternity or dealing with unaging adolescents hardly fits many people's idea of eutopia.

Baum probably recognized the problems with his fairy kingdom — he may be only half joking when he has his narrator in *The Emerald City of Oz* say, "I do not suppose such an arrangement would be practical with us"; and from Baum's viewpoint it may not even be desirable. After all, the narrator of *The Emerald City of Oz* is the Royal Historian of Oz, in other words, a fictitious representation of Baum himself. It seems doubtful that Baum was trying to create the ideal conditions that a eutopia involves, nor was he trying to create a totalitarian society. Critics like Sackett and Zipes, who see Oz as a eutopia, a great, good place, a kind of earthly paradise that Baum created as an antidote for the evils he found in capitalistic America, may be reading their own desires and political viewpoints into Baum's books rather than reading what Baum actually wrote. Rogers notes that Oz is no "fatuously perfect utopia [...]" (248), and Jordan Brotman judiciously writes that Oz has "utopian features," but adds, "There are also contradictions and extravagances that exist side by side with the pieties of utopia, because Oz is a much more human than hypothetical paradise." Brotman also claims that there are in Oz "a multitude of utopias," most of which "are absurd, some are funny, and some are merely the private worlds of animals, monsters, or lonely eccentrics like Miss Cuttenclip" of *The Emerald City of Oz* (66). Like Brotman and Flynn, Robert Scholes also insists that Baum does not create a eutopia in Oz; instead, he writes that Baum "made the great discovery that another world could be the basis for fictions that were not programmatically Utopian but simply pleasing in their combination of strangeness and familiarity" (203). Obviously, then, many readers feel that Oz is not a eutopia. Baum's contradictory ideas about Oz seem enough to keep it from being a eutopia of the sort many critics feel it is.

Any country that involves for its continuation spying apparatus of the sort Ozma and Glinda use does not seem to be the best that humankind can do. It also does not seem to be what Baum wanted. Thus, it is difficult to believe that twentieth- and twenty-first-century critics seriously argue that Oz is a eutopia, an ideal place, an Eden of any sort.

Conclusion

L. Frank Baum's Oz books are richer than most critics recognize. They are also darker. Many critics seem to have allowed Baum's own statements about his intentions in his works to mislead them. He did not always tell the truth about his works. Commenting on his tale that he named Oz when he saw O-Z on a filing cabinet drawer, Katharine M. Rogers quotes Baum's nephew, Henry B. Brewster, as writing about his uncle, "he did love to 'Fairytale,' or as you might say, tell 'white lies'" (89). Two of those "white lies" include his insistence that he wrote only to please children — coupled, of course, with the idea that he wrote only to entertain readers and not to teach morality — and that he took all the nightmares out of his writing.

It is certain that Baum wrote to make money and that, even if his main aim was simply to entertain children, he included moral teachings in his tales. He also undoubtedly noticed that many very popular, very good children's books have nightmares at their centers, and he seems to have quite deliberately worked nightmares into his Oz books. That so many nightmarish episodes could result by accident or that Baum could have been unaware of them or their implications seems preposterous. Most of the nightmares seem intentionally designed to scare readers: his witches, including the wicked Witches of the East and West, Mombi, and Mrs. Yoop; his other threatening figures, including the Kalidahs, the Mangaboos, the invisible bears, the Gargoyles, the caged Mr. Yoop, Ugu the Shoemaker, the Nome King, and Kiki Aru; his dangerous settings, including the deadly desert, the mountains around the tunnel leading to the Nome King's domain, those in which Mr. Yoop is imprisoned, and especially his horribly claustrophobic underground passages; and his frightening episodes in which his child protagonists face real danger and possible death.

Some of the other things readers may find nightmarish, Baum, a creature of his time, apparently did not find at all nightmarish, especially his racism and imperialism. Still, denying that the nightmares are present is one of Baum's "white lies," and believing him is an act of naiveté on the part of adults. Most children, on the other hand, and many adults recognize the nightmares immediately and enjoy being scared by them as long as they know that as they experience them vicariously they are quite safe in the real world outside of Baum's books.

Baum also knew that more adults than children would buy his books for children and then give them and even read them to children. Thus, like most authors of good children's literature, he produced works that children can enjoy on one level and adults on other levels. Really fortunate adults can enjoy the works simultaneously on many levels: they can enjoy the adventures of Nick Chopper in *The Tin Woodman of Oz*, finding Mrs. Yoop frightening and wondering how Baum is going to get his characters out of their predicaments. At the same time, they can find amusing the way that Baum's book mocks epic tradition and the way that the Tin Man is a kind of antihero who, when measured by a yardstick of a true hero, like Odysseus, appears to be terribly lacking. They can also see the book as a kind of mock eutopian novel. Moreover, they can see that in book after book Baum uses variations of the quest, some of which become genuine hero quests and some of which remain relatively trivial. They can also recognize failed or subverted quests in several of his works. Perhaps they can even recognize that his books are not as "unliterary" as many critics suggest.

It is undeniable that Baum was, at times, a careless writer. The many contradictions in his Oz books are the bane of literary critics who work with him. But he is a better craftsman and more sophisticated author than most people give him credit for. In particular, he is a more careful constructor of plots, often modeling the ones in his Oz books on mythic or literary patterns. He also writes in a variety of modes, including picaresque and mock epic. Small children, of course, will not discern those modes, nor will many adult readers. But once aware that Baum uses them, adult readers can find more enjoyment in the Oz books. Moreover, the use of myths and traditional fairy tales as well as literary modes such as mock epic and picaresque help give Baum's books the kind of universality that appeals to child — and adult — readers. Perhaps his use of mythic and other kinds of traditional plots and his echoes of traditional literature help explain in part his lasting popularity with audiences both in America and elsewhere.

In spite of his contradictions, there are some definite generalizations that one can make about the world of Baum's Oz books. First, although Baum claims to be writing "modern" and "American" fairy tales, his works draw heavily on European fairy tales and myths and European literary traditions. The very kinds of things that he writes that he wants to dispense with — "disagreeable incidents," "heartaches and nightmares," and "horrible and blood-curdling incidents" found in the European tales — abound in his Oz books.

Second, Baum's Oz is, from first to last, a fairyland located in the no place of the fairy tale. Thus, it is indeed a utopia, a no place. But it is not a eutopia, a good place, although it may in many ways be better than the America of Baum's day and later. In many ways, however, it is worse. Too many problems occur for it to be Baum's ideal country, and too many nightmares are present. Without those problems and nightmares, the Land of Oz would become stagnant, and children and adults probably would not have clamored and continue clamoring for the books. In spite of Baum's statements in *The Emerald City of Oz* and *The Tin Woodman of Oz* that many critics think make Oz eutopian, the Land of Oz does not seem to represent Baum's ideal for humankind. As he writes in *The Emerald City of Oz*, an arrangement of the sort found in Oz probably would not "be practical with us," especially since that arrangement involves a monarchy and slavery.

The Land of Oz may not even represent Baum's ideal for a fairyland. In his Oz books he creates three different major myths about the origins of present-day Oz, one in *The Marvelous Land of Oz*, one in *Dorothy and the Wizard in Oz*, and one in *The Tin Woodman of Oz*. Each involves a different conception of present-day Oz. If one desires to think of Oz using a term like *eutopia* (often written *utopia*) or good place, one should, as Brotman does, really use the plural: it at best involves a set of eutopias, at least a different one for each of Baum's conceptions of Oz itself. Baum repeatedly, in book after book, rewrites Oz history to produce a different set of mythical backgrounds for his imaginary kingdom. But in the last analysis none of them represent Baum's ideal good place.

Third, in the Oz books Baum consistently values political stability and virtue as much as he values individual contentment, and even though Oz under Ozma seems materially prosperous, Baum and his good characters consistently value contentment over material riches. In many of his Oz books Baum condemns material riches for their own sake; his sympathies often lie with those who are poor in material goods, beginning with Dorothy's family in Kansas in *The Wonderful Wizard of Oz* and running at least to Zella and her family in *Rinkitink in Oz*. In addition, threats to political stability and virtue abound in the Oz books; those threats often result from individual discontent, even that of residents of Oz like General Jinjur, Ann Soforth, Ugu the Shoemaker, and Kiki Aru. In turn, those discontented people cause others to be discontented and have the potential of causing even greater discontent if they succeed in destroying the political stability in Oz. For Baum, the legitimate ruler is concerned with the welfare of her or his people and works toward making them all content, whether that ruler is the Queen of the Field Mice, the Scarecrow ruling over the Emerald City, or Ozma herself. And if that ruler does her job properly, her subjects should be content to let her rule. In Oz the one who can take the throne does not necessarily belong on it. Glinda has more power than anyone else in Oz. In the first Oz book she uses it not for her own benefit but for that of the inhabitants of the Emerald City, the Land of the Winkies, and the forest. In the second book she uses it not to take over rule of the Emerald City but to put Ozma on her rightful throne. In later Oz books she uses it to support Ozma's benevolent rule over the entire Land of Oz.

Fourth, in his Oz books Baum tends to be opposed to armies. He even at times is anti-imperialistic, as long as the persons with imperialistic aims are not Glinda, Ozma, or some other person Baum considers a good ruler or person. It is fine for Glinda to drive Jinjur from the Emerald City and for her to use the Scarecrow to drive King Krewl from his throne. It is also fine for Ozma to drive the Su-dic from his throne. Inga also can drive King Gos and Queen Garee from their thrones. All five are bad rulers. It also seems fine for the Wizard to destroy completely the Land of Naught. But when bad rulers, like Roquat or King Gos and Queen Garee, try to conquer other kingdoms, that is invariably wrong. Baum also prefers settling disputes peacefully rather than militarily, and he especially wants no one to get hurt in settling these disputes, although Nomes' and Mrs. Yoop's getting hurt doesn't seem to bother him. Thus, perhaps in spite of himself, Baum reflects some of the racism and imperialism of his day.

Fifth, in his Oz books Baum seems committed to equal rights for men and women. His first protagonist, Dorothy, is a little girl. Moreover, through most of his books his Land of Oz is a matriarchy, ruled by Ozma with the aid of Glinda. Even in *The Marvelous Land of Oz*, where Baum at times seems to reflect the sexism of his day, he subverts that sexism, eventually putting a female, Ozma, on her rightful throne and repeatedly throughout his Oz books indicating the rightness of keeping her there.

Sixth, in book after book Baum is concerned with getting his protagonists to look beneath appearances to reality. This whole idea is connected with what he treats repeatedly as the worst kind of magic one can perform: transformation. Since transformation makes things appear to be what they are not, he is almost consistently against it. Transformation distorts the individual, and as becomes apparent in *The Marvelous Land of Oz*, it can throw the state into anarchy.

Finally, quests seem central to Baum's Oz books, often supplying their plots and forms. Quests are central to his first and last Oz books and appear in some way in each of his other Oz books. Like so many authors of children's books, Baum uses the pattern of the quest repeatedly to give his books universality as well as power and depth.

Baum's Oz books, then, are richer and more complex than people usually admit. They do indeed please children, but part of that pleasure comes from being scared. And the books please and scare adults who are willing to read them carefully and without preconceptions. Baum did not write the great American novel; he probably did not even try to, but he did write at least one great American children's novel — *The Wonderful Wizard of Oz*— along with a set of Oz books, many of which are of exceptional quality. In his Oz books he left America and the world a legacy. Although the books vary widely in quality, all of them are fun to read; all of them are exciting and suspenseful. Several of them are excellent, showing control of plot, setting, and character. They have the kind of richness, complexity, and depth that have enabled them to pass the test of time and make them enjoyable for adults and children alike. In addition, Baum's books produced and are still producing many imitators and successors, only a few of which have been mentioned in this book. One of these successors, the 1939 movie of *The Wizard of Oz*, still remains extremely popular and effective as an influence on popular culture. Consequently, Baum has a definite place in the canon of American children's literature and even the canon of American literature.

Notes

Introduction

1. See Clark 149–61.

2. See Clark 140–44, for a discussion of Baum's adult readership, which, Clark says, is mostly male.

3. See for example Riley and Rogers, both of whom give useful, extensive plot summaries of many of Baum's works, including all of his Oz novels.

4. See, for example, Earle's book, which focuses on *The Wonderful Wizard of Oz* as both a product of its time and a contributor to later American culture. See Nathanson's book, also, which does an excellent job of exploring the effect of the 1939 movie, *The Wizard of Oz*, on American culture.

5. Discussions of the attempts, mostly by librarians, to protect children from the Oz books appear in many places. Rahn summarizes these attempts in her *Wizard* (15–16) and "Introduction: Analyzing Oz" (xiii–xiv).

6. I assume that Hunt is the main author of the chapter in which this material appears. Whereas other chapters list authors for them, a note to this chapter says, "This chapter has been written with the advice of the Editorial Team, and with contributions from Gillian Avery, Louisa Smith, C. W. Sullivan, III, and Zena Sutherland" (225n).

7. For information on the naming of Oz, see Rogers 89.

8. For a discussion of the sales of Baum's books, see Clark 131–32. On 137 she treats the idea that Baum wrote primarily for money.

9. For one of many discussions of those inconsistencies and an attempt to explain the purpose of some, see Haff. Some critics try to explain away the inconsistencies, arguing that they really involve parts of Oz history of which the reader is unaware. One such attempt is that of David Hulan, who writes Oz books himself. In one of his critical essays he notices the inconsistency between what Ozma says to Dorothy about returning to Oz in *Ozma of Oz* and what Dorothy says Ozma said about returning when Dorothy discusses the matter in *Dorothy and the Wizard in Oz*. Hulan asserts that this inconsistency "suggests that Dorothy may have paid at least one brief unrecorded visit to Oz between those books" (24n5), an assertion for which Hulan provides no evidence and for which I can find none.

I know that when I was a child, I was aware of no inconsistencies in the books. I do remember, however, being bothered by what I considered a lie in the 1939 movie, *The Wizard of Oz*, when Dorothy sings that the witch came "thumbing for a hitch" (Langley, Ryerson, and Woolf 59). I was, of course, even more disturbed by the witch herself.

10. See, for example, Wagner, who calls Oz "the matriarchal utopia envisioned by his [Baum's] mother-in-law in her magnum

opus, *Woman, Church, and State,* published in Chicago in 1893" (10). Zipes at least admits, "Baum's 'socialist' utopia is a strange one since it is *governed* by a princess named Ozma [...]" (129), but he still insists that it is a utopia (or more precisely, eutopia).

11. "The Tiger's Eye" is a genuine horror story about a magician forced to become a tiger's eye. Then, the magician becomes a person's eye and a deer's eye. The eye forces the ones it inhabits to do vicious deeds. Finally, it returns to its original human form, that is, the eye of the magician, and the father of the tiger the eye inhabited devours the magician.

12. I have no idea on what Rogers bases her assertion that "tightly constructed plots" are undesirable especially in works for children.

13. In S. H. Butcher's translation of *The Poetics* by Aristotle the passage Booth apparently refers to reads, "The structural union of the parts being such that, if any one of them is displaced or removed, the whole will be disjointed and disturbed" (sec. viii). Leon Golden translates the passage, "Moreover, it is necessary that the parts of the action be put together in such a way that if any one part is transposed or removed, the whole will be disordered and disunified" (16).

14. I think it only fair to point out that Hourihan devotes most of her book to showing limitations of the traditional quest.

15. O'Keefe writes that each Oz book "contains several loosely connected journeys" (57).

16. In her pioneering study of Oz, Raylyn Moore notices this kind of structure when she writes about Baum's "traditional management of the fairy tale" (135).

17. After the first edition *The Wonderful Wizard of Oz* was renamed *The Wizard of Oz,* and in 1903 it was published by Bobbs-Merrill as *The New Wizard of Oz. The Marvelous Land of Oz* was renamed *The Land of Oz.*

18. Books of Wonder Press has published beautiful hardbound editions of Baum's Oz books that reproduce, with a few changes, the original color and black and white illustrations. In the press's edition of *The Wonderful Wizard of Oz* the page colors are also reproduced, as they are in the press's edition of *The Road to Oz.* Still, these books do not contain authoritative texts, for they on at least one occasion silently change Baum's words

apparently to make them more acceptable to late-twentieth and early-twenty-first century audiences. Compare, for example, the song the phonograph sings on 130 in the Ballantine edition of *The Patchwork Girl of Oz* to the one it sings on 137 in the Books of Wonder edition. This song will be discussed in more detail in chapter 8 that treats *The Patchwork Girl of Oz.*

19. See Rahn's *Wizard* 12–22 and "Introduction: Analyzing Oz."

20 See Rahn's "Beneath the Surface of *Ozma of Oz.*"

Chapter 1

1. In addition to David L. Greene and Martin (12), whose work I mention in my Introduction, see, for example, Brotman 69, Dighe 42n1, and Hearn 6n8. Deborah Thacker entitles one chapter in Thacker and Web "*The Wonderful Wizard of Oz*: Pleasure Without Nightmares," but even she finds in the book "an expression of the uneasiness and anxiety of the *fin de siècle* [...]" (90). Sale implies that Baum fully intended to keep "blood-curdling incident" out of his work, but he occasionally "fell into writing such incidents almost as if without knowing he was doing so" (*Fairy Tales* 238).

2. For statements about and brief studies of the mythic and fairy tale background of *The Wonderful Wizard of Oz,* see Nye 4, Schuman, and Attebery 91–93. Also, for a spoof of the idea of treating Baum's book seriously in terms of myth, see Starr.

3. Campbell italicizes this material, most likely for emphasis. I retain his italics.

4. Culver gives a fascinating reading of *The Wonderful Wizard of Oz,* placing it in the context of Baum's interest in and work with show windows and treating it as a study in advertising, in manipulating what Baum calls "the vagaries of consumer desire" (97).

5. Throughout this study I try to follow Baum's use of capital letters to indicate proper nouns. However, he is often inconsistent within books and from book to book. As a result, I arbitrarily make some decisions about capitalization: for example, unless I am quoting, I do not capitalize words like *witch, queen,* and *king* when they stand alone or the word *wizard* unless it stands for the Wonderful Wizard himself, and I do not capitalize the phrases *wicked witch* (when it stands alone), *great book of records, magic belt, magic picture,*

flying monkeys, china dolls, and similar phrases. Even though in *Tik-Tok in Oz* and *Rinkitink in Oz* Baum uses lower-case for *nome* and *nomes,* in the body of my text I follow Baum's usual practice, thus capitalizing the words.

6. Moore calls Glinda a "supportive mother-figure" and Ozma (who is not in *The Wonderful Wizard of Oz*) the main "mother-goddess figure" in Oz (126–27). Beckwith, however, asserts that Glinda "must not be taken as a mother-symbol" since she is not an "ugly old" woman (241). The logic of this argument escapes me. In connection with Glinda as mother-figure, see my chapter on *Glinda of Oz.*

7. Compare Bettelheim 66–70.

8. Compare Bettelheim 29.

9. Although Edward W. Hudlin's article is excellent in many ways, he makes a factual error when he writes that of the three times the witch uses the monkeys, the second was "to drive the Great Oz (not the wizard but the ancient ruler of Oz) out of the land of the west" (459). I can find no mention or even hint of an ancient ruler of Oz in *The Wonderful Wizard of Oz.* However, the Wizard's reaction to the Scarecrow's threat demonstrates that the witch's second use of the flying monkeys involved the Wizard who confronts Dorothy. Why he went into the West is a question discussed in chapter 2 of this study.

10. Schuman exaggerates when he writes that through Dorothy's "return, Kansas is changed. The land seems less hostile, the family is reconciled. The greenness of Oz has renewed the fertility of the 'normal' world" (303). He presents no evidence to support these assertions. See also Hudlin 462, who writes, "The desert of Kansas is beginning to bloom once again." However, in Oz no one has to water crops. At the end of the book Aunt Em is going to water the cabbages. Dorothy is clearly back in a realm where hard work is necessary to grow crops, whereas in Oz even inanimate objects like the Scarecrow come to life.

11. Griswold's psychoanalytic reading of this section of the book is fascinating: he says that Dorothy's sweeping the brown-sugar-like mess out the door and picking up her silver shoe and cleaning it show that she has "slain the mother, replaced her as housekeeper, filled her shoes, and now has the father all to herself" (38). I'm not sure in what sense Dorothy "has the father all to her-self," but the rest of Griswold's reading makes sense.

12. In *The Wonderful Wizard of Oz,* Dorothy refers to Toto as "a meat dog" (53). In later Oz books people are called "meat" people to distinguish them from non-meat people like the Scarecrow, the Tin Man, and the Patchwork Girl.

13. In *The Tin Woodman of Oz* Baum has the Tin Woodman say that the girl worked for the witch herself (7).

14 In this obvious allusion to "Hansel and Gretel" Baum again shows his indebtedness to European fairy tales.

Chapter 2

1. The permutations the title went through before the book's publication are fairly well known. For a discussion of them in the context of the writing of the book, see Rogers 84–88.

2. In Baum's first Oz book and his second, *The Marvelous Land of Oz, establishing* unity and stability is of paramount importance. In those that follow *The Marvelous Land of Oz, preserving* unity and stability becomes of paramount importance. The foiling of explicit attempts of would-be tyrants to overthrow Ozma's rule is central to a number of the later Oz books.

3. For an excellent discussion of this aspect of *The Wonderful Wizard of Oz,* see McReynolds and Lips 91. Their entire article is instructive in connection with this episode.

4. Treatments of political aspects of Baum's works will be discussed in more detail later in this book. For now, see Littlefield; Erisman, "L. Frank Baum and the Progressive Dilemma"; Cook; Geer and Rochon; and Koupal, "Wonderful Wizard of the West." For a fairly comprehensive, recent treatment, see "The Politics of Oz: A Symposium" that includes Gessel; Koupal, "Add a Pinch"; and Erisman, "L. Frank Baum and the American Literary Tradition." Their main point is that *The Wonderful Wizard of Oz* is not a populist parable and that scholars know far too little of Baum's politics to label him a political discontent or to say that the Oz books reflect that discontent.

5. For a discussion of this point, see Koupal, "Add a Pinch" 159–60; and Dighe 4–9. Incidentally, the long introductory material in Dighe's book is much more sensible than its subtitle indicates. Dighe also

includes a version of the complete text of Baum's first Oz book with annotations directed toward using it as a textbook in economics and economic history.

6. For a discussion of critics who see aspects of the book as anti-imperialistic, see Dighe, especially note 22 on 65–66, note 30 on 78, and note 59 on 122–23

7. Carol Billman also finds that social context helps explain the original popularity of *The Wonderful Wizard of Oz*, but she points to the disappearance of the frontier, the growing separation of social classes, and problems of industrialization (94).

Chapter 3

1. For examples of some of the work done on *The Marvelous Land of Oz*, see Riley 106–07, 154; Griffith and Frey 770; Sackett 215–16; Culver, "Growing Up in Oz"; Vidal 260–62; David L. Greene and Martin 18; and Zipes 128.

2. Riley seems to disagree with Moore and agree with Rogers when he writes, "*The Marvelous Land [of Oz]* is one of the more inconsistent books in the series [...]." Although Riley is mostly concerned with ways that this book differs from other Oz books rather than inconsistencies within the book, there are inconsistencies in the book itself, such as Jellia Jamb's statement that in all "of Oz but one language is spoken" (71) and the protagonal party's inability to understand "the mouse language" (153).

3. Even Rogers writes that Jinjur's revolt in general and these words in particular are "hard to reconcile with" Baum's usual views and adds that in this part of *The Marvelous Land of Oz* he seems to belittle the suffrage movement. Then Rogers tries to explain Baum's words in a fairly typical way: Baum had a stage extravaganza in mind and was catering to the popular taste (125). If Rogers' explanation is correct, then the book has some very serious flaws.

4. See *Marvelous Land* 152, where, before the Queen of the Field Mice allows her subjects to participate in the Scarecrow's plan, she makes sure that it will not harm them.

5. Cannibalism is a repeated motif in Baum's Oz books.

6. This statement points to another of Baum's inconsistencies: in *The Wonderful Wizard of Oz* he writes that the Wizard says

that he had his people build the Emerald City (161).

7. Glinda uses this term in connection with her own desire not to perform transformations. She says that "they are not honest, and no respectable sorceress likes to make things appear to be what they are not" (260). Thus, an important aspect of being "honest" is to appear to be what one really is.

8. Tip/Ozma's quest is notably lacking in violence. For a discussion of the importance of violence in the more traditional hero quest, see Hourihan 98–106.

9. Incidentally, in his ability to nurture even the grotesque Pumpkinhead, Tip makes an interesting contrast with Victor Frankenstein, who, in Mary Shelley's *Frankenstein* (1818), refuses to nurture the grotesque creature he makes.

10. In her study of the idea of Oz in American culture Madonna Kolbenschlag draws a similar idea from the ending of *The Marvelous Land of Oz*: "Real power and identity in men is connected with the release of the authentic feminine in the self and in the body politic. Everything else — all of the typical male masks — are defense mechanisms at best and pathology at worst" (53). Kolbenschlag, however, is commenting on American culture, and in so doing, she, in effect, reverses one of Baum's points: in *The Marvelous Land of Oz* Baum indicates that real power in women involves, among other things, understanding the authentic masculine in the self.

11. In his excellent study of *The Marvelous Land of Oz* Culver apparently disagrees. He writes, "Baum is not anticipating the androgynes of *Nightwood* [by Djuna Barnes] and *Orlando*." His reading of Ozma is that she is basically "unsexed" (625). She may indeed be "unsexed," but she is female; she is not ungendered, and gender issues rather than sexual ones seem to be at the heart of Baum's ideas in this book about identity and fitness for rule. For an excellent discussion different from mine of Ozma's mixture of masculinity and femininity, see Culver's entire essay, "Growing Up in Oz," especially his conclusion on 625.

12. Kolbenschlag sees "the attempt to restore order" as "the dominant motif" in *The Marvelous Land of Oz* (51). Restoring and maintaining order is extremely important in this book and Baum's other Oz books. Central to four of Baum's twelve Oz books later

than *The Marvelous Land of Oz* are would-be tyrants' attempts to overthrow Ozma's rule: see *The Emerald City of Oz*, *Tik-Tok of Oz*, *The Lost Princess of Oz*, and *The Magic of Oz*. In addition, *The Scarecrow of Oz* involves Glinda's attempts to extend Ozma's rule to the inhabitants of a remote corner of Oz, and *Glinda of Oz* involves Ozma's attempts to extend her rule to the inhabitants of another remote corner of Oz.

13 Perhaps Gardner shows his own prejudice when he writes, "albeit prettier."

Chapter 4

1. Sale revises this essay as a chapter in his book, *Fairy Tales and After* (223–43), omitting the comma from the chapter title. However, the material I quote above is not in the book, just the essay. Sale adds to the material about the monsters being based on spoiled or naughty children that all Baum's "monsters, like the Man with the Giant Hammer or Mr. Yoop the Giant, are chained, not free, like Grendel [in *Beowulf*] to wander and pillage" ("L. Frank Baum" 586). This idea, although true of Mr. Yoop, is certainly not true of his wife, Mrs. Yoop, in *The Tin Woodman of Oz*.

2. Baum's Nomes probably involve an American source too. Frank Joslyn Baum and Russell P. MacFall call Christopher Pearse Cranch's *The Last of the Huggermuggers: A Giant Story* (1856) and *Kobboltozo: A Sequel to The Last of the Huggermuggers* (1857) Baum's "prototypes" for his first Oz book (126–27). In the second of these books, Jacky Cable goes underground and encounters a race of gnomes. Jacky's adventures underground are especially significant for one interested in Baum since seven of Baum's fourteen Oz books include underground adventures. In fact, one — *Ozma of Oz* (1907), *The Emerald City of Oz* (1910), *Tik-Tok of Oz* (1914), and *Rinkitink in Oz* (1916) — include adventures in the realm of the Nome King. However, Baum's Nomes are very different from Cranch's gnomes, who pay absolutely no attention to the wanderers from the surface of the earth. Cranch's gnomes are, of course, based in part on those of European folklore.

3. Incidentally, my own interactions, both as a child and adult, with children convince me that children fear "naughty children" and with good reason.

4. Stannard cites several articles by Baum

from South Dakota's *Aberdeen Saturday Pioneer* to prove his point (126–127). In a study of "Ethnic Stereotypes in Baum's Books for Children" Francis B. Randall concludes that Baum's stereotypes "were unmalicious, unfanatical and in the milder range of early Twentieth Century prejudice" (12). Randall, however, completely ignores groups like the Nomes, Munchkins, and wicked witches that have no exact counterpart in the real world. A much more balanced discussion of Baum's incorporation of racist attitudes in his works appears in a long endnote in Rogers' book, where she discusses Baum's "rather shocking" racism in some of his works, especially *Rinkitink in Oz*; in the instances she cites, says that "Baum unthinkingly went along with contemporary attitudes," but she also points out that elsewhere Baum "ridiculed ethnic prejudices" (271–72n34). Interestingly, the passages she cites to support this final assertion are not from Oz books.

5. The film *The Birth of a Nation* came out eight years after *Ozma of Oz*. This film is full of racism of the sort Baum includes in his book: in it male African Americans have childlike exteriors but lust for white women. For an interesting discussion of the role of sex in racial hostility in general and of white men's perception that African-American men lust for white women, see Stember's entire book, especially his chapter on "The Sexual Focus of Racial Hostility" (10–36).

6. In a story in *American Fairy Tales*, entitled "The Queen of Quo," Baum has a ten-year-old king whose mother died when he was a baby. When his chief counselor says that he should "marry a wife," he replies, "Can't I marry a mother instead?" (46). Both the passage in *Tik-Tok of Oz* and the one in "The Queen of Quo" have interesting Freudian implications.

7. I know that when I was a child, I was aware of no racism in *Ozma of Oz*, but that fact may reveal more about me than it does about the book.

8. The books by Baum that I consider darkest all involve underground journeys: *Ozma of Oz*, *Dorothy and the Wizard in Oz*, *Tik-Tok of Oz*, and *The Scarecrow of Oz*. The idea that the underground for Baum is a kind of hell seems clear. However, it may have additional meaning. Like the underground in Lewis Carroll's *Alice's Adventures in Wonderland*, Baum's underground may also represent the dark side of human consciousness. In

this connection see Moore 167. I also guess that something in my own psyche makes most of Baum's underground journeys enjoyably terrifying to me.

Chapter 5

1. I inevitably connect Dorothy's descent with my own nightmares.

2. It is interesting to note that one of Henri Fuseli's most famous paintings is entitled *Nightmare*. It uses chiaroscuro effects to emphasize the horror of the situation. In the picture an incubus sits on the stomach of a sleeping woman clothed in white. In the background is a dark horse, supposedly the representation of the metaphoric idea of a night*mare*. Incidentally, I first came across an allusion to this haunting picture in "The Fall of the House of Usher," one of Poe's works that deals with premature burial.

3. See Thacker's entire essay on "Playful Subversion." Incidentally, in *Queen Zixi of Ix*, an earlier work than *Dorothy and the Wizard in Oz*, Tallydab and Ruffles, a dog that starts to talk, discuss whether they are in a fairy tale. They ironically decide that they are in "real life in the kingdom of Noland" (97).

4. This is another of Baum's contradictions, although a minor one. In *Ozma of Oz* Ozma says that she will look at Dorothy "every Saturday morning" (244).

Chapter 6

1. Sale omits from his book the first of the passages I quote (*Fairy Tales* 236).

2. The soup episode is another of several allusions to cannibalism in Baum's Oz books. Another example occurs in connection with *The Marvelous Land of Oz* when the Woggle-Bug suggests eating Jack's pumpkin head. The topic will be treated in more detail in connection with Mr. Yoop in *The Patchwork Girl of Oz*. See chapter 8 of this study.

3. See, for example, Jack Kerouac's essay "The Vanishing American Hobo" in *Lonesome Traveler* where Kerouac tells about "the Brueghel hobo and the hobo today" being "the same," but the attitudes toward them are different: "In Brueghel's time children danced around the hobo" (174). Kerouac's whole essay pays homage to the hobo (172–83), indicating that many hoboes have none of what Riley calls "deficiencies within" themselves but *choose* to be hoboes. It also dis-

cusses some of Kerouac's own adventures as a hobo.

4. The novels central to Bjornson's study are the anonymously published *Lazarillo de Tormes* (1554); Mateo Alemán's *Guzmán de Alfarache* (1599, 1604); Francisco de Quevedo y Villegas' *El Buscón* (1626); *Simplicius Simplicissimus* (1668) by Hans Jakob Christoffel von Grimmelshausen; *Gil Blas* by Alain René Lesage (parts of which were published in 1715, 1724, and 1735); *Moll Flanders* (1722) by Daniel Defoe; and *Roderick Random* (1784) by Tobias Smolett.

Chapter 7

1. The first to broach the idea that Oz is a eutopia seriously in print was Edward Wagenknecht in *Utopia Americana*. In his first endnote Andrew Karp cites seven works in addition to the essays by Zipes and Wagenknecht that treat Oz as a eutopia (119n1). Incidentally, Karp does use the term *utopia*, but the sources he cites treat it as not what modern theorists would call a *utopia* (or no place) but as a *eutopia* (or good place). In chapter 15 of this study I treat at length the idea that Oz is not a eutopia.

2. In an endnote Rogers briefly sums up what scholars know about Baum's politics and the kinds of readings of the Oz books, especially *The Wonderful Wizard of Oz*, that people have tried to base on what are probably false ideas about his political beliefs (265–66n51). See also the excellent symposium on "The Politics of Oz" in *South Dakota History* that includes essays by Gessel, Erisman ("L. Frank Baum and the American Political Tradition"), and especially Koupal ("Add a Pinch of Biography"). Also relevant is the section in Dighe's *The Historian's Wizard of Oz* that Dighe entitles "Just Because the Book Can be Read as a Populist Allegory Does Not Mean that It was Written as One" (4–9).

3. I write "significantly called the Gale Force" since in Maguire's book Dorothy *Gale* does the decidedly wicked Wizard real favors when her house destroys Elphaba's sister and when Dorothy destroys Elphaba. Maguire also plays on the meaning of Dorothy's last name, since a strong, destructive wind brings her to Oz.

In his sequel to *Wicked*, entitled *Son of a Witch* (2005), Maguire has his protagonist, Liir, encounter a crone with a four-horned cow and a child with her named Tip (180–81). Maguire here draws on *The Marvelous Land of Oz* and thus may indicate that in his version of Oz, Ozma is still alive, transformed into Tip.

4. See *Tin Woodman* 132–34, where, among other things, Baum writes "that the Oz people were as happy and contented as can be" (133). Even though the phrase *as can be* is ambiguous, episodes in *The Tin Woodman of Oz* itself seem to contradict this quotation.

5. In *The Emerald City of Oz* the Flutterbudgets spend their time catastrophizing — playing a game of "what if" — but doing so seems to bring them happiness (239–43).

6. Baum seems to be having fun with the names he assigns to the various groups that become allies of the Nomes. The Grand Gallipoot of the Growleywogs has a sound to it that children and adults find humorous. Still, although a gallipot is a kind of earthen, glazed pot and thus *Gallipoot* probably has no real meaning in Baum's book, *Growleywog* sounds similar to *golliwog*, which according to the *Oxford English Dictionary* means, "A name invented for a black-faced grotesquely dressed (male) doll with a shock of fuzzy hair." The on-line version of the *Oxford English Dictionary* supplies three quotations using *golliwog* from before 1910, when *The Emerald City of Oz* was published, so Baum could have been playing on the racial meaning. John R. Neil's illustrations of the Growleywogs, with their headbands, interestingly enough, make them look like stereotypical — but extremely thin — Native Americans (see 76). Perhaps Baum's racism is at work here too.

7. On 238 Rogers refers to Frank Joslyn Baum's service in France.

8. These words also, incidentally, contradict the Scarecrow's words in *The Marvelous Land of Oz* that "the only people worthy of consideration in this world are the unusual ones," words that he follows with, "For the common folks are like the leaves of a tree, and live and die unnoticed" (177), thus making him look like a snob. It is interesting that in *The Lost Princess of Oz* the Cowardly Lion makes a statement similar to the Scarecrow's (124).

Chapter 8

1. According to Rogers, when first published, *The Patchwork Girl of Oz* sold 17,121

copies, outselling *Sky Island* and *The Sea Fairies*, but not *The Emerald City of Oz* (200).

2. This line of the sign may also be self-parody on Baum's part since he edited a trade magazine for show window dressers and wrote a book on show-window dressing.

3. The sheet music for Sterling's song is part of the University of Colorado Digital Sheet Music collection. Actually, at least one other song about Lulu may have been a source, Lew. Dockstader's "I Want My Lulu." The Books of Wonder edition of *The Patchwork Girl of Oz* silently changes the first line of the song to, "Ah want mah Lulu, mah cross-eyed Lulu" (137), thus apparently attempting to make the words more acceptable for modern audiences. It also changes the rest of the song in similar ways.

Chapter 9

1. In *Tik-Tok of Oz* Baum uses no hyphen between "Shaggy" and "Man," but consistently uses one between "Tik" and "Tok."

2. Moore points to the sexual symbolism in the Nome King's changing Ozga into a fiddle and threatening to change Files into a bow. Still, she feels that the *beau-bow* pun is what interested Baum here rather than sexual connotations (131).

3. I admit that I think I react with greater horror to Baum's underground passages than his words warrant, probably because of something in my own psychology.

4. It seems strange that the captain and Trot express no desire to return to California, even though Trot's mother is there.

5. See Rogers 213–15.

Chapter 10

1. It is a mystery why Baum made Ugu a shoemaker. Baum's only explanation is that once Ugu "made shoes for a living" (148). Perhaps his being a shoemaker is another reference to Cranch's books. In both of them, as his name indicates, Kobboltozo is a shoemaker. He is a huge, jealous, vindictive dwarf (everything on the island of the Huggermuggers grows to enormous size) who is very envious of the Huggermuggers. Cranch writes that Stichkin the tailor says that Kobboltozo "was the cause of Huggermugger's misfortunes and departure. When the giant went away in your [Jacky Cable's] ship, he [Kobboltozo] could not repress his joy"

(*Kobboltozo* 17–18). The connection, however, seems tenuous at best.

2. Ugu's use of illusion to keep the parties out of his castle occupies 233–36. For more on appearance versus reality in *The Lost Princess of Oz* see 181–83 and 201–04, where the Lavender Bear creates "images" of real things.

3. In Baum's Oz being young and pretty is advantageous; being old and ugly is disadvantageous. For an essay that treats this idea along with some ideas about the racism in Baum's first Oz book, *The Wonderful Wizard of Oz*, see St. John.

Chapter 11

1. Even Ozma's spying apparatus apparently has some limitations. However, Glinda's great book of records could tell Ozma why the Tin Man is on a quest.

2. See *Emerald City* 22–25 and *Tin Woodman* 132–34.

3. In Rahn's book entitled *The Wizard of Oz* she traces utopian (that is, eutopian) influences on Baum (33–43).

Chapter 12

1. See Koupal, "Wonderful Wizard of the West" 208.

2. See Baum and MacFall, 193–94, as well as "How the Story of Oz Came to an End," which is chapter 30 of *The Emerald City of Oz*, where Baum writes about the separation of Oz from the rest of the world, "we have no right to feel grieved, for we have had enough of the history of the Land of Oz to fill six story books [...]" (298). Also, see Rogers 166.

3. The china princess and the Queen of the Field Mice may be concerned about their people, but they are hardly strong rulers.

4. In *The Lost Princess of Oz* a similar, brief treatment, both ironic and humorous, of what is natural and unnatural occurs when the Scarecrow and the Tin Man agree that a dishpan "that is yellow is unnatural" and not of much value (277). Both seem blissfully unaware of the unnaturalness of *any* dishpan, much less their own unnaturalness.

5. See David L. Greene and Martin on *The Marvelous Land of Oz*: it lays "the groundwork," they say, "for a fairyland in which women [Ozma and Glinda] [...] are supreme, and men support their supremacy" (18).

6. Allen Eyles theorizes that "Oz has an

absolute ruler [Ozma], but she never takes advantage of her position" (53).

7. That the number of legal practitioners of magic is supposedly limited is a constant in Baum's later Oz books. For example, see *The Lost Princess of Oz* 270, *The Tin Woodman of Oz* 66, 134, *The Magic of Oz* 2; *Glinda of Oz* 8, 222.

8. Sale writes that in later Oz books the Wizard "becomes more prissy and less interesting, an adjunct to the kindly, strong magic wielded by Glinda and Ozma" (*Fairy Tales and After* 227–28).

9. Selma Lanes is partially right when she asserts that in Oz magic "does not reside in persons [...] but in the material abundance of the land and the relatively smooth-running machinery of a government in which all of the inhabitants believe" (98). Apparently, however, magic does reside in some persons, such as Ozma and the Lavender Bear, who have what Glinda calls "fairy magic" (*Glinda* 216). Moreover, as several of Baum's Oz books demonstrate, not all the inhabitants of Oz believe in their government.

10. In some stories Baum nonetheless brings several of his fantastic creations to America; see, for example, *The Woggle-Bug Book*.

Chapter 13

1. Incidentally, critics are by no means unanimous in their praise of *Glinda of Oz*. Roger Sale, for example, calls the book "thin," but does admit that it involves "a fine central situation and [...] one spectacular stretch" ("L. Frank Baum" 585). The "spectacular stretch," Sale asserts, is the part dealing with Reera the Red ("L. Frank Baum" 590–91). In the revised version of this part of his essay Sale does not call the book "thin" (*Fairy Tales and After* 238). Rogers asserts that Baum, writing on his deathbed, was unable "to shape them [the adventures in *Glinda of Oz*] into as sustained and effective a story as usual" (238).

2. Even if she could remember the magic, she could not perform it since in *Glinda of Oz* webbed feet cannot work magic (63), or so the Su-Dic says. This idea may involve one of Baum's inconsistencies: see *The Magic of Oz* in which the Lonesome Duck performs acts of magic (152–54). Still, the Su-Dic may be wrong.

3. See also *Cult of the Mother Goddess*, where E. O. James also treats this myth at length (153–60).

4. See Graves 92, 387. Graves uses the spelling "Core" rather Kore.

5 See *Glinda of Oz* 206–07 especially.

Chapter 14

1. For a sampling of similar statements, see Wagenknecht, *Utopia Americana* 27; Brotman 69–70; Moore 143–44.

2. See Rogers 27 for a discussion of Baum's connection with Methodism and Episcopalianism. For a brief explanation of Theosophy in connection with Baum, see Rogers 50–53 and Hearn xc–xciv.

3. Also see, for example, *Glinda*, where Baum makes a clear distinction between Ozma, a fairy, and Dorothy, whom he calls an "Earth Child" (15).

4. See *Emerald City* 21–25. Also, see my discussion of the whole idea of Oz as a eutopia in chapter 15 below.

5. That the number of legal practitioners of magic is limited by law is a constant in Baum's later Oz books. For example, see *Lost Princess*, 270; *Tin Woodman* 66, 134; *Magic of Oz*, 2; *Glinda of Oz*, 8, 222.

6. For a brief discussion of the relationship between Baum's good witches and good witches in European tradition, see Tuerk, "Good Witches."

Chapter 15

1. In *The Marvelous Land of Oz* Tip fishes (2). In *The Lost Princess of Oz* the Soldier with

the Green Whiskers "went fishing about two months ago, and hasn't come back yet," Button-Bright says (53).

2. See for example *The Emerald City of Oz* 162.

3. Baum usually calls Ozma a princess, but in *The Marvelous Land of Oz* he calls her Queen of the Emerald City. Trying to understand why residents of democracies create so many fantasy worlds that involve monarchy and aristocracy, Hourihan theorizes that the hierarchies in these books "are images of order, and this appears to constitute part of the appeal of these stories," and that "hierarchical societies" in fantasies "are images of an unattainable but longed for systemic security" (65–66). These ideas may help explain Baum's choice of a monarchy for Oz, but they also point to another connected idea: totalitarianism is a possible end result of the political system that appears in most of Baum's Oz books.

4. A similar idea appears in Coleman.

5. See especially *Wizard* 23–25 for a description of the lands of Boq, a Munchkin farmer.

6. See Jefferson's entire chapter entitled "Manufactures" 164–65.

7. See, for example, the end of "To My Readers" in *The Tin Woodman of Oz* (x).

Bibliography

Allen, Graham. *Intertextuality.* New critical idiom. London: Routledge, 2000.

Alter, Robert. *Rogue's Progress: Studies in the Picaresque Novel.* Harvard studies in comparative lit. Cambridge: Harvard UP, 1964.

Anderson, Celia Catlett. "The Comedians of Oz." *Studies in American Humor* 5.4 (winter 1986–87): 229–42.

Aristotle. *Aristotle's Poetics: A Translation and Commentary for Students of Literature.* Trans. Leon Golden. Ed. O. B. Hardison. Englewood Cliffs: Prentice, 1968.

_____. *The Poetics.* Trans. S. H. Butcher. The Project Gutenberg e-text of *The Poetics.* Nov. 1999. 1 Mar. 2004 <http://onlinebooks.library.upenn.edu/webbin/gutbook/lookup?num=1974>.

Attebery, Brian. *The Fantasy Tradition in American Literature: From Irving to Le Guin.* Bloomington: Indiana UP, 1980.

Baum, Frank Joslyn, and Russell P. MacFall. *To Please a Child: A Biography of L. Frank Baum Royal Historian of Oz.* Chicago: Reilly & Lee, 1961.

Baum, L. Frank. *American Fairy Tales.* Introd. Martin Gardner. 1901. New York: Dover, 1978.

_____ [Edith Van Dyne]. *Aunt Jane's Nieces in the Red Cross.* Chicago: Reilly & Britton, 1915.

_____ [Edith Van Dyne]. *Aunt Jane's Nieces in the Red Cross.* 2nd ed. Chicago: Reilly & Lee, 1918.

_____. "The Discontented Gopher." *Animal Fairy Tales.* Introd. Russell P. MacFall. 1905. 2nd ed. [Escanaba, MI]: International Wizard of Oz Club, 1989.

_____. *Dorothy and the Wizard in Oz.* 1908. New York: Ballantine, 1979.

_____. *Dot and Tot of Merryland.* Indianapolis: Bobbs-Merrill, 1901.

_____. *The Emerald City of Oz.* 1910. New York: Ballantine, 1979.

_____. *The Enchanted Island of Yew.* Indianapolis: Bobbs-Merrill, 1903.

_____. *Father Goose: His Book.* Chicago: Geo. M. Hill, 1899.

_____. *Glinda of Oz.* 1920. New York: Ballantine, 1981.

_____. *John Dough and the Cherub.* 1906. [Whitefish, MT]: [Kessinger], [2004].

_____. *The Land of Oz.* 1904. New York: Ballantine, 1979.

_____. *Little Wizard Stories of Oz*. Chicago: Reilly & Britton, 1914.

_____. *The Lost Princess of Oz*. 1917. New York: Ballantine, 1980.

_____. *The Magic of Oz*. 1919. New York: Ballantine, 1981.

_____. [Edith Van Dyne]. *Mary Louise and the Liberty Girls*. Chicago: Reilly & Lee, 1918.

_____. "Modern Fairy Tales." *Advance* 19 Aug. 1909: 236–37. Rpt. in *The Wizard of Oz*. Ed. Michael Patrick Hearn. Critical heritage ser. New York: Schocken, 1983. 137–40.

_____. *The New Wizard of Oz*. Indianapolis: Bobbs-Merrill, 1903.

_____. *Ozma of Oz*. 1907. New York: Ballantine, 1979.

_____. *The Patchwork Girl of Oz*. 1913. New York: Ballantine, 1979.

_____. *The Patchwork Girl of Oz*. 1913. New York: Books of Wonder, 1995.

_____. *Queen Zixi of Ix, or The Story of the Magic Cloak*. 1905. Introd. Martin Gardner. New York: Dover, 1971.

_____. *Rinkitink in Oz*. 1916. New York: Ballantine, 1980.

_____. *The Road to Oz*. 1909. New York: Ballantine, 1979.

_____. *The Scarecrow of Oz*. 1915. New York: Ballantine, 1980.

_____. "The Tiger's Eye: A Jungle Fairy Tale." *American Book Collector* Dec. 1962: 21–24.

_____. *Tik-Tok of Oz*. 1914. New York: Ballantine, 1980.

_____. *The Tin Woodman of Oz*. 1918. New York: Ballantine, 1981.

_____. *The Wizard of Oz*. 1900. New York: Ballantine, 1979.

_____. *The Woggle-Bug Book (1905)*. Introd. Douglas G. Greene. Delmar, NY: Scholars' Facsimiles & Reprints, 1978.

Bauska, Barry. "The Land of Oz and the American Dream." *Markham Review* 5 (winter 1976): 21–24.

Beckwith, Osmond. "The Oddness of Oz." *Children's Literature* 5 (1976): 74–91. Rpt. in L. Frank Baum. *The Wizard of Oz*. Ed. Michael Patrick Hearn. Critical heritage ser. New York: Schocken, 1983. 233–47.

Bettelheim, Bruno. *The Uses of Enchantment: The Meaning and Importance of Fairy Tales*. New York: Knopf, 1976.

Bewley, Marius. "The Land of Oz: America's Great Good Place." *Masks and Mirrors: Essays and Criticism*. New York: Atheneum, 1970. 255–67. Rpt. in L. Frank Baum. *The Wizard of Oz*. Ed. Michael Patrick Hearn. Critical heritage ser. New York: Schocken, 1983. 199–207.

Billman, Carol. "'I've Seen the Movie': Oz Revisited." *Children's Novels and the Movies*. Ed. Douglas Street. New York: Ungar, 1983. 92–100.

The Birth of a Nation. Dir. D. W. Griffith. Perf. Lillian Gish, Mae Marsh, Henry B. Walthall, and Miriam Cooper. Mutual, 1915.

Bjornson, Richard. *The Picaresque Hero in European Fiction*. Madison: U of Wisconsin P, 1977.

Blackburn, Alexander. *The Myth of the Picaro: Continuity and Transformation of the Picaresque Novel, 1554–1954*. Chapel Hill: U of North Carolina P, 1979.

Booker, M. Keith. *The Dystopian Impulse in Modern Fiction: Fiction as Social Criticism*. Contributions to the study of science fiction and fantasy 58. Westport, CT: Greenwood, 1994.

Bradbury, Ray. "Because, Because, Because, Because of the Wonderful Things He Does: A Preface." *Wonderful Wizard Marvelous Land*. By Raylyn Moore. Bowling Green: Bowling Green U Popular P, 1974. xi–xviii.

Brombert, Victor. *In Praise of Antiheroes: Figures and Themes in Modern European Literature, 1830–1980*. Chicago: U of Chicago P, 1999.

Brotman, Jordan. "A Late Wanderer in Oz." *Chicago Review* 18.2 (1965): 63–73.
Campbell, Joseph. *The Hero With a Thousand Faces.* Bollingen ser. 17. 1949. Princeton: Princeton UP, 1968.
_____. *The Masks of God: Primitive Mythology.* New York: Viking, 1959.
Carpenter, Angelica Shirley, and Jean Shirley. *L. Frank Baum: Royal Historian of Oz.* Minneapolis: Lerner, 1992.
Carroll, Lewis. *Alice's Adventures in Wonderland.* 1865. *Alice in Wonderland.* 2nd ed. Critical ed. Ed. Donald J. Gray. New York: Norton, 1992. 2–99.
Clark, Beverly Lyon. *Kiddie Lit: The Cultural Construction of Children's Literature in America.* Baltimore: Johns Hopkins UP, 2003.
Cranch, Christopher Pearse. *Kobboltozo: A Sequel to the Last of the Huggermuggers.* Boston: Phillips, Sampson and Company, 1857.
_____. *The Last of the Huggermuggers: A Giant Story.* Boston: Phillips, Sampson and Company, 1856.
Cohen, Morton N. *Lewis Carroll: A Biography.* New York: Knopf, 1995.
Coleman, Earle J. "Oz as Heaven and Other Philosophical Questions." *Baum Bugle* 24.2 (1980): 18–20.
Cook, Timothy E. "Another Perspective on Political Authority in Children's Literature: The Fallible Leader in L. Frank Baum and Dr. Seuss." *Western Political Quarterly* 36 (1983): 326–36.
Cox, James. "A Hard Book to Take." *One Hundred Years of* Huckleberry Finn: *The Boy, His Book, and American Culture.* Ed. Robert Sattelmeyer and J. Donald Crowley. Columbia: U of Missouri P, 1985. 386–403.
Culver, Stuart. "Growing Up in Oz." *American Literary History* 4.4 (winter 1992): 507–28.
_____. "What Manikins Want: The Wonderful Wizard of Oz and the Art of Decorating Dry Goods Windows." *Representations* 21 (winter 1988): 97–116.
Dighe, Ranjit S., ed. *The Historian's Wizard of Oz: Reading L. Frank Baum's Classic as a Political and Monetary Allegory.* Westport, CT: Praeger, 2002.
Dockstader, Lew. "I Want My Lulu." *The Lester S. Levy Collection of Sheet Music.* Johns Hopkins U. 11 Apr. 2006 <http://levysheetmusic.mse.jhu.edu/>.
Earle, Neill. *The Wonderful Wizard of Oz in American Popular Culture: Uneasy in Eden.* Lewiston, NY: Mellen, 1994.
Egoff, Sheila, G. T. Stubbs, and L. F. Ashley, eds. *Only Connect: Readings on Children's Literature.* Toronto: Oxford UP, 1969.
_____. *Only Connect: Readings on Children's Literature.* 2nd ed. Toronto: Oxford UP, 1980.
Egoff, Sheila, Gordon Stubbs, Ralph Ashley, and Wendy Sutton, eds. *Only Connect: Readings on Children's Literature.* 3rd ed. Toronto: Oxford UP, 1996.
Einhorn, Edward. *Paradox in Oz.* San Diego: Hungry Tiger, 1999.
Eliade, Mircea. *Cosmos and History: The Myth of the Eternal Return.* Trans. Willard R. Trask. Harper Torchbooks, Bollingen lib. New York: Harper, 1959.
_____. *The Sacred and the Profane: The Nature of Religion.* Trans. Willard R. Trask. New York: Harcourt, 1959.
Erisman, Fred. "L. Frank Baum and the American Political Tradition." *South Dakota History* 31 (summer 2001): 162–68.
_____. "L. Frank Baum and the Progressive Dilemma." *American Quarterly* 20.3 (fall 1968): 616–23.
Eyles, Allen. *The World of Oz.* Tucson: HP, 1985.
Flynn, Richard. "Imitation Oz: The Sequel as Commodity." *The Lion and the Unicorn* 20.1 (1996): 121–31.

Frye, Northrop. "The Journey as Metaphor." *Myth and Metaphor: Selected Essays, 1974–1988*. Ed. Robert D. Denham. Charlottesville: UP of Virginia, 1990. 212–26.

Gardner, Martin. Introduction. *American Fairy Tales*. By L. Frank Baum. 1901. Dover: New York, 1978. v–xiii.

———. Introduction. *The Marvelous Land of Oz*. By L. Frank Baum. 1904. New York: Dover, 1969. v–xv.

———. Introduction. *Queen Zixi of Ix, or The Story of the Magic Cloak*. By L. Frank Baum. 1905. New York: Dover, 1971. v–xiii.

———. Introduction. *The Surprising Adventures of the Magical Monarch of Mo and His People*. By L. Frank Baum. New York: Dover, 1968. v–xi.

Geer, John G., and Thomas R. Rochon, "William Jennings Bryan on the Yellow Brick Road." *Journal of American Culture* 16.4 (winter 1993): 59–63.

Gessel, Michael. "*The Wizard of Oz* as Urban Legend." *South Dakota History* 31 (summer 2001): 146–52.

Gilead, Sarah. "Magic Abjured: Closure in Children's Fantasy Fiction." *PMLA* 106 (Mar. 1991): 277–93.

Glassman, Peter. Afterword. *The Patchwork Girl of Oz*. By L. Frank Baum. New York: Books of Wonder, 1995. 342–46.

"Golliwog." *Oxford English Dictionary: The Definitive Record of the English Language*. 2nd ed. 1989. 11 Jan 2006 <www.oed.com>.

Graves. Robert. *The Greek Myths*. 2 vols. Baltimore: Penguin, 1955.

Greene, David L. "L. Frank Baum's Later Oz Books: 1914–1920." *Baum Bugle* 16.1 (1972): 17–20.

Greene, David L., and Dick Martin. *The Oz Scrapbook*. New York: Random, 1977.

Greene, Douglas G. Introduction. *The Woggle-Bug Book (1905)*. Delmar, NY: Scholars' Facsimiles & Reprints, 1978.

Griffith, John W., and Charles H. Frey, eds. *Classics of Children's Literature*. 3rd ed. New York: Macmillan, 1992.

Griswold, Jerry. *Audacious Kids: Coming of Age in America's Classic Children's Books*. New York: Oxford UP, 1992.

Haff, James. "Magic Belt Mysteries." *Baum Bugle* 20.3 (1976): 18–20.

Hansen, Linda. "Experiencing the World as Home: Reflections on Dorothy's Quest in *The Wizard of Oz*." *Soundings* 67 (Spring 1984): 91–102.

Hearn, Michael Patrick, ed. *The Annotated* Wizard of Oz. Centennial ed. New York: Norton, 2000.

Heuscher, Julius E. *A Psychiatric Study of Fairy Tales: Their Origin, Meaning and Usefulness*. Springfield, IL: Thomas, 1963.

Homer. *The Odyssey*. Trans. Samuel Butler. 1925. Vol. 15 of *The Works of Samuel Butler*. Shrewsbury ed. Ed. Henry Festing Jones and A. T. Bartholomew. New York: AMS, 1968.

Hourihan, Margery. *Deconstructing the Hero: Literary Theory and Children's Literature*. London: Routledge, 1997.

Hudlin, Edward W. "The Mythology of *Oz*: An Interpretation." *Papers on Language & Literature* 25 (1989): 443–62.

Huddleston, Robert S. "Baroque Space and the Art of the Infinite." *The Theatrical Baroque*. Ed. Larry F. Norman. Chicago: David and Alfred Smart Museum of Art, 2001. 13–19.

Hulan, David. "Are You a Good Ruler or a Bad Ruler? An Inquiry into the Quality of Ozma's Governance." *Baum Bugle* 48.1 (spring 2004): 24–28.

Hunt, Peter. *An Introduction to Children's Literature*. Oxford, ENG: Oxford UP, 1994.

Hunt, Peter, and others. "Children's Literature in America: 1870–1945." *Children's Literature: An Illustrated History.* Ed. Peter Hunt. Oxford, ENG: Oxford UP, 1995. 225–51.

James, E. O. *The Cult of the Mother Goddess: An Archaeological and Documentary Study.* New York: Barnes, 1959.

Jefferson, Thomas. *Notes on the State of Virginia.* Ed. William Peden. Chapel Hill: U of North Carolina P for Institute of Early American History and Culture at Williamsburg, Virginia, 1955.

Karp, Andrew. "Utopian Tension in L. Frank Baum's 'Oz.'" *Utopian Studies* 9.2 (1998): 103–21.

Kelly, Richard. *Lewis Carroll.* Twayne's English authors ser. 212. Boston: Twayne, 1977.

Kerouac, Jack. *Lonesome Traveler.* 1960. New York: Grove, 1970.

Knoepflmacher, U. C. "Roads Half-Taken: Travel, Fantasy, and Growing Up." *Proceedings of the Thirteenth Annual Conference of the Children's Literature Association.* Ed. Susan R. Gannon and Ruth Anne Thompson. Kansas City: U of Missouri, Kansas City, 1988.

Kolbenschlag, Madonna. *Lost in the Land of Oz: The Search for Identity and Community in American Life.* San Francisco: Harper, 1988.

Koupal, Nancy Tystad. "Add a Pinch of Biography: Seasoning the Populist Allegory Theory with History." *South Dakota History* 31 (summer 2001): 153–62.

_____. "The Wonderful Wizard of the West: L. Frank Baum in South Dakota." *Great Plains Quarterly* 9.4 (fall 1989): 203–15.

Kovaly, Pavel. "Marxism and Utopia." *Utopia/Dystopia?* Ed. Peyton E. Richter. Cambridge, MA: Schenkman, 1975. 75–92.

Lanes, Selma. *Down the Rabbit Hole: Adventures & Misadventures in the Realm of Children's Literature.* New York: Atheneum, 1971.

Langley, Noel, Florence Ryerson, and Edgar Allan Woolf. *The Wonderful Wizard of Oz: Screenplay.* [N.p.]: [n.p.], 1939.

Leach, William. *Land of Desire: Merchants, Power, and the Rise of a New American Culture.* New York: Pantheon, 1993.

Lewis, C. S. "On Three Ways of Writing for Children." *Proceedings* of the Bournemouth Conference, 1952. Rpt. in *Only Connect: Readings on Children's Literature.* Ed. Sheila Egoff, G. T. Stubbs, and L. F. Ashley. 2nd ed. Toronto: Oxford UP, 1980. 207–20.

Littlefield, Henry M. "The Wizard of Oz: Parable on Populism." *American Quarterly* 16.1 (spring 1964): 47–58.

Luthi, Max. *Once Upon a Time: On the Nature of Fairy Tales.* Trans. Lee Chadeayne and Paul Gottwald. Introd. Francis Lee Utley. New York: Ungar, 1970.

MacFall, Russell P. Introduction. *Animal Fairy Tales.* By L. Frank Baum. 2nd ed. [Escanaba, MI]: International Wizard of Oz Club, 1989. 5–12.

Maguire, Gregory. *Son of a Witch.* New York: Harper, 2005.

_____. *Wicked: The Life and Times of the Wicked Witch of the West.* New York: Harper, 1995.

Marder, Herbert. *Feminism & Art: A Study of Virginia Woolf.* Chicago: U of Chicago P, 1968.

McReynolds, Douglas J., and Barbara J. Lips. "A Girl in the Game: *The Wizard of Oz* as Analogy for the Female Experience in America." *North Dakota Quarterly* 54.1 (winter 1986): 87–93.

Miller, Stuart. *The Picaresque Novel.* Cleveland: P of Case Western Reserve U, 1967.

Monteser, Frederick. *The Picaresque Element in Western Literature.* Studies in the humanities 5, lit. University: U of Alabama P, 1975.

Moore, Raylyn. *Wonderful Wizard Marvelous Land.* Bowling Green, OH: Bowling Green U Popular P, 1974.

Nagel, Joane. *Race, Ethnicity, and Sexuality: Intimate Intersections, Forbidden Frontiers.* New York: Oxford UP, 2003.

Nathanson, Paul. *Over the Rainbow:* The Wizard of Oz *as a Secular Myth of America.* McGill studies in the history of religions. Albany: State U of New York P, 1991.

Neumann, Erich. *The Great Mother: An Analysis of the Archetype.* Trans. Ralph Manheim. Bollingen ser. 47. Princeton: Princeton UP, 1955.

Nodelman, Perry. "Introduction: On Words and Pictures, Neglected Noteworthies, and Touchstones in Training." *Picture Books.* West Lafayette, IN: Children's Lit. Assn., 1989. 1–13. Vol. 3 of *Reflections on the Best in Children's Literature.* [Ed. Perry Nodelman]. 3 vols. 1985–89.

Nye, Russell B. "An Appreciation." *The Wizard of Oz and Who He Was.* [Ed.] Martin Gardner and Russell B. Nye. East Lansing: Michigan State UP, 1957. 1–17.

O'Keefe, Deborah. *Readers in Wonderland: The Liberating Worlds of Fantasy Fiction.* New York: Continuum, 2003.

Papanikolas, Zeese. *Trickster in the Land of Dreams.* Lincoln: U of Nebraska P, 1995.

Pendexter, Hugh, III. "The Magic of Baum." *Baum Bugle* 21.1 (1977): 2–9.

––––––. "Magic in Post-Thompson Oz." *Baum Bugle* 24.1 (1980): 2–6.

Rabkin, Eric S. "Atavism and Utopia." *No Place Else: Explorations in Utopian and Dystopian Fiction.* Ed. Eric S. Rabkin, Martin H. Greenberg, and Joseph D. Olander. Carbondale: Southern Illinois UP, 1983. 1–10.

Rahn, Suzanne. "Beneath the Surface of *Ozma of Oz.*" *Baum Bugle* 46.1 (spring 2002): 25–30.

––––––. "Introduction: Analyzing Oz." *L. Frank Baum's World of Oz: A Classic Series at 100.* Ed. Suzanne Rahn. Children's Lit. Assn. centennial studies 2. Lanham, MD: Children's Lit. Assn. and Scarecrow, 2003. ix–xxxviii.

––––––. The Wizard of Oz: *Shaping an Imaginary World.* Twayne's masterwork studies 167. New York: Twayne, 1998.

Randall, Francis B. "Ethnic Stereotypes in Baum's Books for Children." *Baum Bugle* 28.1 (spring 1984): 8–12.

Return to Oz. Dir. Walter Murch. Perf. Fairuzo Balk, Nicol Williamson, Jean Marsh, Piper Laurie, and Matt Clark. Disney, 1985.

Richter, Peyton E. "Thinking Utopian." *Utopia/Dystopia.* Ed. Peyton E. Richter. Cambridge: Schenkman, 1975. 1–17.

Riley, Michael O. *Oz and Beyond: The Fantasy World of L. Frank Baum.* Lawrence: UP of Kansas, 1997.

Robinson, Henry Peach. *Pictorial Effects in Photography Being Hints on Composition and Chiaroscuro for Photographers.* Introd. Robert A. Sobieszek. 1896. Pawlet, VT: Helios, 1971.

Rogers, Katharine M. *L. Frank Baum: Creator of Oz.* Cambridge, MA: Da Capo, 2002.

Rudman, Masha Kabakow. "An Overview." *Children's Literature: An Issues Approach.* Ed. Masha Kabakow Rudman. Lexington: Heath, 1976. 1–11.

Russell, David L. *Literature for Children: A Short Introduction.* 5th ed. Boston: Pearson, 2005.

Sackett, S. J. "The Utopia of Oz." *Georgia Review* 14 (1960): 275–90. Rpt. in *The Wizard of Oz.* Ed. Michael Patrick Hearn. Critical heritage ser. New York: Schocken, 1983. 207–21.

Sale, Roger. *Fairy Tales and After: From Snow White to E. B White.* Cambridge, MA: Harvard UP, 1978.

_____. "L. Frank Baum, and Oz." *Hudson Review* 25 (winter 1972–73): 571–92.

Schiller, Justin G. "An Appreciation." *L. Frank Baum's* The Wonderful Wizard of Oz. Illus. Barry Moser. West Hatfield, MA: Pennyroyal, 1985. 257–68.

Schmidt, Gary D. "'So here, my dears, is a new Oz story': The Deep Structure of a Series." *Children's Literature Association Quarterly* 14.3 (winter 1989): 463–65.

Scholes, Robert. *The Crafty Reader.* New Haven: Yale UP, 2001.

Schuman, Samuel. "Out of the Fryeing Pan and into the Pyre: Comedy, Myth and *The Wizard of Oz.*" *Journal of Popular Culture* 7 (1973): 302–04.

Slochower, Harry. *Mythopoesis: Mythic Patterns in the Literary Classics.* Detroit: Wayne State UP, 1970.

Smith, Henry Nash. *Mark Twain: The Development of a Writer.* New York: Atheneum, 1972.

St. John, Tom. "Lyman Frank Baum: Looking Back to the Promised Land." *Western Humanities Review* 36.4 (1982): 349–59.

Stannard, David E. *American Holocaust: Columbus and the Conquest of the New World.* New York: Oxford UP, 1992.

Starr, Nathan Comfort. "The Wonderful Wizard of Oz: A Study in Archetypal Mythic Symbiosis." *Unicorn* 2.4 (Summer 1973): 13–17.

Stember, Charles Herbert. *Sexual Racism: The Emotional Barrier to an Integrated Society.* New York: Elsevier, 1976.

Sterling, Andrew B. "Ain't You My Lulu." *The Laughable Song Ain't You My Lulu.* Music by Geo. Hamilton. New York: W. B. Gray, 1900. 3–5. *University of Colorado Digital Sheet Music Collection: Music Library.* 2004. U of Colorado. 11 Jan. 2006 <http://ucblibraries.colorado.edu/>.

Thacker, Deborah. Introduction. *Introducing Children's Literature: From Romanticism to Postmodernism.* By Deborah Cogan Thacker and Jean Webb. London: Routledge, 2002. 1–10.

_____. "Playful Subversion." *Introducing Children's Literature: From Romanticism to Postmodernism.* By Deborah Cogan Thacker and Jean Webb. London: Routledge, 2002. 139–50.

_____. "*The Wonderful Wizard of Oz*: Pleasure Without Nightmares." *Introducing Children's Literature: From Romanticism to Postmodernism.* By Deborah Cogan Thacker and Jean Webb. London: Routledge, 2002. 85–90.

Thalmann, William G. *The Odyssey: An Epic of Return.* Twayne's masterwork studies 100. New York: Twayne, 1992.

Tolkien, J. R. R. "On Fairy-Stories." *Tree and Leaf.* 1956. London: Unwin, 1964. 11–70.

Tuerk, Richard. "Dorothy's Timeless Quest." *Mythlore* 63.1 (1990): 20–24.

_____. "Good Witches in *The Wonderful Wizard of Oz.*" *Roundtable* ns 11 (Spring 1999): 1–5.

Ulanov, Ann, and Barry Ulanov. *The Witch and the Clown: Two Archetypes of Human Sexuality.* Wilmette: Chiron, 1987.

Updike, John. "A Critic at Large: Oz is Us: Celebrating the Wizard's Centennial." *New Yorker* 25 Sept. 2000: 84–88.

U. S. Census Bureau. "Table 13. Population of Largest Urban Places: 1900." U. S. Bureau of Census. 15 June 1998. 29 Dec. 2005 <http://www.census.gov/population/documentation/twps0027/tab13.txt>.

Vidal, Gore. "On Rereading the Oz Books." *New York Review of Books* 13 Oct. 1977: 37–42. Rpt. in *The Wizard of Oz.* Ed. Michael Patrick Hearn. Critical heritage ser. New York: Schocken, 1983. 256–70.

Vivante, Paolo. *Homer.* New Haven: Yale UP, 1985.

Wagenknecht, Edward. *As Far As Yesterday: Memories and Reflections.* Norman: U of Oklahoma P, 1968.

_____. *Utopia Americana.* Seattle: U of Washington Book Store, 1929.

Wagner, Sally Roesch. "The Wonderful Mother of Oz." *Baum Bugle* 47.3 (winter 2003): 7–11.

Wellbank, Joseph H. "Utopia and the Constraints of Justice." *Utopia/Dystopia?* Ed. Peyton E. Richter. Cambridge, MA: Schenkman, 1975. 29–41.

The Wizard of Oz. Dir. Victor Fleming. Perf. Judy Garland, Frank Morgan, Ray Bolger, Bert Lahr, Margaret Hamilton, Jack Haley, and Billie Burke. MGM, 1939.

Woolf, Virginia. *Orlando: A Biography.* New York: Harcourt, 1928.

Yolen, Jane. *Touch Magic: Fantasy, Faerie & Folklore in the Literature of Childhood.* Expanded ed. Little Rock: August House, 2000.

Zipes, Jack. *Fairy Tales and the Art of Subversion: The Classical Genre for Children and the Process of Civilization.* New York: Wildman, 1983.

Index